Access, delivery, performance

the future of libraries without walls

Access, delivery, performance

the future of libraries without walls

A Festschrift to celebrate the work of
Professor Peter Brophy

Edited by
Jillian R. Griffiths and
Jenny Craven

facet publishing

PEFC
PEFC/16-33-111
CATG-PEFC-052
www.pefc.org

Published by Facet Publishing,
7 Ridgmount Street, London WC1E 7AE
www.facetpublishing.co.uk

Facet Publishing is wholly owned by CILIP: the
Chartered Institute of Library and Information
Professionals.

British Library Cataloguing in Publication Data
A catalogue record for this book is available from
the British Library.

ISBN 978-1-85604-647-3

First published 2009

Text printed on PEFC accredited material. The
policy of Facet Publishing is to use papers that are
natural, renewable and recyclable products, made
from wood grown in sustainable forests. In the
manufacturing process of our books, and to
further our policy, preference is given to printers
that have FSC and PEFC Chain of Custody
certification. The FSC and/or PEFC logos will
appear on those books where full certification has
been granted to the printer concerned.

Typeset from author/editors' disks by Facet
Publishing in 10.5/14pt Bembo and Nimbus
Sans.
Printed and made in Great Britain by
MPG Books Ltd, Bodmin, Cornwall.

Contents

Contributors

Professor David Baker is Principal, University College Plymouth St Mark and St John. He was born in Bradford, West Yorkshire, in 1952. His first love was the church organ, and by the time that he was 16, he was an Associate of the Royal College of Organists, gaining his Fellowship the following year. In 1970 he was elected Organ Scholar of Sidney Sussex College, Cambridge, graduating with a First in Music three years later. He took an MMus degree from King's College London in 1974. He then moved into library and information services, taking a Master of Library Studies degree in 1976 and a PhD in 1988 from Loughborough University. He became Chief Librarian of UEA Norwich in 1985, being promoted to Director of Information Strategy and Services in 1995, and Pro-Vice-Chancellor in 1997. He became Principal of University College Plymouth St Mark and St John in 2003 and, in addition, was appointed Professor of Strategic Information Management there in 2006. He has published widely in the field of library and information studies, with 13 monographs and some 100 articles to his credit. He has spoken at numerous conferences, led workshops and seminars and has undertaken consultancy work in most countries in the European Union, the Middle East and Africa. A particular professional interest has been the strategic management of technology. He gained an MBA degree from the Open University in this subject area in 2002. He is a member of the Board of the Joint Information Systems Committee (JISC) and chairs its Content Services Committee, also having led a number of large technology-based projects in digital and hybrid library development and content creation for teaching and learning. His other key professional interest and expertise has been in the field of human resources, where he has been active in major national projects.

Michael Buckland is Professor Emeritus, School of Information, and Co-Director, Electronic Cultural Atlas Initiative, at the University of California, Berkeley. He started library work at the Bodleian Library of Oxford University and, with a diploma in librarianship from Sheffield University, joined University of Lancaster Library in 1965, where from 1967 to 1972 he was responsible for a series of studies in the Library Research Unit for studies on book usage, book availability and library management games. His PhD dissertation from Sheffield University was published as *Book Availability and the Library User* (1975). In 1972 he moved to the USA to be Assistant Director of Libraries for Technical Services at Purdue University, then Dean of the School of Library and Information Studies at Berkeley, 1976–84. He was Assistant Vice President for Library Plans and Policies for the nine campuses of the University of California from 1983 to 1987 and Co-Director of the Electronic Cultural Atlas Initiative since 2000. He was President of the American Society for Information Science in 1998. His writings include *Emanuel Goldberg and his Knowledge Machine*, a biography (2006), *Library Services in Theory and Context* (1983; 2nd edn, 1988), *Information and Information Systems* (1991), and *Redesigning Library Services* (1992). Professor Buckland's interests include library services, information retrieval, cultural heritage and the history of documentation. Since 1990 he has worked on a series of projects to make bibliographical searching easier and more effective through search support for unfamiliar metadata vocabularies, translingual search, cross-genre searching between numeric and textual resources, improved geographical search, enhanced biographical resources, and moving reference resources into the digital library environment. For more see http://people.ischool.berkeley.edu/~buckland.

Brenda Chawner is Senior Lecturer, School of Information Management, Victoria University of Wellington (VUW), New Zealand. She has been employed at VUW since 1997, and teaches courses on electronic publishing and business information sources in the Master of Library and Information Studies programme. She has a BSc and an MLS from the University of Alberta in Edmonton, Canada, and is currently a PhD candidate at Victoria University of Wellington. She has worked as a librarian, project analyst, systems analyst, team leader and lecturer. Her research interests are best described by the phrase 'all things open' – her PhD project involves an investigation of factors that affect participant satisfaction with open source software, and she is also interested in open access publishing and open standards used in information management. Brenda is currently experimenting with the use of open access wikis and blogs to support her courses.

Jenny Craven is Research Associate, Centre for Research in Library and Information Management (CERLIM), Manchester Metropolitan University (MMU). She is a Chartered librarian and has worked as a Research Associate at the for over ten years. She has worked on a variety of research projects, mainly concerned with web accessibility and usability, with a particular focus on access to information by blind and visually impaired people, and has facilitated workshops on this topic in Chile, Mexico, Vietnam, Brazil and Sabah. She has published widely on this topic, and most recently edited *Web Accessibility: practical advice for the library and information professional*, Facet Publishing, 2008. Jenny contributes to teaching and supervision of undergraduate and postgraduate students within the Department of Information and Communications at MMU. She is a trustee for ForceUK, a charity that seeks to improve access to information and library materials by blind, visually and print impaired people, and is on the Standing Committee of the IFLA Section of Libraries for the Blind.

Rowena Cullen is Associate Professor and Director of Research, School of Information Management, Victoria University of Wellington (VUW), New Zealand. She teaches in the Master of Library and Information Studies and Master of Information Management programmes. She has a PhD from VUW, and an MLitt from the University of Edinburgh. She is a longstanding member of the Board of the Northumbria International Conference on Performance Measurement in Libraries and Information Services, and the associated journal *Performance Measurement and Metrics*. Rowena is on the editorial board of the *Journal of Academic Librarianship*, and co-editor of the International Perspectives column for the journal. Rowena is also a member of the health libraries community, having served as Secretary of the Health and Biosciences section of IFLA for some years, and currently is Regional Associate Editor for *Health Information and Libraries Journal*. She was joint editor of a special issue of the journal in 2007, on the impact of information services in the health sector. With an ongoing interest in the evaluation of information services, Rowena is currently (with co-author Brenda Chawner) investigating the development of and academic attitudes to institutional repositories throughout the higher education sector in New Zealand. Rowena has been a keynote speaker at several international conferences, and has published over 100 articles, book chapters and conference papers. She has recently published the monograph *Health Information on the Internet*, and *Comparative Perspectives on E-government* with Peter Hernon.

John Dolan OBE was formerly Head of Library Policy at the Museums, Libraries and Archives Council (MLA). At MLA (2006–2008) he managed a major consultation of the future priorities for public libraries leading to the MLA libraries plan, 2008–13. He worked on strategic public library developments in health, skills for life, library design, research and for young people. Through the British Council he supported developments overseas, notably in Bulgaria and India. In Birmingham (1990–2006) he held several posts latterly as Assistant Director with responsibility for the youth service, adult education, family learning and early years provision, and as Head of Birmingham Libraries and the City Archives. John led on creating the original concept for the new city library, the Library of Birmingham, exploring worldwide the powerful influence of town and city central libraries on learning, social cohesion, community identity and urban regeneration. In St Helens (1986–90) he managed libraries, archives and museum services following his earlier career in Manchester, first as a graduate trainee, then in both the Central and Community libraries, notably in east and north Manchester, actively developing new approaches to library and information services for diverse urban communities. John was Project Leader (1997) for the strategy to bring internet access to all UK public libraries. The People's Network transformed libraries through a £170m lottery investment in infrastructure, content and staff training, which attracted exciting, new and more diverse audiences to libraries. John was awarded the OBE for services to libraries and information provision in 1999. He now works independently.

Juliet Eve is Principal Lecturer, University of Brighton, School of Computing, Mathematical and Information Sciences. She is currently Head of the Division of Information and Media Studies, and has previously been Course Leader for the MA in Information Studies. She specializes in (and enthuses about) teaching research methods, and is passionate about bringing together research and library practice. She has been a member of the Library and Information Research Group since 2000, and is currently newsletter editor. Her research interests are in the role of public libraries in society (previous research projects include evaluating the role of ICTs in UK libraries and public libraries as supporters of lifelong learning across Europe) and research into practice. Before moving to Brighton, Juliet taught in the Department of Information and Communication at Manchester Metropolitan University, where she had previously been a Research Fellow in CERLIM.

Jillian R. Griffiths is Research Associate, Centre for Research in Library and Information Management (CERLIM), Manchester Metropolitan University (MMU). Since joining in 1999 she has worked on a number of projects focused on academic use (student, lecturer and researcher of UK higher education institutions) of electronic information sources (and identification of their information needs) and on information systems performance and usability. She has published widely on these subjects, most recently as an invited speaker at the *17th Conference of Greek Academic Libraries: academic library evaluation as a measure of institutional quality assessment* and to *Libraries Without Walls* 7 (Facet, 2008). Current research includes work in the m-learning area, students' information literacy with her colleague Bob Glass as part of the HEFCE-funded LearnHigher CETL at MMU and the Higher Education Academy funded project Building Curricula for the 21st Century Learner – a Tool Kit for Diversity Review led by Liz Marr. Jill's teaching within the Department of Information and Communications at MMU at undergraduate and postgraduate level is research led and focuses on research methods; information retrieval, including information seeking behaviour; evaluation of IR systems; and organizing information. She also supervises at undergraduate and postgraduate level.

Professor Richard J. Hartley is Head of the Information and Communications Department, Manchester Metropolitan University. He has experience in academic, national and public libraries, and was previously a Lecturer at the Department of Information and Library Studies, University of Wales Aberystwyth, and Principal Lecturer and Reader at the University of Northumbria at Newcastle. He has been a Visiting Professor in the Department of Library Studies, TEI, Thessaloniki, Greece. He was a member of the Librarianship, Archives and Information Science Panel of the AHRB from 1997 to 1999. He has been an invited reviewer for LIS education in Greece (1999) and Estonia (2001). He is joint editor of *Education for Information*. He is on the editorial board of the electronic journal *ITALICS* and the *Library Review*, and will become a senior associate editor of the *Journal of Information Science and Technology*. Dick is also a Fellow of the Chartered Institute of Library and Information Professionals (FCLIP). His research interests are information retrieval, with a particular interest in OPACs image retrieval and how users search retrieval systems, and the application of information technology in Greek libraries.

Alan F. MacDougall is Visiting Professor, Department of Information and Communications, Manchester Metropolitan University. He is currently a management consultant who specializes, nationally and internationally, in the areas of strategic and operational library management, reviews and evaluation of service, planning of new and refurbished library and learning resource buildings, and mentoring at chief executive level. He has spent over 30 years in the library and information profession. His career has included posts at the University of London Library and at Loughborough University; subsequently he held the posts of Director of the UK Library and Information Statistics Unit, Director of Library Services at Dublin City University and Director of Information Services and Systems at King's College London, retiring in 2003. He has taught library and information science at Loughborough University and was a visiting professor at University of Central Lancashire where CERLIM was to be established. He is now a visiting professor at Manchester Metropolitan University where he has continued to work closely with Professor Peter Brophy on such matters as European projects, various consultancies, lecturing and the planning and delivery of the biennial Libraries Without Walls conference held in Greece. He has been actively involved in research, holds a doctorate in the area of strategic management and has published widely in the library and information field. He also now devotes increasing time to being a magistrate and to pursuing his love of London by providing interpretative guiding and lecturing on a range of historical subjects to specialist organizations.

Charles R. McClure is the Francis Eppes Professor of Information Studies and Director of the Information Use Management Policy Institute at the College of Information, Florida State University. He completed his PhD from Rutgers University and prior to his position at Florida State University had been a distinguished professor at the School of Information Studies, Syracuse University. He was one of the two founding editors of *Government Information Quarterly* and currently serves as the journal's associate editor. With John Carlo Bertot, he has conducted the national survey of public libraries and the internet since 1994, which is currently funded by the Bill & Melinda Gates Foundation and the American Library Association. He has written extensively on topics related to the planning and evaluation of information services, federal information policy, information resources management and digital libraries.

Gill Needham is Head of Strategic and Service Development at the Open University Library and Learning Resource Centre. She is responsible for leading and co-ordinating the Library's development projects and initiatives. Since joining the Open University in 1998 she has taken a leading role in developing the Library's electronic services to its 200,000 students, has launched and developed an information literacy strategy for the University and has been a major author on three Open University courses. She was awarded a National Teaching Fellowship in 2006. Previously she worked for 15 years in the National Health Service, initially as a librarian and subsequently as an R&D specialist in public health, responsible for promoting evidence-based practice and public involvement in healthcare decision making.

Sue Roberts is University Librarian, Victoria University of Wellington, New Zealand. Prior to moving to New Zealand in early 2007, she was Dean of Learning Services at Edge Hill University in Lancashire (UK) and the Director of SOLSTICE, a Centre for Excellence in Learning and Teaching with a focus on supported online learning. Sue has also researched and published in the fields of learner support roles and teams, leadership and management, continuing professional development, digital library development and e-learning, and is the co-author of *Managing Information Services* (Facet Publishing, 2004), *Developing the New Learning Environment* (Facet Publishing, 2005) and *Leadership: the challenge for the information profession* (Facet Publishing, 2008).

Jennifer Rowley is Professor of Information and Communications, Department of Information and Communications, Manchester Metropolitan University. She has previously held a number of other academic posts in the UK. Her research and publication activities are extensive and cover information management, knowledge management, e-business and related disciplines. Key books include *Organizing Knowledge* (4th edn with Richard J. Hartley, Ashgate, 2008); *Leadership: the challenge for the information profession* (with Sue Roberts, Facet Publishing, 2008); *E-Business: principles and practice* (Palgrave, 2002); and *Information Marketing* (2nd edn, Ashgate, 2006). She is editor of the *Journal of Further and Higher Education*, and has completed a major JISC-funded project on the use of digital information resources in further and higher education.

John T. Snead is Research Associate, Information Use Management and Policy Institute, College of Information, Florida State University. His areas of interest include evaluation of networked services and resources, outcomes assessment, and information policy research; his research background includes five years of evaluation of the Florida Electronic Library (online digital library), development of the Evaluation Decision-Making System (online instructional system), evaluation of the Public Library Geo-database (GIS system), and e-government research initiatives. In addition, he is a doctoral candidate at the College of Information and his dissertation research is focused on access for individuals through federal websites to executive agency records that contain personal data.

Nicky Whitsed is Director of Library Services at the Open University. She has led the development of library services to the Open University's 200,000 students. To ensure the delivery of the Library's new vision a purpose-built state of the art building has recently been opened. A new feature of the building is the Digilab, a creative space for developing the application of new technologies to learning and teaching. Nicky's current remit includes University Archives and University Records Management as well as support to learning and teaching, research and the University's e-business. Before joining the Open University, Nicky was Information Manager at SmithKlineBeecham where she was involved in a major culture change programme, and Librarian of Charing Cross and Westminster Medical School (University of London) where she pioneered the introduction of end-user databases for clinicians and students. Nicky has an MSc in Information Systems and Technology and is a Fellow of the Chartered Institute of Library and Information Professionals (CILIP). Nicky is a Board Member of the South East Museums Libraries and Archives Council (MLA: SE) and a member of the *Health Information and Libraries Journal* (*HILJ*) editorial team. She is a director of the Digital Preservation Coalition and a member of the Higher Education Funding Council (HEFCE) Digitisation Advisory Group. Nicky is convenor of the Milton Keynes Libraries Network (MKLCLN).

1

Introduction

ALAN F. MacDOUGALL

This Festschrift celebrates and commemorates the work and career of Professor Peter Brophy, who retired in 2008 as the Director, Centre for Research in Library and Information Management (CERLIM), Department of Information and Communications at Manchester Metropolitan University. It both identifies and honours his contribution and acknowledges his distinguished career over more than 30 years in the field of libraries, information management and information science. The collection of writings in this work is written among others by: close academic colleagues, those who worked for and with him, people whom he inspired and peer colleagues of high international repute. It weaves an impressive account of achievement and respect for his abilities. It also gives an insight into his character.

In an introduction of this kind the requirement to reflect on Peter's career and achievements might unwittingly seem more like an obituary, or Gedenkschrift, rather than a Festschrift. On the contrary, Peter retires from his post at the zenith of his career, indeed, he constantly likes to remind me, and anyone who will listen, that he is actually younger than me (only four days though!).

I begin this introductory chapter on a personal note but with some reason. To be asked to write this introduction is a privilege and an honour. I am equally aware that contributors to this book were eager to honour Peter and his importance in the profession, and to record his achievement, which will stimulate the next generation, their research and their practice.

The second chapter in this work refers to the time before I knew him. It provides an insight to Peter's contribution during the early days of his career from 1971 to 1973. Written by Michael Buckland, the eminent professor, it is worthy of note that he should describe Peter as having a 'distinguished career'. The chapter introduces us to the innovative work of the Library Research Unit at Lancaster University, which Buckland headed and where Peter was a research associate. It is a timely commentary both as a review of the work of that Unit and Peter's role in its success, and as an introduction to his professional career. It was to be the formative period for the way he was to think, challenge, analyse and deliver quality throughout his career. At this stage he was encouraged to go beyond the status quo to enquire why things are done, how they are achieved, why they are achieved and, significantly, to carry out the research to discover how any activity could be informed and improved. In essence, this process involved re-examining traditionally held thoughts and proposing new ideas within a context of continuous improvement.

Buckland then makes reference to Peter's leaving Lancaster in 1973 to become the Library Systems Officer at Strathclyde University, where he worked until 1975. A measure of the man can be deduced when one realizes that it was only a further eight years until he was appointed, aged 33, to the post of Librarian of Bristol Polytechnic (subsequently renamed University of the West of England). In those intervening eight years he was successively a subject librarian and Deputy at Teesside Polytechnic.

After six years, in 1989, Peter left Bristol to return back North, not to 'God's Own County' and the county of his birth (Yorkshire) but to Lancashire. He became the Head of Learning Resources at University of Central Lancashire. I can still remember meeting him (with a sinking heart) at breakfast on the morning of the interview; I was one of the candidates!

Unfortunately because of space limitations this volume could not accommodate additional chapters on his outstanding success in the two practically based professional posts of University Librarian; strictly this Festschrift has concentrated on his academic record.

If Lancaster University was to be the place where he served his research apprenticeship then it was at the University of Central Lancashire that he began to practise his research craft as a master. In 1993, while still the Director of Learning Resources and achieving outstanding results, he set up the Centre for Research in Library and Information Management (CERLIM), which until the present day has continued to be so influential in the profession. He was recognized as one of the leading and most influential university librarians and also as an acknowledged leader, carrying out research in information management, which could be fed directly back in to the library world and to the benefit of his community.

The research output was impressive but during the following few years it became clear that something had to give. While Peter pondered the possibility of a full time career in research, Professor Dick Hartley, the Head of Department of

Information and Communications at Manchester Metropolitan University, who has contributed a chapter to this volume, approached Peter with an offer for the team to come to Manchester. It was an inspired thought. After some discussion he managed to encourage Peter to come to Manchester with the CERLIM team in 1998. It turned out to be to the benefit of Manchester Metropolitan University and to the Department (enhanced research assessment exercise rating followed) by enriching the research environment. It clearly also suited Peter and the CERLIM staff, who went from strength to strength, providing high level and much needed research in the profession. Subsequent findings emanating from CERLIM continued to play a part in influencing the way that libraries and their services were being developed. Peter, as Professor of Information Management, devoted himself primarily to the pursuit of research, albeit with teaching commitments.

The above paragraphs outline the progression of Peter's career but do not convey the influence, range and extent of the research and original contribution to knowledge. The remaining chapters in this book illustrate the main themes of his research interest over the past 30 years or more. A more comprehensive treatment of the themes would merit a multi-volume work.

The first area of these research interests is associated with libraries and learning, including distance learning – an area with which I became associated through European projects, particularly the project entitled BIBDEL (Libraries Without Walls: the delivery of library services to distant users). Gill Needham and Nicky Whitsed chart the progression and contribution of the Library at the Open University to the needs of the distant learner and acknowledge Peter who 'has been such an inspiration to us working in this field'. The chapter neatly illustrates how the challenge ten years ago was to overcome the physical distance to give the best support to distance learners; now the challenge is to overcome the virtual distance and understand different virtual spaces so as to position and provide services for the future. The chapter by Professor David Baker, who had a similarly fast track career, reflects on the history, development, application and future of information and communication technology in the field of learning and teaching, with special reference to UK higher education. One of the most influential library bodies in the UK has been the Joint Information Systems Committee (JISC), which has contributed to the shape and direction of the future of information provision. It is no surprise that Peter has been closely associated with carrying out major consultancy work on behalf of JISC.

The second theme is that of widening access to information. It illustrates Peter's ability to influence matters beyond the boundaries of academic libraries and especially to public libraries. The chapter by Jenny Craven, a fellow colleague in CERLIM, illustrates the thinking and research carried out in the area of widening access to library services for people with print impairments. It emphasizes the requirement of ensuring equality of delivery for all. Chapters by John Dolan, one of the most respected leaders in this area, on widening access and public libraries, and Juliet Eve (a former fellow academic at Manchester) on Web 2.0, both emphasize this perspective.

The third theme is the changing direction of information delivery. Under this heading, contributions include a chapter by Rowena Cullen and Brenda Chawner at the School of Information Management, Victoria University of Wellington, which provides a comprehensive view of institutional repositories and illustrates the rapidly evolving thinking about storage and dissemination. Professor Richard J. Hartley, in his chapter, also refers to Peter as having a distinguished career, reminding us of Peter's commitment to networking and dissemination, especially the conference series entitled 'Libraries Without Walls', of which Peter was the creator. It came out of the European research and dissemination process for the BIBDEL project. This conference has been repeated every two years since the 1990s and I can testify that its continued success is primarily due to Peter. Time and time again I have been informed by attendees that the reason for their attendance is to have the opportunity to talk to him about developments and seek advice.

The final theme is performance and quality, areas with which I became associated through becoming a partner in various European projects directed by Peter. Two examples are Eqlipse (Evaluation and Quality in Library Performance: Systems for Europe) and its follow-on project entitled Equinox. In the 1970s and 1980s the library profession was only beginning to gather and articulate its thoughts about matters related to quality. Peter acted as a catalyst and, along with the professional bodies, helped to stimulate timely research. As the years passed and the influence of digitization began to be noted he, and his team, began to focus on electronic provision and how it might be evaluated. Professor Charles R. McClure, a highly regarded US scholar, and his colleague John T. Snead discuss web-based evaluation decision-making systems. Chuck McClure's input symbolizes Peter's commitment and involvement in pursuing international solutions. Jill Griffiths, a colleague of Peter's in CERLIM, reflects on some of the work on quality attributes thinking in her chapter. Also under this theme Professor Jennifer Rowley (fellow academic at Manchester Metropolitan University) and Sue Roberts (Victoria University of Wellington) write on influential leadership. The authors mark Peter's contribution as an information leader 'who has over many years, in differing contexts, and playing different roles, been a leader not only in the specific job roles that he has held, but also to the profession as a whole. He has been an exemplar of the influential leader . . . on some occasions unwittingly as a consequence of a seemingly unrelated action'. A sentiment widely held and endorsed by the library and information community.

Conclusion

This Festschrift clearly illustrates Peter's contribution to the profession in terms of original thinking; original research; contribution to knowledge; the acknowledgement of his peers by having been made a Fellow of several bodies; the numerous requests for him to carry out consultancies particularly for the British Council; the recognized influence he has had on those who have worked with him; and, significantly, the wider international audience that Peter would have no idea of and may never have met.

One only need look at Peter's voluminous publishing output as further evidence of his contribution (see the Bibliography at the end of the volume). A glimpse at three of his major works: *The Library in the 21st Century* (2nd edn, 2007), *Measuring Library Performance* (2006) and *The Academic Library* (2nd edn, 2005) offers some indication of his academic rigour, structured thinking, intellectual grasp and incisiveness.

Peter's work exhibits a continuing desire for improvement and equity; this also extends to the way he conducts not only his professional but also his private life. Many people have remarked on Peter's ability to inspire and enthuse them and comment on the manner in which he has helped to provide marvellous opportunities for their career development; these sentiments have been particularly emphasized by the present and former staff in CERLIM.

What many people will not know is that he has an equally successful parallel life. He has been a magistrate (and was very helpful in introducing me to the magistracy), and has deep spiritual convictions. It is often the case that behind a successful person is another very important individual; Peter's position is no different. There is no doubt that his highly successful career is influenced in no small part by his family: his daughter Jenny, and Alison. It has been my pleasure to know his librarian wife, Alison, and it is abundantly obvious that she is a wonderful support. It will be no surprise to learn that she is an accomplished counsellor.

It only remains to thank the contributors for their timely and thoughtful chapters and for their perceptive words about Peter, which so accurately reflect his abilities. I am convinced that when he learns of, and reads the content of, this book he will be genuinely surprised that his colleagues have wanted to bring these chapters together in his honour. He will also find it difficult to accept the words of praise, but this is a measure of the man and his genuine modesty. He deserves the praise and the recognition; the information profession is much the stronger and richer for the contribution of Professor Peter Brophy.

2

The Library Research Unit at the University of Lancaster, 1967–1972: a memoir

MICHAEL BUCKLAND

Introduction

Peter Brophy entered librarianship by a thoroughly unorthodox route. He was one of the first students to take the BSc in Information Science developed by B. C. ('Bertie') Brookes at University College, London, graduating in 1971. He then moved into full-time research on library problems at the Library Research Unit at the University of Lancaster Library before moving on in 1973 to library automation and eventually library management. At the time both his undergraduate degree and the Library Research Unit were radical departures from conventional practice. This memoir, written mainly from memory, provides an account of the Lancaster Library Unit in which Brophy's professional career began.

A new university at Lancaster

The University of Lancaster was one of the 'new universities' founded in the 1960s to help accommodate the rapid expansion of university education in the UK. Charles F. Carter, the founding Vice-Chancellor, an economist and a Quaker, was concerned that the University address real-world problems as well as regional needs. Lancaster had the first department of operational research in the UK, the first department of marketing, and, also a first, a department of systems engineering with special interest in optimization in chemical industries. The ethos of the new university was very similar to that of the land grant universities in the USA. Currently, the University's website opens with the slogan 'Learning for the real world' (www.lancs.ac.uk).

Among the very earliest appointments was the University Librarian, A. Graham Mackenzie, who had graduated in Classics from the University of Glasgow. His handle-bar moustache and his enthusiasm for machines were both attributed to his service in the Royal Air Force. He liked to recall how when he was interviewed he was taken south of Lancaster to a grassy, windswept hillside, the Bailrigg site, where he was abruptly asked what a first-rate university library would be like in 20 years. His interviewers said that they wanted one on this site and that the first students would be arriving in 18 months. It was a challenge to which he responded with enthusiasm and boldness. It was clear that the planned library would have to be developed quickly and be both economical and effective. Initially the library service was provided in temporary quarters in Lancaster and the first phase of the new library building opened in January 1967. Mackenzie spent a large amount of time working with the architect on the design of the new building, which had a pleasant, functional and economical design.

Innovation in British university libraries

The 'new universities' generated a pulse of new life and created opportunities for librarians like Graham Mackenzie to become library directors in their prime instead of having to wait for dead men's shoes. What was striking about the University of Lancaster library was the range of innovation. In addition to the new and well designed library building, a novel three-part staffing structure was adopted comprising:

- senior library assistants, professionally qualified librarians, responsible for all professional tasks for which subject expertise was not necessary, such as acquisitions, cataloguing and lending services
- assistant librarians, with academic qualifications in addition to professional qualifications, responsible for liaison with teaching staff, collection development, bibliographic instruction, classification and advanced reference
- support staff for clerical and technical activities.

Library automation was just beginning in the mid-1960s and was not yet cost-effective. A Friden Flexowriter, a punched paper-tape typewriter, was programmed to mechanize catalogue card production. The catalogue records were saved on punched paper tape for a future online catalogue. In the early 1970s a computer was used to maintain a simple listing of books on reserve and a 'hybrid' circulation system was implemented that combined a minicomputer at the service desk with overnight updating on a mainframe (Buckland and Gallivan, 1972; Gallivan, Bamber and Buckland, 1972).

Bibliographic instruction, relatively undeveloped in British university libraries, was emphasized and tailored guides were developed (for example, Buckland, 1967, 1968). Meanwhile the new National Lending Library for Science and Technology (later the British Library Document Supply Centre) was able to satisfy an increasing proportion of interlibrary loan requests overnight. The 1960s and early 1970s were a golden era for British academic librarianship. Other university libraries were also adopting these kinds of innovations, but Lancaster adopted them more completely than elsewhere. Even more unusual was Graham Mackenzie's push for the library to have a substantial research programme. In January 1965 he and Vice-Chancellor Carter submitted an ambitious grant proposal to the Department of Scientific and Industrial Research. It began 'In considering future policy for the development of libraries and of library techniques, it seems to us that there is a serious gap in present knowledge. Not enough is known about the ways in which people use a store of knowledge.'

Formation of the Lancaster Library Research Unit

The case for the research programme was based on the argument that although much was known about the past and present of libraries the government's very large outlay in creating and maintaining new university libraries justified an investigation of how library services could be made more effective. Mackenzie and Carter asked for government funding for a large, multidisciplinary team, with a highly paid project leader, for five years and funding was approved. It is hard, now, to appreciate how radical this initiative was in the UK in 1965. There was no tradition of serious research into practical library problems. Doctoral study related to libraries was rare and dealt with historical bibliography or library history. The main exception was Aslib's research and consulting service, concerned mainly with special libraries, science information and information retrieval.

Since it was unclear what would be done or who could do it, an international competition, based on architectural competitions for major building projects, was announced. Anyone interested in leading the project at Lancaster was invited to submit a proposal outlining what they thought should be done and why they were qualified to do it. Two applicants were commissioned to develop more detailed proposals, which were then reviewed by a jury of distinguished senior figures. At this point the scheme collapsed because the senior figures did not like either of the two commissioned proposals. There was some irony in this. If the leadership in academic librarianship had been engaging competently in such research, there would have been little need for a major new project.

The failure of the planned research programme was deeply disappointing, but the funding agency, the Office of Scientific and Technical Information (OSTI, which later became the British Library Research and Development Department) offered a small grant to fund 1.5 persons for a single year and a Library Research Unit was formed within the University Library. I had joined the library as an assistant librarian in July 1965 and was re-assigned full time to the project. Ian Woodburn, an applied statistician, became the other half-person. The Department of Systems Engineering wanted to hire him as a lecturer, but could afford only half his salary. In this way Ian Woodburn was able to get the academic position he wanted, but at the price of having to work half-time with me on the library's new project.

The project was entitled 'Systems Analysis of a University Library'. The distant vision was clear: to find out what a really good university library ought to be in 20 years and show how to move to that state rapidly. It is fair to say that nobody involved had any real idea what would be done or how, and I had a bad dream in which the final report was composed of sheets of blank paper. However, the direction was soon clarified: the development of mathematical models in order to understand and manage library services better. The first publishable idea was the insight that two well known empirical patterns of the use of scholarly literature – obsolescence (the decline in use over time) and scattering (the skewed dispersal of articles on any topic across different journals) – could be combined to create theoretical 'p% library' models of the optimal collection and retention policies for journals in any given subject area in any given situation (Buckland and Woodburn, 1968b). The approach was too idealized for direct application, but some intriguing aspects of these empirical patterns were examined later (Buckland, 1972a; Buckland and Hindle, 1969b).

Book availability

The central fact of library logistics is that the demand for books is highly skewed: a very few titles are in high demand, accounting for much of the actual book use, and very many titles are used little or not at all. Libraries tend to form hierarchical structures with heavily used books located near to users and the residual demand for rarely requested books absorbed by larger libraries (Woodburn, 1969). Prior quantitative research, especially in the USA, had been heavily concentrated on how to deal with the many least-used books, which dominate libraries' storage costs. The desire to reduce libraries' space costs had diverted attention from the management of the most-used books, which necessarily dominate the quality of service for library users. Whatever else academic libraries do, they exist to make books available for readers and this is especially important when many students need the same text at the same time and the library has only one or very few copies. So the next investigation was a collaboration with the service desk staff to examine the actual patterns of demand for, and the actual availability of, books placed in the short loan reserve collection. What were the relationships between the level of demand, the length of the loan period, the number of copies, and, as a standard of service, how often a copy was available when requested? These four factors are related like a cat's cradle: each influences and is influenced by the other three. In the relatively simple situation of a reserve collection, queuing theory could be applied and some practical guidance provided (Buckland and Woodburn, 1968a, 1969).

These initial efforts justified an extension of funding at the same level for a second year. Full-time funding for Ian Woodburn's teaching appointment had still not been found, so he continued half-time in the Library Research Unit. By this time a member of the academic staff in the Department of Operational Research, Anthony ('Tony') Hindle, had become increasingly involved. He was unusual in being interested in public services, in having a background in industrial psychology as well as ergonomics and cybernetics, and in having just the right aptitude for what needed to be done in the library.

An obvious next step would be to extend the examination of the availability of books in the short term reserve collection to the rest of the collection, but the dynamics of the use of the books shelved on the open shelves were little understood and too complex for queuing theory. There had been complaints that books were too often unavailable when needed despite the generous book budget and skilled selection. The Library Research Unit was mandated to investigate and to make recommendations if need be. During 1967 and 1968 a series of measurements were undertaken which showed that library users could find the books they were looking for about 6 times out of 10; that the major cause of non-availability was that the book was out on loan to someone else; that borrowed books tended to remain out for the full length of the loan period; that in practice a loan period was determined not by written policies but by when overdue fines began; that disappointed would-be borrowers did not often avail themselves of the procedures for recalling books back from loan; and that in-library book use tended to have a stable relationship to circulation in any given library (Hindle and Buckland, 1978). A Monte Carlo simulation was used to avoid the limitations of queuing theory. A flow chart of borrowing activities was programmed so that a computer could simulate the sequence of users seeking a single book, its repeatedly being borrowed and returned, and how often a copy was not available when sought. The simulation was flexible enough to show the effects of changes in the pattern and level of demand, in the length of the loan period, and/or of changing the number of copies of that book.

Diversification

At this promising juncture, during 1968, disaster struck. The Lancaster Library Research Unit was not the only small library-related research unit in Britain. There was the Project to Evaluate the Benefits of University Libraries (PEBUL) at Durham University led by John Hawgood and Richard Morley, and a group led by J. N. Wolfe at the University of Edinburgh interested in economic analyses. A misguided application of the 'centres of excellence' principle induced the funding agency, the Office of Scientific and Technical Information (OSTI), to discontinue support for small units and to concentrate their funding at a new and larger centre for library management research to be established at Cambridge University. To this end I received a personal telephone call from London asking me to agree to transfer to Cambridge. I had no desire to leave Lancaster; I did not believe that Cambridge would be a suitable environment and declined. The funding went to Cambridge anyway for a library management research unit under Leonard Schofield and was later transferred to Loughborough University of Technology. Lancaster received a six-month extension to complete and document its work.

For the unit to survive, new funding was urgently needed and some was found in a pair of sub-contracts from the National Libraries Automated Data Processing (ADP) Project led by Maurice B. Line. The degree of overlap in the titles in different libraries is important. A high degree of overlap is needed to make collaborative cataloguing cost-effective; a low degree of overlap makes union catalogues important for resource sharing. We took stratified samples of pre-1968 imprints from the catalogues of 23 different libraries, including all the largest, and edited the records into a consistent form with codings for date and language. Analysis of the samples gave us a profile of the collections by age and language. Then a sub-sample of records was searched for in the catalogues of each of 18 of the libraries. It was a laborious exercise, but it enabled us to estimate the overlap between any pair of libraries or within any group of libraries. We projected how the cumulative number of different titles increased as libraries were added to a consortium (in any given order) and estimated the total number of different titles in all British libraries combined (University of Lancaster, Library Research Unit,

1971b). A related study examined how far there was duplication in the current acquisition of foreign books (University of Lancaster, Library Research Unit, 1971a). Overlap has other important applications, for example in examining the coverage of literature by abstracting and indexing services. Therefore, the numerous methodological problems were examined with some thoroughness and illustrated with some of our findings (Buckland, Hindle and Walker, 1975).

Library management games

OSTI was almost the only UK source of funding for library research and development and more funding for library management studies was precluded by the Cambridge initiative. However, OSTI's funding programme was compartmentalized, so could our work be considered in some other category than 'library management'? Our answer was that mathematical models of library services could yield instructive insights even when not directly applicable. The 'p% library' model was a good example. So pitching our work as a contribution to *library education* rather than *library management* allowed access to a different funding programme within OSTI and resulted in grants in 1971 and 1972 to develop educational library management games. Two games were developed. A library technical services management game was based on two trade-offs in library technical services. First, the balance in funding between the cost of the books and the cost of staff to process them. Second, the optimal deployment of labour of different kinds at each stage of acquisitions, cataloguing, binding and preparation for the shelves. Outcomes include the number of books reaching the shelves and the length of time it takes them to get there. Insufficient and/or poorly assigned staff leads to chronic delays. Increasing staffing reduces the number of books that can be afforded. (The underlying model is given in Mackenzie, 1970b.)

The second game drew directly on the book availability studies. Players had to choose and implement loan and duplication policies and the likely consequences of cost and demand as predicted by the simulation. Realism could be enhanced by adding a concurrent in-tray exercise whereby players were subjected to the kind of memos, crises and distractions that library managers receive. Evaluative workshops were held in Morecambe in 1972 and Bowness in 1973 and game kits were published. Teaching staff from seven different library schools were attached to the Library Research Unit for varying periods (Brophy and Buckland, 1972; Brophy et al., 1972; Buckland and Hindle, 1971; Daly et al., 1976). This work was honoured by the conferral by the [British] Library Association of the Robinson Medal 'for invention in library technology or administration' in 1972.

As the work expanded, Eileen Morris provided secretarial support and two young researchers were hired, Peter Brophy and Veronica Pogson (later Veronica Brett).

The dynamics of library use

In the meanwhile, studies of the availability of books in the main collection had led to the adoption of two measures: *immediate availability* (the chances that the next person to look for a book will find a copy on the shelf) and *collection bias* (the degree to which the most-popular books are available). The relationships between these two measures and different combinations of loan and duplication policies were quantified using computer simulations for different levels of demand. Then the number of books at each level of demand was estimated in order to calculate the immediate availability and collection bias for the library as a whole. The simulation also estimated the number of books out on loan at any given time, a figure which could also be calculated from the circulation system records. The close match found provided some assurance that the simulation results really did approximate reality. The analyses allowed us to provide detailed guidance to the Library Committee. The immediate availability was around 60%. Increasing it to 80% could be achieved either by spending the entire next year's book budget on duplicate copies of in-demand titles or by shortening the loan period for the 9% most-borrowed books to one week for all borrowers even if loan could be renewed or by a combined strategy (Buckland, 1972d, 1975; Buckland and Hindle, 1969a and b). Further, since past use tended to predict future use and since demand for any title would be spread across all copies, specific recommendations for loan length and for duplication could be based on circulation data on a volume by volume basis.

At the time, the number of dates stamped on any book's 'date due' was counted. Later Peter Brophy, the head of the Service Desk, R. N. ('Bill') Bamber and others worked on deriving feedback from automated circulation systems (Brophy and Moorhouse, 1984; Richardson and Bamber, 1985). So any set of policies could be implemented swiftly and economically and, better yet, subsequent inspections could lead to further adjustments on a volume by volume basis thereby making library collection continuously and efficiently adaptive as demand changed. This adaptiveness proved to be even more important than expected. Per capita library use at Lancaster, already higher than at any other

British university library, doubled in the year after the new policies to increase availability were implemented. Of course, increased demand required increased response from a now-adaptive library. Library use was evidently far more sensitive to immediate availability than had been expected. Data from Lancaster and elsewhere suggested a homeostatic balance, with demand adjusting to 60% immediate availability. These issues were discussed more fully in a doctoral dissertation and eventually in a book (Buckland, 1972b, 1975).

Some overviews of the work of the Library Research Unit were published (Mackenzie, 1971) and a variety of other activities were undertaken more or less incidental to the funded projects. An international conference was organized (Mackenzie and Stuart, 1969); a tutorial on operations research for librarians was published in a reader (Brophy, Buckland and Hindle, 1976; Hindle, Buckland and Brophy, 1976); and some literature surveys were a by-product of research done (Buckland, 1978; Buckland and Kraft, 1976; Mackenzie and Buckland, 1972).

The Library Research Unit existed in two legal forms: as a department in the Library and also a division of Uldeco, the University's development company, which increased administrative flexibility. Also, we hoped to be the first library ever to confer a PhD. At Lancaster the Library was formally an academic department and so there were no obstacles when a very suitably qualified candidate (Peter Brophy) was enrolled as a PhD student in the Library itself.

Our primary concern, however, was to understand the dynamics of library provision and use. In particular, the substantial increase in demand in response to improved availability revealed the need to investigate the dynamics of library user behaviour. We had modelled the response of the collection to demand, but now we knew that we also needed to model the response of the users to the collection. In 1971 the Council on Library Resources, Inc., of Washington DC, generously provided funding for a project called 'Fundamental research on factors affecting the use of library services'. An early product was a major literature review (Ford, 1973). The idea was that demographics, personality traits and task characteristics (such as time pressure) might yield a predictive model of user behaviour. A stratified sample of students were paid to participate, their demographic characteristics were noted, and they were given a battery of tests for motivation, attitude to the library, the Terman Concept Mastery Test, and the Eysenck Personality Inventory. At intervals they were given a pair of forms to be completed on their next visit to the library. On arrival at the library they wrote down on one form what they intended to do in the library during this visit. On the other form they wrote a chronicle of what they actually did do. Qualitative analysis of these records yielded some interesting ideas about categorizing library users as 'searchers', 'workers' and 'shirkers', but the variety and fluidity of activities in the library defied reduction to quantitative models. A by-product of this work on task characteristics was an analysis showing that differences in the types of searches performed provided a plausible explanation of the substantial differences between public, special and university libraries.

Eventually a new grant was received for a project entitled 'Acquisitions, stock holding, stock control and discarding policy in libraries', which attempted to combine the work on book availability with models of acquisitions, book processing and user behaviour (Buckland and Hindle, 1976; Hindle, 1977).

In retrospect

There never would have been a Library Research Unit without the imagination and determination of Graham Mackenzie, the University Librarian. Nor would it have survived without his strong protection. He was the principal investigator for all the grants. At the same time, he had neither the time nor the background to do the kind of research that needed to be done. Tony Hindle provided most of the methodological expertise, but he had limited time to spare. I was in the middle, working in the Unit full time, and so in a position to take care of the varied and often time-consuming tasks that needed to be done, including much of the writing. Each of us was entirely dependent on the other two – and knew it – and an exceptionally effective partnership resulted.

In March 1972 I left Lancaster and was succeeded by Geoffrey Ford. The Library Research Unit continued the work on library management games, the attempt to model user behaviour, and, later, another grant was received to develop a more complete and integrated approach to library collection management combining acquisitions, stock control and discarding policies. Tony Hindle remained active at Lancaster. Graham Mackenzie moved to the University of St Andrews in 1976, retired in 1986, and died in 2005. All of us were grateful to Brian Perry and Sir Frank Francis and their colleagues at the British Library Research and Development Department (previously OSTI) and at the Council on Library Resources (now Council on Library and Information Resources) respectively for their willingness to support what was unconventional work.

Peter Brophy left the Library Research Unit in the summer of 1973 to become Systems Librarian at Strathclyde University. His responsibilities kept him too busy to become the first PhD (Library) graduate and his career showed that he did not need a doctorate. He paid tribute to his Lancaster years both in words (Brophy, 1986) and, more importantly, in developing his own very active and successful research unit, CERLIM. It is very fitting that his distinguished career ended as it had begun, energetically engaged in a lively library research unit.

References

Brophy, P. (1986) *Management Information and Decision Support Systems in Libraries*, Gower.

Brophy, P. and Buckland, M. (1972) Simulation in Education for Library and Information Science Administration, *Information Scientist*, **6** (3), 93–100.

Brophy, P., Buckland, M. and Hindle, A. (eds) (1976) *Reader in Operations Research for Libraries*, Information Handling Services.

Brophy, P. and Moorhouse, P. (1984) The Operation of a Variable Loan Policy Within an Automated Library System, *Program*, **18** (2), (April), 166–9.

Brophy, P. et al. (1972) *A Library Management Game: report on a research project*, University of Lancaster Library Occasional Papers 7, University of Lancaster Library; available as ERIC Report ED 071 700. Also issued as *Computer-aided Instruction in Scientific and Technical Systems Management: report to OSTI on project SI/14/67*.

Buckland, M. (1967) Sources of Information for Operational Research Studies, *Operational Research Quarterly*, **18** (3), 297–313.

Buckland, M. (1968) British Sources of Information for Marketing Studies. In Kelley, W. T. (ed.), *Marketing Intelligence*, Staples Press.

Buckland, M. (1972a) Are Scattering and Obsolescence Related?, *Journal of Documentation*, **28** (3), 242–6; also at www.sims.berkeley.edu/~buckland/obscat.html.

Buckland, M. (1972b) *Library Stock Control*, PhD thesis, Faculty of Social Sciences, Sheffield University.

Buckland, M. (1972c) Library Systems and Management Studies at Lancaster University. In *Proceedings of the 35th Annual Meeting, Washington, 1972*, American Society for Information Science.

Buckland, M. (1972d) An Operations Research Study of a Variable Loan and Duplication Policy at the University of Lancaster. In Swanson, D. R. and Bookstein, A. (eds), *Operations Research: implications for libraries, 35th Annual Conference of the Graduate Library School, August*, Chicago University Press. Also in *Library Quarterly*, **42** (1), 97–106.

Buckland, M. (1975) *Book Availability and the Library User*, Pergamon Press.

Buckland, M. (1978) Ten Years Progress in Quantitative Research on Libraries, *Socio-Economic Planning Sciences*, **12**, 333–9.

Buckland, M. (1979) On Types of Search and the Allocation of Library Resources, *Journal of the American Society for Information Science*, **30**, 143–7.

Buckland, M. and Gallivan, B. (1972) Circulation Control: off-line, on-line, or hybrid, *Journal of Library Automation*, **5** (1), 30–8.

Buckland, M. and Hindle, A. (1969a) Loan Policies and Duplication. In Mackenzie, A. G. and Stuart, I. M. (eds), *Planning Library Services: proceedings of a research seminar*, University of Lancaster Library Occasional Papers 3, University of Lancaster Library; available as ERIC Report ED 045 173.

Buckland, M. and Hindle, A. (1969b) Library Zipf: Zipf's law in libraries and information science, *Journal of Documentation*, **25** (1), 52–7. See also letter in *Journal of Documentation*, **25** (2), 154.

Buckland, M. and Hindle, A. (1971) The Case for Library Management Games, *Journal of Education for Librarianship*, **21** (1), 92–103.

Buckland, M. and Hindle, A. (1976) Acquisitions, Growth and Performance Control Through Systems Analysis. In Gore, D. (ed.), *Farewell to Alexandria: solutions to space, growth, and performance problems of libraries*, Greenwood Press, 44–61.

Buckland, M. and Kraft, D. H. (1976) *A Bibliography on Operations Research in Libraries*. In Brophy, P., Buckland, M. and Hindle, A. (eds), *Reader in Operations Research for Libraries*, Information Handling Services.

Buckland, M. and Woodburn, I. (1968a) *An Analytical Approach to Duplication and Availability*, University of Lancaster Library Occasional Papers 2, University of Lancaster Library; available as ERIC Report ED 022 516.

Buckland, M. and Woodburn, I. (1968b) *Some Implications for Library Management of Scattering and Obsolescence*, University of Lancaster Library Occasional Papers 1, University of Lancaster Library; available as ERIC Report ED 022 502. Revised as Buckland and Woodburn (1969).

Buckland, M. and Woodburn, I. (1969) An Analytical Study of Library Book Duplication and Availability, *Information Storage and Retrieval*, **5** (1), 69–79. Revised version of Buckland and Woodburn (1968b).

Buckland, M., Hindle, A. and Walker, G. P. M. (1975) Methodological Problems in Assessing the Overlap Between Bibliographical Files and Library Holdings, *Information Processing and Management*, **11** (3/4), 89–105.

Buckland, M. et al. (1970) *Systems Analysis of a University Library: final report on a research project*, University of Lancaster Library Occasional Papers 4, University of Lancaster Library; available as ERIC Report ED 044 153.

Daly, J. et al. (1976) *The Use of Gaming in Education for Library Management: final report on a research project*, University of Lancaster Library Occasional Papers 8, University of Lancaster Library.

Ford, G. (1973) Research in User Behaviour in University Libraries, *Journal of Documentation*, **29**, 85–106.

Gallivan, B., Bamber, R. N. and Buckland, M. (1972) *Computer Listing of a Reserve Collection*, University of Lancaster Library Occasional Papers 6, University of Lancaster Library.

Hindle, A. (1977) *Developing an Acquisitions System for a University Library*, BLR&DD Report 5351, British Library.

Hindle, A. and Buckland, M. (1976) *Towards an Adaptive Loan and Duplication Policy for a University Library*. In Brophy, P., Buckland, M. and Hindle, A. (eds), *Reader in Operations Research for Libraries*, Information Handling Services.

Hindle, A. and Buckland, M. (1978) In-library Book Usage in Relation to Circulation, *Collection Management*, **2** (4), 265–77.

Hindle, A., Buckland, M. and Brophy, P. (1976) The Techniques of Operations Research. In Brophy, P., Buckland, M. and Hindle, A. (eds), *Reader in Operations Research for Libraries*, Information Handling Services.

Mackenzie, A. G. (1970a) Bibliotheconomics: or, library science revisited, *An Leabharlean*, **28** (3), 97–105.

Mackenzie, A. G. (1970b) Systems Analysis of a University Library. In Foskett, D. J., de Reuck, A. and Coblans, H. (eds), *Library Systems and Information Services: Proceedings of the Second Anglo-Czech Conference of Information Specialists*, Archon Books, 35–43. Reprinted in Brophy, Buckland and Hindle (1976), 293–306.

Mackenzie, A. G. (1971) Library Research at the University of Lancaster, *Library Association Record*, **73**, 90–2.

Mackenzie, A. G. (1973) Systems Analysis as a Decision-making Tool for the Library Manager, *Library Trends*, **21** (4), (April), 493–504.

Mackenzie, A. G. and Buckland, M. (1972) Operational Research. In Whatley, A. H. (ed.), *British Librarianship and Information Science, 1966–70*, Library Association. Reprinted in Brophy, Buckland and Hindle (1976), 349–54.

Mackenzie, A. G. and Stuart, I. M. (eds) (1969) *Planning Library Services: Proceedings of a Research Seminar*, University of Lancaster Library Occasional Papers 3, University of Lancaster Library, multiple pagination; available as ERIC Report ED 045 173.

Richardson, I. S. and Bamber, R. N. (1985) Variable Loan Policy at University of Lancaster Library, *Program*, **19** (2), (April),176–80.

University of Lancaster, Library Research Unit (1971a) *Foreign Books Acquisitions Study: report to the [British] National Libraries ADP Study*, University of Lancaster Library.

University of Lancaster, Library Research Unit (1971b) *National Catalogue Coverage Study: report to the [British] National Libraries ADP Study*, University of Lancaster Library.

Woodburn, I. (1969) A Mathematical Model of a Hierarchical Library System. In Mackenzie, A. G. and Stuart, I. M. (eds), *Planning Library Services: Proceedings of a Research Seminar*, University of Lancaster Library Occasional Papers 3, University of Lancaster Library.

Theme 1

Libraries, learning and distance learning

3

Alice in www.land: reflections on ten years of developing library services for distance learners

GILL NEEDHAM AND NICKY WHITSED

Introduction

This story begins in 1998 at a time of tremendous change and challenge in the provision of library services to distance education students. At the Open University Library we were embarking on a journey which at the outset appeared to have a relatively clear route and destination. Universities are, however, large and complex organizations and operate in a volatile and increasingly political context. The journey had more than a few twists and turns along the way and we are taking the opportunity of writing this chapter to reflect on our progress and some of the challenges we have encountered. This is particularly appropriate in a volume dedicated to Peter Brophy, who has been such an inspiration to all of us working in this field.

A tale of two Alices

In the beginning it was all about equity and access for distance learning students. This was both an ethical issue – the rights of these learners to have an equivalent service to that enjoyed by campus students – and an issue about academic standards and 'graduateness'. The challenge was to abolish, or at least minimize, *distance* for those learners. It was characterized at the time by a tale of two Alices.

The Follett Report of 1993 (the Joint Funding Councils' Libraries Review Group, 1993) reviewed the provision of library services in UK higher education and made some important recommendations about investment, particularly regarding information technology, with the plan to set up the Joint Information Systems Committee (JISC). The report predicted the importance of the virtual library and presented a series of scenarios in this context, one of which introduces Alice, an undergraduate student of the future: Alice has just received feedback, online, from her tutor on her latest assignment:

He suggests two further references. Alice switches to the library catalogue. Fortunately one reference is available on the campus textbook server: she requests it for printing in the hall of residence. The other reference takes longer to locate: it is an electronic journal article and will cost £10 for immediate transmission. . . . She calls up the abstract/front page option on screen, decides it will be worth reading, swipes the credit card and in a few seconds the article is on screen, transmitted over the networks from an electronic document delivery exchange in Colorado.

(Joint Funding Councils' Libraries Review Group,1993, 60)

In 1998 the British Library published the results of five linked studies looking at the role of libraries supporting distance education students (Unwin, Stephens and Bolton, 1998). Based on the recorded experiences of postgraduate distance education students, the book introduces another Alice, one who is struggling to locate and access library materials she needs to support her studies on a postgraduate course she is studying at a distance. She visits her local university library where the subject coverage doesn't match the demands of her course and then contacts her own university where she . . .

finally spoke to the subject librarian at her own university who was prepared to admit that, yes, DL students have a problem, and, yes, as a special concession to her she would personally photocopy a couple of references and send them, along with a key monograph, by post, as long as she was able to pay the return postage. . . . She looked forward to the day when DL students could search databases from home and make e-mail requests for materials to be sent by post. She said that the university had an experimental project looking at just this.

(Unwin et al., 1998, 199–200)

As well as highlighting distance learners' need for access to library resources and services, the Unwin et al. study (1998) also highlighted the importance of supporting the development of information skills: 'All students, including undergraduates, need to develop more effective library and information retrieval skills and should receive training' (112).

The lack of skills and experience in information handling had been identified by many researchers as an obstacle to effective learning and in particular to the development of independent learning. This was particularly the case for distance learners:

A major problem for DL students is that they can arrive at the library with a similar or lesser skills level than the new undergraduates or nursing students but they do not benefit from any organised induction sessions or instruction in library use, and then they are expected to produce work of degree level or higher straight away.

(Coles, 1994, 3)

This posed a significant challenge for libraries in the sector, and one for which there was no relevant body of experience to draw on.

The Open University

The Open University (OU) is the largest university in the UK, with around 200,000 students. It is recognized as a pioneer in open and distance education and until the mid-1990s with the exception of the University of London's extension programme was the only large scale provider in the UK. The University developed a very successful model of supported open learning, whereby students study in their own homes or workplaces, with the support of a personal tutor who provides optional tutorial sessions and marks their work. For the majority of OU students, libraries played no part whatsoever in their experience of higher education. Instead, their course materials provided an alternative experience comprised of a rich array of print, audio and video or broadcast material – everything needed to complete a degree programme successfully. Generations of students graduated without the help of a library. While the majority of students may have been content with this, a survey of OU students in 1999 (Bremner, 2000) found that, like the postgraduate students surveyed by Unwin and colleagues (1998), a significant proportion of students either used libraries to supplement their work or considered it important to do so. A third of the students surveyed had used their local public library to find material to support their studies and 15% had used local university libraries. There were, in short, many Alices studying at the OU.

In 1998 the world of higher education libraries was changing. The impact of the Dearing Report (1997) with its emphasis on the strategic use of ICT and skills for lifelong learning was beginning to be felt. Of particular note were the Libraries without Walls conferences from 1995. Campus universities were beginning to offer courses to distance learners (albeit not on the scale of the Open University) and their libraries set up special services for these groups (Sheffield Hallam, Leicester and Surrey are good examples). Like some of the smaller open universities around the world (for example, Athabasca and OU

Hong Kong), as well as engaging with technology, these libraries were able to offer postal versions of their standard library services. Many provided postal loans, photocopying services and searches. In 1995 the Open University Library was asked by the University to begin to develop and deliver services to students. The challenge was hardly comparable to that taken up by universities with a few thousand distance learners. How could we deliver services to around 200,000 students and their 8000 tutors?

Phase 1 – Equity and access
The vision for Alice

The solution for the Open University in addressing these challenges had to lie with the rapid development of networked technology. Indeed the vision for the future was far closer to the Alice portrayed in the Follett Report, with her own computer and her access to online collections, than Unwin et al.'s Alice whose greater interest lay in a physical library offering her 'freedom to browse' (200). Two-thirds of the students surveyed by Bremner (2000) wanted online access to the Open University Library. Respondents to the survey also said that they wanted to learn how to use libraries: they had little, if any, experience. The challenge the Library faced was therefore twofold: to develop an effective library service for students and to help students learn to use it, without being able to offer the traditional library induction session available to conventional university libraries.

In 1999, following some successful small-scale experimental projects providing electronic resources to several postgraduate courses, a five-year Learner Support Strategy was produced by the Library and endorsed by the University. The Strategy's aim was:

> to ensure that OU students receive maximum benefit from their studies in terms of access to high quality information resources and that they develop the skills and confidence in information management to equip them as lifelong learners.

The document provided a framework for the phased development of a comprehensive service for Open University students. It comprised three strands: one on *support* – outlining the development of a helpdesk service using a range of communication technologies; a second on *resources* – an ambitious plan to build up an extensive collection of electronic library resources to meet the needs of the OU curriculum including electronic journals, electronic books and online databases; and a third on *skills* – which involved the development of generic information skills programmes and materials for staff and student use.

The University invested in this strategy, providing resources for building the e-collections and the recruitment of a team of learner support staff to develop and provide the service, while the subject specialist librarians were responsible for working with course development teams. Short term project funding was also forthcoming for specific developments.

Challenges and diversions

With the support of the University and an injection of new funds, the development of the new service was on its way. There were, however, a few hurdles to negotiate. One of the University's fundamental principles was, and continues to be, 'openness to people' and at this time less than half of our students had access to the internet. How could we justify offering library services which the majority would be unable to access? This reflected a significant issue for the University as a whole as it developed its post-Dearing Learning and Teaching Strategy. How long would it be before the University could realistically expect all students to be online so that they could embrace Dearing and make effective use of technology for learning? How equitable was it to offer services to what might be considered a privileged group who happened to have access to the technology?

Gradually a small number of courses (mainly postgraduate initially) began to require students to have computers and internet access. This gave the Library the opportunity to work with those courses to develop an appropriate collection of databases and electronic journals and make these available to the students. This was indeed the beginning of a long term strategy for the Library, which continues today.

While the major barrier to progress would seem to have been the take up of access to technology (the digital divide), a more difficult and enduring one has been the University's highly successful model for teaching at a distance. Many academics found the introduction of online library services challenging to their traditional ways of working. The idea of students being able to find their own resources and use them in their work was alien to those used to a model where all resources were 'prescribed' and provided by the course team. Surveys carried out by the Library in 2001 and 2003 showed that the majority of students were not encouraged to use or refer to any resources other than their course materials. Although many students had no problem with this – distance learning students are notoriously time poor and will therefore take a pragmatic stance – some felt that they were missing out: they wanted to feel like real students. Many OU academics who were concerned about student workload and had little experience of the developments in the centrality of libraries in conventional universities were still to be convinced that students should need to use a library or library resources to support their studies.

The Learning and Teaching Strategy

Following initial investment by the University in staff and electronic resources, support for the development of a comprehensive online library service for students came at strategic level through its incorporation into the University's first Learning and Teaching Strategy in 2000. The strategy endorsed the importance of information literacy skills and placed these in the broader context of transferable skills for lifelong learning in the manner of Dearing. Through its collection of electronic resources, the Library offered courses with one of the first opportunities to engage students using technology. Despite official support and endorsement, however, there was still some concern in the faculties. Some academic staff were reluctant to engage with the internet and all it offers. They were concerned that students using the web would find unsuitable or poor quality material.

In response to this concern the Library developed a service whereby quality websites were selected and evaluated by academic and library staff together for particular courses. These were annotated and stored in a database searchable by course code or subject. This was attractive to the academics who had misgivings about the internet because we were able to persuade them that their students would be introduced to quality materials in a controlled environment. This service was called ROUTES (Needham, O'Sullivan and Ramsden, 2000) and for many students this was one of the only online services available to them. It gave the Library the opportunity to engage with faculties and course teams and to raise the Library's profile. Faculties and course teams were able to show that they were meeting the University's strategic priorities by offering their students online services. The service flourished as more and more courses took it up, and the database grew to include resources for 200 courses. This became a major industry for the Library and formed a significant component of the new e-library. Open Library was launched in 2000, comprising the ROUTES database, the growing collection of e-journals and databases as well as information literacy materials.

The success of the ROUTES service, however, turned out to be a double edged sword. Although the number of courses in the database grew steadily, the level of use by students was disappointingly low. An investigation (Kirkwood, 2006) confirmed our suspicions: Open University students, notoriously time poor, are unlikely to spend time on any additional activities unless they form an integral part of the course or, in particular, they are assessed. Courses where ROUTES was used as part of assessed activities showed a significantly higher level of usage than those where it was merely offered as an extra resource to enhance experience. Ironically the Library was working extremely hard and providing an excellent service, highly valued by course teams as they were able to show that they were offering students the opportunity to work online, but the majority of students were not reaping the benefits we had envisaged.

A similar story was true of the Library's significant collection of electronic journals and bibliographic databases. Library staff worked with academic colleagues to identify and then purchase collections and resources which support both research and teaching. Nevertheless the level of use of these resources by undergraduate students did not meet our expectations.

Information literacy materials provided by the Library suffered a similar experience. With the availability of online databases and electronic journals to the postgraduate courses for students working online, library staff (subject specialists) had produced comprehensive subject-based guides to resources and literature searching. For the first few years these were produced in print, which meant that they were difficult to keep up to date with inevitable changes in services and interfaces. There was then a gradual shift to online versions with their increased versatility. A debate began (which still rages today) about the merits of subject specific versus generic information skills. Developing subject specific guides in every area and keeping these up to date is extremely labour-intensive. Additionally, because these guides had been adapted from print versions, they generally contained a lot of lists of resources in the subject area – information which could be more effectively presented and maintained as part of the Library website.

A generic online information skills tutorial, SAFARI (Skills in Accessing Finding and Reviewing Information), was developed by a team of library staff with academic colleagues acting as critical readers. This resource, with its interactive online activities and built in portfolio functionality, was at the time in the forefront of e-learning development at the university. The idea was that any course could use it and link to it at appropriate points. Over the years SAFARI has proved extremely popular both in the University and externally – with many universities developing similar resources and many others linking to SAFARI, which is freely available on the web. Despite the availability of SAFARI and the online subject specific guides, take-up by students was less than expected. An investigation revealed that the majority of courses were offering these to students as optional extras – not a core part of the learning. This was despite the fact that the Library had developed an information literacy strategy in 2003 and disseminated this widely with support from senior management. Clearly a new approach was required.

Phase 2 – Integration and mainstreaming

Integration

After five years of activity and not inconsiderable investment the Library had, to a significant extent, minimized the impact of distance and given Alice access to a library service, to an impressive online collection, and to opportunities to develop and practise her information literacy skills. But this wasn't enough. For all the historical and cultural reasons described, Alice and her equally busy fellow students weren't using the library because, however wonderful, it required optional extra work and they just didn't have time. So the next phase of our journey was all about *integration*.

The library staff who support course development have concentrated their energies and resources since 2003 to try and achieve this. The strategy has been to endeavour to ensure that library resources, ROUTES websites and information literacy materials are integrated into the core learning activities of courses. We define integration as either use for core learning activities in the course or, better still, for assessment purposes. This has been (and continues to be) a tremendous challenge, involving intensive work with all new course teams. Interestingly the integration of online library resources and materials into the curriculum has become a cornerstone in the University's move to e-learning and this has led to one of the Library's performance measures being the number or percentage of courses with this kind of integration. Since the beginning of 2003 the Library has provided a quarterly report to the Pro-Vice-Chancellor Learning and Teaching on the number of courses integrating e-resources and the number with specific information literacy activities. There has been considerable progress year on year, restricted mainly by the rate at which OU courses are renewed and replaced.

Information literacy

The work on information literacy has enabled the Library to extend its role and credibility in the University. Working with colleagues in the University's Centre for Outcomes Based Education a framework (OU Centre for Outcomes Based

Education, 2005) was developed to help faculties identify appropriate information literacy learning outcomes at each level of study, to ensure consistency and progression. This is being adopted gradually within faculties, but many students will not experience this kind of continuity as the older courses are less likely to have information literacy embedded. Where the skills are integrated, there are different approaches to delivery: in some courses, students are referred to carry out learning activities in the SAFARI tutorial, in others new activities are authored by librarians in conjunction with their academic colleagues, although the latter approach is less attractive in a changing financial climate.

OU Alice at last found herself taking a course where she was helped to develop some information skills. One of her assignments involved learning how to carry out a simple literature search and how to organize what she found into a bibliography (something students in conventional universities have been doing since the 1970s). She thought this would be very useful in the next course she took but unfortunately this was not the case. Sadly her next course was an older one and required no use of the Library. Her friend, Mary, was enrolled on the social work programme and her experience was entirely different. The information skills element built gradually through each year of the programme, so that by the end of the third year she was confident to find, evaluate and organize information on any topic independently (Open University Library, 2007).

The integration of information literacy activities and the use of library resources has greatly increased the demand for staff development. Once these kinds of activities are required and assessed within a course, the tutors who are responsible for supporting the students and marking their assignments need to be confident and knowledgeable themselves. As the 8000 tutors (all part time) employed by the University are geographically dispersed, the provision of an effective staff development programme has been challenging. Library staff have always responded positively to requests to deliver training sessions (mainly at weekends) for tutors in the OU's 13 regional centres, but these are limited by budget and staffing capacity. Successful experiments have been carried out to identify different effective means for extending our reach. The first has been a three-year project to investigate the logistics of using sophisticated web conferencing software to deliver staff development to small groups of geographically scattered tutors. Sessions are advertised via the tutors' website and once sufficient numbers have signed up, a one- to two-hour session is provided. The software uses voice, text, whiteboard, voting and application sharing and has proved generally popular with participants. This project has enabled library staff to build up considerable expertise in the effective pedagogical use of this technology, and this has informed a strand of the University's virtual learning environment (VLE) development.

A related project has taken a 'people-based' approach, which involves training a group of tutors in each region to become trainers, hence embedding skills in the community and building capacity. The 'trainers' are given intensive training and support, as well as a portfolio of learning and teaching materials. This cascade model has so far proved to be very powerful in that the tutors have a far better understanding of the needs of their community and are able to develop and tailor their presentations accordingly. It also offers the potential to continue to cascade skills after the duration of the project. The Library's role would then be to keep materials up to date and to offer occasional refresher sessions.

Personalization and the virtual learning environment

While the Open University has possessed most of the elements of a VLE for many years (course websites, online conferencing and so on) the implementation of a fully integrated VLE is relatively recent. The decision to adopt Moodle was taken in 2005/6 and a two-year multi-strand development and implementation programme is reaching completion in 2008. The advent of the VLE has been eagerly anticipated by the Library. Only too aware of restrictions on students' time to engage with the resources offered by the Library, we decided in 2002 to pursue the idea of a personalized library, where students had all the resources relevant to their course in one convenient online space, and which could be customized to suit their individual needs and interests. A two-year internally funded project resulted in the development of 'MyOpenLibrary', a personalized library, using open source software (MyLibrary) developed in the United States at Notre Dame University. This was the first personalized library to be developed in the UK and one of the earliest personalization services at the OU. It was, however, only intended as a short term solution as it was expected that a VLE would provide this kind of functionality, would integrate the Library into students' learning and would relieve the Library of the task of maintaining a separate system. In the event, far from being a small and short term pilot, the MyOpenLibrary service has been extremely popular with faculties and students alike. The number of courses using the service has grown exponentially since its inception but sadly, as with other library services, not all courses use MyOpenLibrary and students may lose their MyOpenLibrary facility when they move from one course to another.

There has been a lot of discussion in the library community about the relationship between libraries and VLEs. While on the one hand the VLE may be an opportunity to introduce library resources more effectively into a course, on the other hand they create a 'walled garden', which may well deter the learner from engaging freely with the Library. Our concern was to ensure that the functionality of MyOpenLibrary enjoyed by so many students would be reproduced and improved within the VLE. Library integration is one of the main project strands of the VLE implementation, led by a member of the library staff. The first phase of the project involved the development of an RSS feeds tool, which delivers library links into Moodle course websites. The second phase is considerably more ambitious as we aim for an integration which would enable students to identify relevant resources from library or other collections, tag and annotate them and organize them in their personal portfolios to be published when required. We hope to take the work forward in the near future and are currently seeking a technical solution, which will eventually allow us to replace MyOpenLibrary.

Phase 3 – All about learning

If Phase 2 was all about integration and mainstreaming it is by no means complete. There are many legacy courses which still do not require students to use the Library or to develop skills in information handling. These will not change until the courses reach the ends of their lives (in the OU this can be anything from five to ten years). We do believe, however, that there is a significant change of emphasis and that this is having, and will increasingly have, a major impact on the role of the Library. There is a gradual realization by our colleagues in the organization that the Library's role is all about learning. Our expertise on information literacy has allowed us to carry out activities like the development of two successful short courses – Making Sense of Information in the Connected Age and more recently Beyond Google – as well as the development of an information management toolkit designed to support the University in rolling out a document management system.

These projects have demonstrated that library staff have skills and knowledge in learning and teaching which are considerably broader and more generic than the specific area of information literacy, although this remains the focus. The work with curriculum development is changing and evolving. Although we may still have to account for numbers of courses or students using library resources and numbers teaching information literacy, there is a shift to considering the impact and outcomes of this work. The impact of the sustained advocacy around information literacy should mean that eventually it becomes embedded in the course authoring process and will not require the same kind of input from library staff. The librarian then becomes a mainstream member of the course team, offering a range of expertise and knowledge and making suggestions about the creative use of resources for learning, rather than having to focus solely on a specific mission. This model is infinitely more sustainable.

The shift to resource-based learning

The University as a whole is reviewing the way it teaches and the way it develops courses, influenced only partially by the advent of the VLE. New pedagogic models for courses are emerging with greater emphasis on resource-based learning and use of personal portfolios. For these models the Library will play the central role in the student experience, which it has aspired to over the last ten years. Although this shift may be helped by economic considerations, as faculties begin to understand that it is cheaper to use materials already bought by the Library than to author from scratch or purchase rights from third parties, we would prefer to believe that we may have had a role in influencing this gradual shift.

How is the Library adapting to allow us to assume this altered role? From the beginning of the University's move to e-learning, the Library has assumed a change management role, legitimized at strategic level. This has been underlined by the Library having a central role in the development and implementation of both the VLE (library staff were seconded as project managers) and also a new system for digital asset management. Library staff have worked with colleagues in other units to develop services and resources to help encourage the creative use of technology for learning. Most notable is the DigiLab, a creative play space in the library building for course developers to experiment with technologies such as mobile devices and gaming. Library staff are having to undergo significant staff development themselves, particularly in the areas of pedagogy, educational technology and learning design. We have employed an educational technologist as an e-learning specialist for 18 months to help to develop and embed knowledge, confidence and skills in the team of learning and teaching librarians. As well as delivering an intensive staff development programme, she is working with them to develop templates and processes for authoring highly effective learning activities. Library staff are involved in e-learning groups, projects and developments throughout the University to an extent that would have been unthinkable ten years ago.

Where is Alice now? She is a few years older and still studying with the OU. Life is different though as, like so many of us, she now lives in the world wide web, using it for her job, hobbies and, whenever she can, OU studies. Her current course is delivered through the VLE and it includes a number of journal articles provided by the Library. As these are delivered into her course website in the VLE she isn't really aware that they are from the Library, which has become increasingly invisible. She is, however, able to use her information skills to find valuable material in the Library when it comes to her final project. Alice's daughter, Amy, has just joined the OU. Amy is a NetGen student. Alice has told her about the wonderful online library, but Amy insists that she won't need it as she is pretty confident she will be able to find anything she needs using Google and Wikipedia. If she can't, she guesses she will just have to MSN some friends.

The next challenge

Is this the next challenge for libraries such as ours? A recent study (CIBER, 2008) has suggested that this group of 'Google learners may feel pretty confident that they can find information on any topic, but in fact their information skills are lacking in a way which will put them at a disadvantage in their academic studies'. How are we to help them? We suspect that the tools and materials we have so proudly developed over the last few years are not the answer, as they are not written in a way that will prove attractive to this particular generation who do not recognize a need for learning these skills in the first place, nor are they presented in a manner likely to satisfy a generation used to visual and experiential approaches. Like many libraries, we at the OU Library are experimenting with providing Web 2.0 services – inviting users to comment on and interact with content and services, building communities around the Library. To what extent will this appeal to Amy and her friends? What, if anything, will entice them to come and live in a space created by the Library, when they have plenty of spaces of their own, where they are comfortable and feel in control?

There is an interesting dilemma for libraries and their future. Should we focus our efforts on strengthening the brand, proudly promoting our services, launching every new collection with a fanfare? Or will we be more effective if we allow our separate identities to fade as we quietly and strategically insinuate our resources and services into all those places where they have the most impact on the would-be recipients? So, just as the Library has become largely invisible but nevertheless a crucial presence, inside the VLE, so will its tentacles appear in Amy's Facebook toolbox and in her online portfolio, where a clever little application helps her to organize her references and the material she has generated herself for her assignments? And perhaps, because of all the investment we have made in staff development and change management, information literacy will be so much part of the academics' thinking that we don't need to worry any more – it will be an integral strand in every area of the curriculum.

The invisible library scenario is certainly attractive in the context of adapting to changing user needs, but potentially problematic in the context of defending our library budgets and status within our corporate environment. We would have to find new ways of evaluating and articulating the impact of our services and this would be difficult. What is the alternative? Perhaps a fiercely assertive Library with increasingly sophisticated and innovative services and exciting new collections can reinvent itself, out-Google Google and win over Amy and her gang to think the Library itself is an exciting place to be?

Ten years ago the challenge was to overcome physical distance to best support and serve our distance learners. It would appear that the future challenge is to overcome virtual distance in order to understand the different virtual spaces in which our students now live, study and work and where best to position our services for Alice and for Amy.

References

Bremner, A. (2000) Open University Students and Libraries Project 1999, *Library and Information Research News*, **24** (76), Spring, 26–38.

CIBER (2008) Information Behaviour of the Researcher of the Future, University College London, www.jisc.ac.uk/media/documents/programmes/reppres/gg_final_keynote_11012008.pdf.

Coles, B. M. (1994) *The Loneliness of the Long Distance Learner*, paper presented to the Medical Health and Welfare Group of the Library Association, Annual Conference, Manchester, UK.

Dearing, R. (1997) *Higher Education in the Learning Society*, The National Committee of Inquiry into Higher Education, NCIHE Publications, www.leeds.ac.uk/educol/ncihe.

Joint Funding Councils' Libraries Review Group (1993) *Report* (Follett Report), Higher Education Funding Council for England.

Kirkwood, A. (2006) Going Outside the Box: skills development, cultural change and the use of on-line resources, *Computers and Education*, **47** (3), 316–31.

Needham, G., O'Sullivan, U. and Ramsden, A. (2000) ROUTES: a virtual collection of resources for Open University teachers and students. In Brophy, P., Fisher, S. and Clarke, Z.(eds), *Libraries Without Walls 3: the delivery of library services to distant users*, Library Association Publishing, 115–20.

Open University Centre for Outcomes Based Education (2005) *Undergraduate Levels Framework*, Open University.

Open University Library (1999–2004) *Learner Support Strategy*, Open University.

Open University Library (2001) *Information Literacy Strategy*, Open University.

Open University Library (2007) *Integrating Information Literacy into the Curriculum*, Practical Pedagogy series, Open University.

Unwin, L., Stephens, K. and Bolton, N. (1998) *The Role of the Library in Distance Learning: a study of postgraduate students, course providers and librarians in the UK*, Bowker Saur.

4

Putting the 'e' into libraries and learning: study, pedagogy, content and services in the digital age

DAVID BAKER

Introduction

This chapter focuses on the history, development, application and future of information and communications technology (ICT) in the field of learning and teaching with special reference to UK higher education (UKHE). The work of the Joint Information Systems Committee (JISC) in improving the take-up of ICT is highlighted.

Background

Just over ten years ago, a report was produced by the Higher Education Funding Council for England (HEFCE, 1997) that looked at the reasons behind the low take-up of ICT in learning and teaching activities within UK HE. Although technology was already pervasive in higher education institutions (HEIs), its usage at that time had been primarily for administrative or 'housekeeping' activities rather than the delivery of teaching or the support of learning. This was despite the fact that there had been a significant investment in the development of ICT-based teaching and learning aids (courseware, computer-assisted or computer-based learning packages, websites, portals and gateways, virtual and managed learning environments – V/MLEs) notably through a series of national initiatives within the higher education (HE) community, and primarily – at the time – the Computers in Teaching Initiative (CTI), the Teaching and Learning Technology Programme (TLTP) and a whole series of projects commissioned and funded by the JISC. The Dearing Report on the future of higher education published that same year (National Committee of Enquiry into Higher Education, 1997) stressed the significant knowledge gap in HEIs with regard to ICT, including at the most senior levels, where a 'deep understanding' of the key issues seemed to be sadly lacking.

In the 1990s, ICT applications were seen as a way of gaining productivity and maintaining quality at a time when there were fewer members of teaching staff because of economic cutback, though the *Summative Evaluation of Phase 3 of the eLib Initiative* (Whitelaw and Joy, 2001) subsequently concluded that there had been no real cost savings as a result of the Follett Report (Joint Funding Councils' Libraries Review Group, 1993); rather there had been both an increased functionality and an increasing empowerment of the user, at least in terms of learning and teaching. Follett also recognized that it was important not to graft new technologies onto old (as has happened in previous ICT-based learning and teaching programmes and projects to some degree) but to look afresh at the issues and the appropriate applications as a whole. The JISC's *Guidelines on the Production of an Information Strategy* (1995) suggested such an approach. The *Guidelines* have since been acted on in a large number of HEIs, not least because the dominant stakeholder (in this case the Funding Councils) required that this be the case. However, there continued to be a seeming lack of payback on the significant investment in ICT-based learning and teaching, despite the many initiatives. In retrospect, it was felt that there was not enough linkup or co-ordination with learning and teaching initiatives, and insufficient engagement with end users; the conclusion was that projects and initiatives must always keep in mind how work will be applicable in the 'classroom' (Whitelaw and Joy, 2000). By the end of the 20th century, much still needed to be achieved in terms of culture change within higher education:

> We can create new environments offering richer access and more meaningful and relevant resources, but how can we stimulate and engender engagement with them? This is not just an issue for the JISC but for all members of the higher and further education (FE) community (and beyond) who aim to maximize the benefits of access to digital resources.   (JISC, 2002a)

'Attitudes and behaviours among professional librarians, academics and students continue in many instances to be a barrier to the effective embedding of [digital] products and services' (ESYS Consulting, 2001). The INSPIRAL bibliography (http://inspiral.cdlr.strath.ac.uk/resources/bibliography.html) and the ANGEL (www.ariadne.ac.uk/issue30/angel/) project's initial formative evaluation provided a clear insight into the issues surrounding the implementation of digital learning environments (Harris, 2001). Transatlantic delivery brought its own significant change management issues, as discussed, for example, in the GATS report (Knight, 2002).

Recent trends and developments

Already, however, the seeds of change had been sown. The Follett Report of 1993 changed UK HE forever. Follett stimulated the development of an integrative model for scholarly communication within an increasingly distributed digital environment and related the need to develop new methods of learning and teaching delivery to the pressures of increased and more demanding markets and reduced financial resources. In the 1990s, UK HE alone spent some £60 million on research into new ways of provision and delivery, though for much of the decade, the emphasis was perhaps on content and services to support research rather than learning and teaching. Scholarly communication now spans everything from primary data through various versions to final product; the electronic journal article or fragments of articles (rather than the journal or the journal issue itself) is the primary unit of publishing or usage in many areas. The move to date has been principally to e-journals, with students now making extensive use of them, preferring the ease of use and additional facilities not available with hard-copy (*THES*, 2005), though e-books – heralded since the 1990s as a major breakthrough in textbook provision and other mass market areas (at least in non-fiction publishing) – are at last beginning to be seen as a real alternative to, if not replacement for, traditional print-on-paper publication (Higher Education Consultancy Group, 2006). Mass digitization programmes such as those managed and largely funded by the JISC have helped to create a rich critical mass of valuable material.

Libraries have been significantly transformed by the advent of the internet and the ability to provide resources to people who may never visit a physical building, but use resources intensively in their own homes or offices. At the University of Warwick, for example, only 2.7% of the library footfall is academic staff (Warwick University Librarian, private communication); yet there is no question of that institution's high rating in research and scholarly activity. Ultimately the vast majority of libraries will be digital and not linked to a physical space or a single organization. Where there is a physical library, it will be significantly different in design, layout and usage from the basic 20th-century model (www.jisc.ac.uk/whatwedo/programmes/elearning_sfc/sfc_blended.aspx).

The first decade of the 21st century, then, has seen a significant increase in the take-up of ICT in teaching and learning throughout UK HE, though it could still be written in 2007 that the further education sector was lagging behind in terms of the integration of e-resources and e-learning into normal practices (www.jisc.ac.uk/publications/publications/pub_valueofjisc2007.aspx). Much has been achieved thanks to the JISC. One of the Committee's strategic aims is to help UK HE to 'provide positive, personalized user learning experiences and aid student progression', the argument being that 'central to successful education and research sectors and therefore to a successful UK economy is an ICT infrastructure of the highest quality as well as innovative programmes to exploit the full potential of technology' (www.jisc.ac.uk/publications/publications/pub_ valueofjisc2007.aspx), for example by developing learning environments and facilitating communication through key projects arising initially from the e-Library Programme and subsequent projects (www.ukoln.ac.uk/services/elib/papers/ other/summative-phase-3/elib-eval-summary.pdf).

The resulting developments in the information environment such as improved accessibility, interoperability and open access to educational materials, including institutional repositories, have made it much easier and more attractive for individuals and organizations to be involved in ICT developments in teaching and learning and elsewhere. The JISC *Value for Money Report* (Tardivel, 2006), for instance, revealed that development calls were regularly oversubscribed, showing a sector 'that wants to be involved', not least because of institutional and individual high-quality access to a wide range of resources through the Joint Academic Network (JANET), an internationally renowned infrastructure that is technically sound, reliable, trustworthy, available and pervasive (with access from schools, as well as HEIs), performs well and has a low cost per connection, being three times cheaper than a commercial provider. Although the 2006 report criticized JANET's lower level of innovation compared with similar services elsewhere in Europe, it also noted that the ATHENS (Access management) system that has underpinned it in recent years is the largest of its kind, facilitating world class digital library access, to, among other things, over 15 million accesses to some 60 e-resources through JISC alone in 2004/5, many of which were either free or heavily subsidized within the UK HE community.

As well as providing significant savings, the national-level approach provided for by JISC has ensured that 'the use of e-resources is now embedded in the work process, the resources are well used and there is evidence that e-resources are accessed more frequently than their paper equivalents' (Tardivel, 2006). This has improved study and teaching by allowing greater use of primary materials and literature searches, allowing people to keep up to date with new research, and providing cheaper access to resources. JISC regional support centres and advisory services provide advice on the integration of ICT and e-learning into education and business activities, aiming to 'remove some of the barriers to the application of ICT in teaching and learning'. It should be noted, however, that the increasing use of e-resources has made it easier to commit plagiarism. For some, this has been a negative aspect of ICT applications, especially because one of the effects of increased plagiarism is the loss of reputation for UK HE and the idea of a product of lower quality internationally.

But, on the whole, e-learning is now generally recognized as important for the general wellbeing of UK HE, as learning and teaching develops and changes to take account both of the technology push of new systems, tools and services, and the market pull of student choice and demand, especially as we have entered the era of the Google generation. Thanks to the new 'dominant design' of simple, pervasive, popular end-user services like Google, the emphasis is moving from provider to consumer on the internet in a number of ways: 'users need to feel in control, and the trend is towards personalisation and customisation; but personalisation doesn't mean being or working alone, and facilitation of group work and social interaction – whether physically or virtually – is always likely to be a prerequisite of good information systems design as well' (Baker, 2006).

Much emphasis is now being placed on flexible or blended learning as the student body becomes increasingly diversified (for example more part-time students and more work-based learning activity) and internationalized, with education being only one part of people's lives, but a part that needs to be fully integrated with all other aspects (JISC, 2002b). The idea of *distributed* learning has also become increasingly fashionable, with distance learning being only one subset of such an approach. A range of flexible and customized learning opportunities are crucial: change is required because more students, many of them less 'traditional' learners, want tailored learning and teaching methods and institutions need assessment methods that fit into those new types of learning and teaching (Stiles, 2008).

BlendEd, a JISC-funded project

BlendEd (www.jisc.ac.uk/whatwedo/programmes/elearning_sfc/sfc_blended. aspx) aimed to tackle such issues as high assessment loadings, falling demand for full-time courses, the desire for integration of continuous professional development with mainstream learning and the improvement of retention and attainment levels. The same core requirements emerged: the need for staff development and support, quality assurance mechanisms and integration into the wider learning environment. An additional problem was the delivery of the blended learning, with the need to update infrastructure – physical and technological – being a crucial element in the success of any non-traditional learning and teaching.

The vision, then, is learner-centred, driven as it is by the needs of the sector and learners and enabled by technology. ICT can complement a wide range of modes of delivery, though beginning students' expectations of university are still remarkably straightforward when it comes to teaching in HE, and emphasize face-to-face contact (Ipsos MORI, 2007). It is therefore crucial – as the BlendEd project found – to be clear what the purpose of new forms of learning actually is, and what is expected of the student who will be using the technology, supported by definitions of how the technology is meant to improve the learner's experience.

Virtual and managed learning environments

The last ten years have seen the development and implementation of the concept of virtual and then managed learning environments. The virtual learning environment (VLE) focused on learning management, the course content and the tools; the managed learning environment (MLE) was about the wider facilitation of the learning experience through the integration of a wide range of activities such as enrolment, record-keeping and publication of content (Stiles, 2008). This integration has been taken further as library services have also been included, all courses, whether or not e-based, requiring learning resources of some kind (for example, the 4i project www.jisc.ac.uk/whatwedo/programmes/programme_divle/project_4i.aspx). But e-use of the library requires a contextual view of the service dependent on the courses on which a student is enrolled, and on the ability to link individuals in an institutional VLE not just to the personalized resources that they need but also to the additional support and service provision in those areas that, for example, the library may provide. This is but one way in which the pressure to produce accurate student data is increased, in this case accurate and integrated user profiling being paramount. But then, so too is the active involvement of academic staff, both with those who create and supply the content and those who use it. Communications between learners and teachers can be much enhanced through ICT, but the human element of communication, whatever the method, is still of paramount importance. Nor should it be forgotten that, at institutional level, the development of a VLE – and especially an MLE – will most likely change many aspects of interaction with students.

Exchange for Learning

Exchange for Learning was the title of a JISC-funded programme that ran from 2002 to 2005 (www.jisc.ac.uk/whatwedo/programmes/programme_x4l.aspx) and aimed to ensure that the exchange of learning materials and knowledge took place effectively. A number of issues were identified as being barriers to the development of e-learning. These included the sharing of content between VLEs and other platforms, including questions of copyright and open access, and, just as crucial, interoperability; the need to be able to guarantee quality; and the need for expertise in repurposing content, especially at a local (institutional) level.

One of the key challenges of e-learning in recent years has been the wish to create quality content 'once only', but then to facilitate its being customized and repurposed, thereby making it useful and accessible to larger numbers of people, increasing efficiency and reducing duplication of effort. As so often with ICT applications, culture change is at the heart of the hoped-for transformation process, for example the willingness of lecturers to share materials: 'there would need to be a cultural shift where sharing is seen as [a] positive thing [and] there were benefits associated with sharing, and safeguards to prevent misuse' (Baldwin, 2004). But the materials themselves need to be of the requisite quality and deemed to be valuable by learner and teacher alike. There is still also the issue of the extent to which the material needs to be repurposed and the level of adaptation that teachers can be expected to do. Intellectual property rights issues also take time to resolve, though the sector is becoming more experienced at identifying the need to deal with it, and knowing where to go for advice, but more support is still required (www.jisclegal.ac.uk/ipr/IntellectualPropertyLinks.htm).

All this potentially creates an overhead for the institution, which will need to ensure that teachers are trained to best effect not only to repurpose material but also to minimize the extent to which repurposing is required anyway. The more material is repurposed, the greater the chance that it cannot easily be transferred between groups of users or institutions; repurposing may be in a very specific manner, meaning that anyone else wishing to use the content will have to undertake further repurposing (or is it de-purposing?) before being able to use the material in a suitable fashion. Re-using is therefore as important a consideration as repurposing. In this context, it should be noted that teacher workloads are not necessarily going to be reduced, merely changed in nature. In some areas to date, experience has shown that it has been difficult to find existing content – time has to be spent either locating it or, if necessary, actually creating it.

Reference was made earlier in this chapter to the need for a holistic approach. The creation, re-creation, re-purposing and use of e-content is almost inevitably focused at the level of the individual teacher and, indeed, the individual learner. This very localized approach has to be moderated by the institution if the curriculum is not to have a disjointed feel to it, but rather provides a true learning experience that both makes sense and matches the learning outcomes expected from the courses. The emphasis, then, has been on the development and implementation of *institutional* strategies, as encouraged by JISC and other agencies since the 1990s. Most recently, this approach has manifested itself in the creation of central or institutional repositories, which may or may not be specific to one institution; indeed, even some larger HEIs have joined together to create a shared repository (www.jisc.ac.uk/programme_rep_pres.aspx) while the JORUM initiative (www.jorum.ac.uk/) has provided the basis for a major central resource. A good central repository will be easily searchable, full of quality content across a range of areas, contain information about the relevant copyright issues and be capable of linking to other repositories.

The e-portfolio

One development that has supported the greater penetration of ICT in learning and teaching in UK HE has been the e-portfolio. Given the transfer of emphasis from teacher to learner, the e-portfolio is a way of helping the student to plan their learning, understand what and how they are learning more fully, monitor and review their strengths and weaknesses as learners, and identify a wider range of learning and development opportunities. This will only be the case, of course, where the e-portfolio process is fully integrated into core learning activity. The hope also with the e-portfolio is that it will integrate the student into the institution and prepare them not only for life after study, but also for continuing study and professional development. The idea of a lifelong portfolio is an attractive one, though it requires significant interoperability and the potential for the learner to 'take' the portfolio with them. Teachers and the institution are also meant to be helped by the use of e-portfolios by developing learners who are more independent (and therefore need less support) and have wider academic skills that can more easily be demonstrated, including for assessment purposes. There is perhaps an added attractiveness for the institution of e-portfolios with the increased emphasis on the acquisition of skills, and employability, with the approach providing the potential for better links between academic activity and career guidance. Nor should it be forgotten that the use of technology can provide a useful back-up to traditional learning, especially where there are issues of access to, for example, the standard lecture, with e-sources being useful as a way of catching up if required.

The use of e-portfolios has been tested in projects such as ISLE (Individualized Support for Learning through E-portfolios; www.jisc.ac.uk/whatwedo/programmes/elearning_sfc/sfc_isle.aspx). ISLE aimed 'to use e-portfolios to help develop a common practice of PDP both among staff and students', and proved that the pedagogical model drives the e-portfolio tool rather than the other way round. In other words, e-learning (of whatever kind) has to be underpinned by strategic thinking. The project seemed to be particularly successful at facilitating the learning process well through encouraging questioning and reflection by the learner and the better ordering of information and experiences, but it proved hard to improve the underperformance of learners, though this might have been the result of short timescales rather than any problems with the approach itself.

Physical space

As noted earlier, the internet has had a profound effect on space used for learning and teaching, and traditional library space in particular. Much thinking has gone into (re-) designing physical space in recent years in order to ensure that there is a new integration with ICT and a best fit with the longer-term strategic implications of the new modes of learning and teaching described here. Again, a holistic approach is required as the design of our learning spaces should become a physical representation of the institution's vision and strategy for learning – responsive, inclusive and supportive of attainment by all (www.jisc.ac.uk/whatwedo/programmes/elearning_innovation/eli_learningspaces.aspx).

It is interesting to note how the new requirements for physical space point to, and sum up, the new virtual learning and teaching environments now being developed. There is a need for space to be flexible and reconfigurable, so that it can be used for different purposes as needs change and landscape develops; it must also be multi-functional to take into account the variety of types of learning being undertaken. Space management techniques have to respond to the challenge of embedding technologies while balancing their use against other considerations of space, for example noise levels and quiet learning, providing space of different types to support the different aspects of learning 24/7, in an integration of the real and the virtual that puts the learning centre at the hub of the academic and the social life of the HEI through bold, creative and enterprising approaches.

The transformation of learning and teaching

How can learning, teaching and assessment practices be changed through ICT? The TESEP (Transforming and Enhancing the Student Experience through Pedagogy) project (www.jisc.ac.uk/whatwedo/programmes/elearning_sfc/sfc_tsep.aspx) has suggested that the key is transformation: not just a move from paper systems and old technologies to new ones but using the same approaches and practices. There is, of course, the suspicion that many of the ICT applications that have been regularly in use in HE and FE to date are really only old forms of teaching delivered electronically. If this is happening, can it really be said that ICT has helped to transform and develop teaching and learning, or is it just an alternative way of delivering the same aspects? (Stiles, 2008).

TESEP argues that it is the pedagogy that has to drive the strategy, enabled through ICT, and underpinned by a holistic approach that results in active learners with a focus on peer learning, personalized learning tasks and technology as enabler in a way that engages students in active and self-directed learning at the earliest possible opportunity, as at induction or even before they arrive to start their university courses. This is then reinforced by the use of technology to aid formative assessment, by use of voting pads, e-assessment software, simulations and inbuilt responses to online surveys and quizzes, and the engagement with peers and access to materials, with an encouragement also to develop tools such as blogs and wikis, thus helping peer engagement. Moreover, linking institutional VLEs to the new social software tools found in Web 2.0 applications, and making these accessible via various tools such as personal digital assistants (PDAs) and mobiles (not just computers) are seen as ways of making ICT in learning and teaching both pervasive and ubiquitous. This approach encourages the development of user created content and the ability to find content created by others by developing and sharing material created, required and accessed by a group. Crucial to success is the provision of learning support and staff development that facilitates and encourages teachers in the use of technologies and enables them to achieve the best fit between the technologies and the various, and most appropriate, styles of teaching and learning. Above all, though, learning technology must support and underpin quality enhancement if it is to be truly successful and central (Stiles, 2008).

The approaches described in TESEP fit well with the results of research into what the end users think. *In Their Own words: exploring the learner's perspective on e-learning* (JISC, 2007) has produced some 'striking insights into the way 21st-century digital learners select and use technologies for learning, revealing some important implications for institutional IT provision, academic practice and learning support'. Technology is not seen as a separate activity – instead, it is (or should be) totally integrated into normal learning practices, not least because communication among learners, teachers and more generally is increasingly taking place using ICT in a whole range of ways that cannot – and should not – be controlled. All forms of ICT-based communication should be used in learning; perhaps it is almost a case of 'if you can't beat them, join them' when it comes to the provision of ICT-based learning and teaching systems, content and services.

Again, the emphasis is on personalization and individual control, with the end user having a feeling of being in charge of the learning environment, able to select materials of relevance and importance. But the effective judgement of what is relevant and important can be a challenge. For the individual, it may often be linked to their expectations of technology, which will have been shaped through previous experiences of technology more broadly; there may be generational issues here, with younger students perhaps having more demands, especially of fast-moving ICT. This leads to the issue of ICT competence among staff and students. In the case of the latter, *In Their Own Words* was 'concerned by the level of support for students undertaking assignments which depend on the use of software, since those who are technically more competent may be able to exploit the software to enhance their performance, while those who lack the necessary skills can be disadvantaged'. This requires that everyone has the skills to exploit digital sources, it not being fair to 'create a situation where ignorance of technology, rather than ignorance of the subject, is the difference between those who get good marks and those who don't'. *In Their Own Words* also noted an increasing 'divide' between the needs, expectations and wishes of the learners and the expectations of the teachers, who were more 'traditional' and perhaps not engaged with e-learning in the same way. As noted earlier, staff development programmes continue to be crucial in helping teachers to integrate ICT into their work and, more broadly, to help explore the changing role of the teacher. Nor should cultural differences be overlooked. International students – and staff – for example, may have different cultural attitudes towards learning, and also towards technology, which might cause some difficulties when providing ICT-based systems and services.

For both students and staff, a major issue is the ease of access to, and availability of, material on the internet. Although there is a general expectation of seamless availability, there is also a widespread temptation to use the easiest rather than the pedagogically soundest sources. The phenomenon of 'satisficing' is already well known and understood, not least thanks to work undertaken by Peter Brophy (Brophy, et al., 2004; Griffiths and Brophy, 2005; Griffiths, Johnson and Hartley,

2007). Increased time pressures on learners – and teachers – do not help, with a perceived reduction in reflective and critical thinking pushing the drive to package content and information in bite-sized chunks or diverse formats, with less and less time or requirement to focus on the meaning behind what is accessed.

Again, the emphasis is placed on integration as a way of redressing the balance, in this case developing ways in which e-learning can promote critical reflection, for example the development of e-portfolios and forms of assessment that include evaluating the worth and validity of online sources. But any system is only as good as its weakest link, and one of the problems found to date is the lagging behind of administrative systems, which are not always as fast as students would like them to be: instant access in other areas raises expectations of real-time updates to information and administrative material that does not necessarily materialize in HEIs. This has been a long-standing problem, with many universities and colleges finding that they do not always have sufficient expertise to remedy the issues (Whitelaw and Joy, 2001).

Future technology take-up in teaching and learning: taking the 'e' out again

There have been significant developments in ICT-based learning and teaching since the early 1990s. The pressures brought about by dwindling resources and increased student numbers consequent upon the development of a mass higher education system meant that technology applications were seen as a way of improving efficiency, maintaining quality and, perhaps, preserving a degree of personalization that would otherwise have gone with the demise of the old, élite systems. JISC (2002b) has summed up the key ways in which ICT has to be applied to learning and teaching if it is to work to best effect. The learner (not finances!) must be at the centre, and learning tools need to be useful and innovative in order to create the essential active and interactive learning community that is able to enjoy a joined-up learning experience across all systems involved. This will only really be achieved if there is a robust underlying strategy for moving towards ICT-based learning; that strategy has to be translatable into practical application, otherwise the potential will never be fully or properly realized: 'I'm afraid that generating masses of electronic content, whilst potentially useful if you do have a strategy, is not a substitute for a planned approach aimed at meeting institutional goals.' That planned approach has to be focused both on pedagogy generally and the development of learners and teachers in particular. JISC (2002b) concludes that there must be engagement, not just interaction, and outcomes, not just content; that peer collaboration is more important than electronic discussion; and that ICT should add value to the learning experience rather than simply be used for its own sake.

The work continues, for example through the JISC's e-Learning Programme (www.jisc.ac.uk/elcapital.html, www.jisc.ac.uk/elearning_pedagogy.html, www.jisc.ac.uk/elp_designlearn.html). The Programme recognizes that learners have a different perspective from their tutors on the technologies available to them, and their use in learning situations. Learners' perspectives are likely to be influenced by their expectations, motivations, prior experiences and attitudes towards technology and learning. In addition, learners are a diverse group living complex lives with different priorities, preferences and approaches to learning and different requirements for support. Their relationships to technology are constantly changing. They make use of technologies – and learning opportunities – they encounter in their daily lives as well as those offered to them by institutions.

To date learners have been under-represented in e-learning research (Smith, et al., 2005), but the e-Learning Programme has sought to address this gap (www.jisc.ac.uk/elp_learneroutcomes.html, www.heacademy.ac.uk/4884.htm). The first phase of studies attempted to determine factors that enable students to be effective in learning with technology. The studies to date have suggested that elements of effectiveness might include how learners cope with the emotional quality of the experience of learning with technology, fit learning around their life, operate in online social networks and communities and conceive of and understand the role of technology in learning. However, these studies offered only a snapshot of each learner's experience. It has been recommended that follow-up studies should look at a longer period in the life of a learner, in order to understand how learners' perceptions of technology and learning change through key experiences such as the transition to higher education, or the introduction of new learning environments and technologies. Learning for our constituents in post-16 education increasingly takes place within a context of designed learning environments, managed assessment and institutional technology agendas. It is not yet clear what impact these contextual factors have on the student experience, although it has been suggested that both courses and institutions may need to change radically if they are to support truly transformative learning experiences. It is important that any such developments evolve through an iterative process, which makes use of student feedback and involves learners in its design.

Much is still to be achieved, but much has been achieved in a relatively short space of time. The effort to date has clearly been sector wide, with a strong central facilitation by JISC in the wake of the e-Library Programme and similar initiatives having begun a long-term transformation process that has not only responded to major economic, societal and technological pulls, but also actually pushed UK HE to the forefront of e-learning to the point where the 'e-' prefix is redundant in a way unimaginable even ten years ago.

References

Baker, D. (2006) Digital Library Futures: a UK HE and FE perspective, *Interlending and Document Supply*, **34** (1), 4–8.

Baldwin, C. (2004) *X4L Review Final Report*, www.jisc.ac.uk/media/documents/programmes/x4l/x4lreview.doc.

Brophy, P., Fisher, S., Jones, C. R. and Markland, M. (2004) *EDNER: final report*, CERLIM (Centre for Research in Library and Information Management). [Online]

ESYS Consulting (2001) *Summative Evaluation of Phase 3 of the e-Lib Initiative: final report summary*, ESYS Consulting.

Griffiths, J. R. and Brophy, P. (2005) Student Searching Behaviour and the Web: use of academic resources and Google, *Library Trends*, (Spring), 539–54.

Griffiths, J. R., Johnson, F. and Hartley, R. J. (2007) User Satisfaction as a Measure of System Performance, *Journal of Librarianship and Information Science*, **39** (3), 142–52.

Harris, N. (2001) Managed Learning? *Ariadne*, www.ariadne.ac.uk/issue30/angel/.

Higher Education Consultancy Group (2006) *A Feasibility Study on the Acquisition of e-Books by HE Libraries and the Role of JISC: final report*, unpublished.

Higher Education Funding Council For England (1997) *Information Technology Assisted Teaching and Learning in Higher Education*, HEFCE.

Ipsos MORI (2007) *Student Expectations Study*, www.jisc.ac.uk/publications/publications/studentexpectations.

Joint Funding Councils' Libraries Review Group (1993) *Report* (Follett Report), Higher Education Funding Council for England.

Joint Information Systems Committee (1995) *Guidelines on the Production of an Information Strategy*, JISC.

Joint Information Systems Committee (2002a) *Information Environment: development strategy, 2001–2005 (draft)*, JISC.

Joint Information Systems Committee (2002b) *Staying on Track, JISC Inform* (issue 1), www.jisc.ac.uk/publications/publications/pub_inform1.aspx.

Joint Information Systems Committee (2007) *In Their Own Words: exploring the learner's perspective on e-learning,* www.jiscinfonet.ac.uk/publications/in-their-own-words/.

Knight, J. (2002) *Trade in Higher Education Services: the implications of GATS,* Observatory on Borderless Education.

National Committee of Enquiry into Higher Education (UK) (1997) *Higher Education in the Learning Society* (Dearing Report), TSO.

Smith, H. J. et al. (2005) Interactive Whiteboards: boon or bandwagon? A critical review of the literature, *Journal of Computer Assisted Learning,* **21** (2), 91–101.

Stiles, M. (2008) *Effective Learning and the Virtual Learning Environment,* www.staffs.ac.uk/COSE/cose10/posnan.html.

Tardivel, J. (2006) *Value for Money Report,* www.jisc.ac.uk/media/documents/aboutus/aboutjisc/vfm210906.pdf.

Times Higher Education Supplement (2005) THES, 23 December 2005.

Whitelaw, A. and Joy, G. (2000) *Summative Evaluation of Phases 1 and 2 of the eLib Initiative: final report,* www.ukoln.ac.uk/services/elib/info-projects/phase-1-and-2-evaluation/elib-fr-v1-2.pdf.

Whitelaw, A. and Joy, G. (2001) *Summative Evaluation of Phase 3 of the eLib Initiative: final report summary,* www.ukoln.ac.uk/services/elib/papers/other/summative-phase-3/elib-eval-summary.pdf.

Theme 2
Widening access to information

5

Library services for visually impaired people: a UK perspective

JENNY CRAVEN

Introduction

As Head of the Library and Learning Resource Service (LLRS) during the 1990s at the University of Central Lancashire in the UK, Peter Brophy was involved in developing the delivery of services for students with disabilities offered within the LLRS through the Specialised Learning Resource Unit (SLRU). The work of the SLRU continues to offer a range of specialist services to provide students with disabilities the opportunity to access the same library resources as everyone else, the aim being to promote 'an accessible and inclusive university' (www.uclan.ac. uk/slru/mission.html). It is interesting to note that the SLRU was developed before existing disability legislation had come into force, thus showing a commitment to social inclusion driven by moral beliefs rather than legal requirements. This belief in the importance of social inclusion is evident throughout Peter Brophy's career, not least in the significant contribution he has made to improving library and information services for people with visual impairments.

As Director of the Centre for Research in Library and Information Management (CERLIM), research projects he has led such as Resources for Visually Impaired Users of the Electronic Library (REVIEL) (www.cerlim.ac.uk/projects/reviel/index.php), Non-Visual Access to the Digital Library (NoVA) (www.cerlim.ac.uk/projects/nova/index.php) and more recently the European Internet Accessibility Observatory (EIAO) (www.cerlim.ac.uk/ projects/eiao/index.php) are good examples of how research has fed into good practice and advice in this field.

This chapter will start with a brief look at the general provision of library services for visually impaired people, primarily in the UK but with reference to other countries and then to a more global perspective, and then look more specifically at developments in the provision of electronic access to the digital library, with a particular focus on access by visually impaired people.

A note on terminology: the term 'visually impaired person' is used in this chapter to refer to someone with a serious sight problem. This could include total blindness, partial sight or low vision, as well as cognitive impairments such as dyslexia, which may result in a print impairment.

Mainstream libraries

At a basic level, mainstream library services for visually impaired people (whether via a public, higher education, college or community library) should include provision of help with searching the catalogue and retrieving items on the visually impaired person's behalf, provision of large print and audio materials, provision of library guides and help sheets in large print and on the library website as well as being prepared to consider the provision of other formats (such as audio or Braille). Library catalogues can be enhanced for visually impaired people by providing additional information such as which titles are provided in accessible formats, location and availability (see for example http://librarycatalogue. rnib.org.uk). Other services could include transcription, and providing personal readers and note-takers.

Library services should include a collection of reading aids and equipment to enable visually impaired people to access the library's print and media collections, catalogues and databases (Machell, 1996). Reading aids could include magnifying glasses or optical lenses; Fresnel lenses, which provide a low level of magnification over a wide area (such as a TV or computer screen); video magnifiers or closed circuit TV (CCTV) devices, which significantly enlarge text; computers with speech output (for example screen readers); electronic Braille bars; and scanners that read out printed material. These are often referred to as assistive, adaptive or accessibility aids, or enabling technology.

Standard PCs in the library can also be adjusted to make them more accessible to people with disabilities, for example by applying stickers with larger text to the keyboard or a larger text overlay to the keyboard. The mouse can be adjusted to provide larger pointers, coloured pointers, mouse trails that highlight the movement of the mouse, or a locator to give a visual indicator of the position of the mouse on the screen. Large monitors can replace standard computer screens, and on-screen adjustments to standard PCs can include enhancement of font size and style, screen resolution, size of the scroll bar, borders and icons, and colour schemes (for example to invert colours of text and background).

The library website should be designed according to accessibility guidelines, such as the World Wide Web Consortium (W3C) Web Content Accessibility Guidelines (WCAG) (www.w3.org/TR/WCAG10/). It should provide information about opening times, services offered and contact details. It should also offer accessible access to the catalogue, online journals, abstracts and contents pages, and provide online access to borrower details, renewal and reservation services. The provision of full text journal articles and the development of e-book provision can provide increased opportunities to access library services remotely. This will be further enhanced by the continued implementation of copyright legislation, which allows alternative formats designed for people with visual or other impairments to be produced from digital files.

Looking towards the future of mainstream library provision for visually impaired users, the Digital Accessible Information System (DAISY) is an important development in the provision of digital talking books and in improving library services to print-impaired people. DAISY is 'an international standard for digital talking books, which is now becoming a multimedia standard', providing a 'multimedia representation of a print publication' (Tank and Frederiksen, 2007) and offers improvements over analogue format through its accessible, feature-rich and navigable format.

Special libraries

Although library services for visually impaired people can be provided via mainstream libraries (for example through services offered by the LLRS as described above), they are often provided via specialist libraries such as those which are referred to as 'libraries for the blind'. The most common scenario is that there is one specialist library for the blind in each country (sometimes several specialist libraries), which provides books and materials in accessible formats, meeting the needs of different audiences (children, students and so on). Libraries for the blind:

- deliver services to a remote user group
- assist users with the selection of books and information
- provide support and a sense of community (Brazier, 2007, 866).

Governance and funding arrangements for these specialist libraries are hard to generalize because the model is different in each country. For example:

- In the UK and Canada libraries for the blind are run as charities or voluntary sector organizations. In the UK, the Royal National Institute of the Blind National Library Service (RNIB NLS) also gets funding from local government in the form of Talking Book subscriptions.
- In Asia and Africa libraries for the blind were established by missionaries, or grew out of rehabilitation agencies.
- In the USA the government took responsibility for training and educating blind people. Legislation requires the provision of equitable public library services with support from the National Library Service for the Blind and Physically Handicapped.
- In Sweden library services for the blind are guaranteed by legislation. The Talking Books and Braille Library (TPB) are a separate entity but are integrated into state-funded mainstream library services as part of the public library system.
- In South Africa the library for the blind is part of the national library service (Brazier, 2007, 865).

The situation in the UK is interesting because whereas equality of service provision is covered by disability legislation such as the Disability Discrimination Act (DDA, 1995), and the Disability Equality Duty (DDA, 2005), which contains a new public sector duty to promote equality, such as the procurement of goods that meet accessibility standards to ensure all public bodies 'pay "due regard" to the promotion of equality for disabled people in every area of their work' (www.dotheduty.org/), there is still a reliance on specialist services such as those offered by the RNIB NLS. This problem is not a new one. Owen reports that by the 1960s, 'public libraries had totally handed over all responsibility for library service provision for blind people to the two main national charities in this field' (Owen, 2007, 812), these being the RNIB and the National Library for the Blind (now the RNIB NLS), together with other voluntary sector agencies such as the Calibre Cassette Library. Therefore a more integrated approach is needed to encourage collaboration and partnerships across the library sectors. This will be discussed in the following section.

Cross sector working

In 1989 an organization called Share the Vision (STV) was established in the UK with the aim to 'improve the quality and availability of library and information services and products which provide for the reading and information needs of visually impaired and other print disabled people' with the vision of 'a voluntary, public, and professional sector partnership across the United Kingdom' (Owen, 2007).

Among STV's many early achievements were:

- to develop with the RNIB the National Union Catalogue of Alternative Formats (NUCAF)
- to publish (with the then UK Library Association, now Chartered Institute of Library and Information Professionals) *Library and Information Services for Visually Impaired People* (Machell, 1996).

In 1998 the Department of Culture Media and Sport (DCMS) awarded STV a grant of £200,000 with a remit to improve library and reading services for visually impaired people. To meet this remit, STV commissioned a number of research and development projects, including a survey of current provision for visually impaired people in UK public libraries (Kinnell, Liangzhi and Creaser, 2000); the publication of *Library Services for Visually Impaired People* (Hopkins, 2000); and REVEAL, which saw the development of the already established National Union Catalogue of Alternative Formats (NUCAF) into the REVEAL catalogue of alternative formats, or Revealweb (http://librarycatalogue.rnib. org.uk/).

STV's commitment to address the needs of visually impaired people continues, with a vision of what might be achieved by 2013, including the following features:

- Throughout their life visually impaired people will be able to access a continuum of library and information services that is equal to those available to sighted people but which meets their personal needs.
- Library and information services (LIS) will be available in their preferred accessible formats via their preferred contact point.
- LIS will ensure their policies and practices are reviewed in order to put the needs of their visually impaired users first.
- LIS will reaffirm and adapt their tradition of co-operating and sharing resources in order to ensure maximum access to content for visually impaired people.
- LIS, whatever sector, will support the creation and ongoing operation of a one-stop national referral agency, which can advise and assist visually impaired people and those serving them.

- All LIS will provide access to the wider range of services from other non-LIS agencies, which can assist the life opportunities and quality of life for visually impaired people.
- LIS will ensure there are enhanced opportunities to access content either remotely or on site via the accessible design of websites, online public access catalogues, digitization and the provision of assistive technology.
- LIS staff will have basic training to enable them to assist the achievement of this vision (Owen, 2007, 827–8).

Current developments: the digital library
Web-based services and resources

The interface of choice for digital library services is the world wide web (the web), and although significant changes are taking place in web technologies, this style of graphical user interface looks likely to remain for some time. Access to the digital library and thus electronic resources via the internet and web are now familiar to most people. Those born after 1993, often referred to as the 'Google generation', will not remember the time when the web did not exist! For them, the web (in the developed world, at least) is just another medium from which to access, interact with, store and share information and data. Predictions are that by 2017 the internet will have come of age for all ages and be completely integrated into most homes (Ciber, 2008).

People with visual impairments have a variety of ways to access digital information, ranging from adjustments to the desktop or browser view (enlarged font size, colour contrasts and inversions), to the use of assistive technologies such as screen magnification, screen readers or Braille output. These can be applied to whichever device they are using, such as desktop computer, laptop or mobile device. Whereas the issue of accessibility was less of a problem in the early years of the web (as the design of websites was mainly text based, which enabled fairly successful access and interaction using assistive technology software), a number of web design developments have taken place, which have presented barriers for people with visual disabilities. The main developments include:

- increased use of images and graphics (the graphical user interface)
- the arrival of web content creation software (authoring tools such as FrontPage and Dreamweaver), which allows unstructured use of HTML
- web browsers moving away from web standards (Howell, 2008, 58–9).

These developments have had a negative impact on the accessibility of websites, particularly for people with visual impairments and those who are using assistive technology software, for example:

- Failure to provide a text alternative for images and graphics will be a problem for people who use screen reading software because it cannot interpret images or graphics (it will simply read out 'image' 'image' 'image', etc.).
- Unstructured use of HTML may look quite acceptable on screen (for example, a misuse of heading levels) but makes navigation difficult for people using screen reading software.
- Web browsers that allow non-standard web coding will display websites even if the coding is poor, and this can be a problem for assistive technology compatibility.

Relevant studies

Widening access for visually impaired people has been the focus of a number of studies undertaken by CERLIM, looking at electronic access, and more specially web accessibility, for people with visual impairments. In 1999 the British Library and Joint Information Systems Committee (JISC) funded a study to look at electronic access to the digital library, with a particular focus on people with visual impairments. The aim of the Resources for Visually Impaired users of the Electronic Library (REVIEL) project (Brophy and Craven, 1999) was to provide a summary of the issues that needed to be considered and addressed if library and information services were to become fully accessible. The project final report revealed that accessibility of electronic services, and in particular accessible web design, was only in the early stages of development, displaying low levels of accessibility in the websites that were assessed.

The main recommendation of the REVIEL project was for the creation of a National Accessible Library Service (NALS), which would be a co-operative enterprise drawing on the strengths of all sectors to serve all citizens. The focus of the NALS would be to encourage content providers and brokers to take accessibility seriously and to facilitate access to materials in appropriate formats. These recommendations were explored in the work commissioned by STV in 1998, such as the development of Revealweb, which enables visually impaired people to make informed choices about what to read by giving access to over

170,000 items available for loan and/or sale in audio, large and giant print, Braille and Moon.

The recommendation for a NALS also influenced developments at the UK National Library for the Blind (NLB) and encouraged co-operation, and ultimately the merger, between the NLB and the RNIB to create a more comprehensive, easy to use service for customers through the RNIB NLS.

Following on from the REVIEL project, the Non-Visual Access to the digital library (NoVA) project (funded by JISC and the Library and Information Commission/Resource) was undertaken by CERLIM to explore the usability of web-based resources in digital libraries and with a particular focus on blind and visually impaired users (Craven, 2003; Craven and Brophy, 2003). The overall objective of the project was to develop an understanding of the searching or browsing behaviour of visually impaired users who could not read or interact with a screen without the aid of assistive technologies. To achieve this, a series of search and retrieval experiments were undertaken in order to map their approaches and to highlight usability issues.

The usability tests undertaken for the NoVA project provided an insight to the type of problems faced by users. Interestingly, although the focus of the project was on the information-seeking behaviour of blind and visually impaired people, the control group of sighted users also had usability problems, which were not necessarily the same as those experienced by the experimental group, thus reinforcing the importance of involving all types of user in any design and development project.

The study showed that although awareness of web accessibility was increasing, all types of user could be faced with navigational problems. Some of the problems observed in the study were caused by accessibility and usability conflicts such as inappropriate or unhelpful use of alternative text, or poor use of language. Other problems resulted from lack of understanding of the different ways users interact and navigate around web-based resources. The study concluded that careful consideration must be given not only to ensure that conflicts between accessibility and usability are addressed, but in the layout and navigation of a site and to the ways different assistive technologies interact with them. The study revealed that different assistive technologies presented different problems for the users and that success in navigation might depend not only on experience in searching, but also on experience in the use of assistive technology – which raises training issues both for users and trainers.

Web accessibility

The REVIEL and NoVA projects were very timely in relation to other important work on accessibility taking place around this time. Probably the most well known is that of the W3C Web Accessibility Initiative (WAI) (www.w3.org/WAI/), set up in 1999 to raise awareness of web accessibility and to provide guidelines for creating accessible websites (the Web Content Accessibility Guidelines (WCAG)), as well as for creating accessible authoring tools (ATAG, the Authoring Tool Accessibility Guidelines) and browsers (UAAG, the User Agent Accessibility Guidelines). Since the creation of WCAG, some countries and organizations have developed their own guidelines (usually based on WAI principles). For example, the British Standards Institute produced guidelines on commissioning accessible websites (BSI, 2006), which include advice on steps that should be taken to commission accessible websites; how the W3C guidelines and specifications should be adopted; and the role of the guidelines and specifications, software tools and user testing within the development life cycle.

The WAI WCAG are currently being updated from version 1.0 (which has been available since 1999) to version 2.0. The aim of this revised version is not to change the thinking about web accessibility drastically, but to provide guidelines that are more easily understood and that provide more flexibility than the prescriptive list of checkpoints offered by version 1.0. WCAG 2.0 will cover issues relating to web accessibility and, where they have an impact on accessibility, usability issues will be addressed. Four principles of web accessibility are proposed, which are referred to as the POUR principles:

- to be perceivable: content must be perceivable to each user
- to be operable: user interface components in the content must be operable by each user
- to be understandable: content and controls must be understandable to each user
- to be robust: content must be robust enough to work with current and future technologies.

Other activities that have helped to improve accessibility include the e-Europe accessibility action plan to address the i2010 strategy for creating a 'European society for growth and employment' (European Commission, 2005) by 2010, which places a particular emphasis on accessibility requirements for public procurement of ICT, accessibility certification, and web accessibility assessment methods and tools.

Accessibility statements and policies have also been developed by organizations to inform visitors to their website of how accessibility has (or has not) been addressed. For example, the Office for Information Technology Policy (OITP) of the American Library Association (ALA) has published advice on how to develop an accessibility policy, for example 'Listen to the community so as to establish its needs and any perceived barriers', 'Examine other organizations' policies in this area to see if they contain good ideas that could be adapted and adopted', 'Write an overarching statement of intent that sets out what the library is committing itself to', 'State who is responsible', 'State how information on accessibility will be disseminated' (Brophy, 2008, 100–2).

Recommendations have also been provided for the digitization of information using accessibility standards and specifications such as those created by the Centre for Educational Technology and Interoperability Standards (CETIS) and the IMS specification for e-learning technology standards.

Future prospects
New models for library service provision

In 2007 a large scoping study, funded by the British Library, the International Federation of Library Associations and Institutions (IFLA), and the Museums Libraries and Archives Council of England (MLA), was undertaken to compare different approaches to the funding and governance of library and information services for visually impaired people. The study collected information from 11 countries (Australia, Canada, Croatia, Denmark, Japan, Korea, Netherlands, South Africa, Sweden, UK and the USA). The key findings were that there was 'no single "best practice" model for providing library and information services to visually impaired and print impaired users: the situation varies greatly from country to country' but that a number of common elements were identified 'that would form the basis of policy and practice when combined in appropriate ways' (Rights.com, 2007). The report included the following recommendations for provision of:

- tools for focusing service providers' and their representative bodies' activities; this could include the provision of appropriate, comparable performance indicators
- tools for influencing government strategy and policy-making; this could include copyright exceptions related to functional requirements of visually impaired and print impaired people; a recommendation was also made that

governments should provide policy and financial support to all organizations that provide library and information services
- tools for involving content providers and rights holders; for example, publisher provision of digital files for content available for conversion.

Despite the Rights.com report findings that there was 'no single best practice model' of service provision, examples of good practice in library service provision for visually impaired people can be found. For example, a report by Brophy (2004), based on a survey of 149 English library authorities (78% response rate), conducted in October 2003 contains evidence of the impacts that the People's Network in the UK (see Dolan, Chapter 6, page 78) was having on end-users. It provides evidence that many positive impacts were being felt around the country.

In relation to social inclusion, examples of good practice in UK libraries included:

- South Tyneside – for using Speakout, a software package for people with dyslexia
- Swindon – for using Cicero to scan documents and output them as Word documents for visually impaired people
- Lancashire CC – with funding from the DCMS/Wolfson Challenge Fund set up the SMILE service to help ensure children with special needs or learning difficulties can make full use of the library services, and provided materials in alternative formats such as Braille
- Portsmouth Libraries – set up an IT suite with adaptive software (assistive technologies) within the library, offering free IT classes for visually impaired people. A blind member of staff ran the sessions and provided tuition and support for visually impaired members of the community.

The global digital library

The global digital library is a new and ambitious initiative to widen access to library services for visually impaired people, not just nationally, but on a global level. The project will be owned jointly by IFLA Libraries for the Blind Section (IFLA/LBS) and the DAISY Consortium, and will be project managed by the DAISY Consortium. A joint steering committee will be established to provide governance, oversight and direction to the project. The 'global library' project will be included in both organizations' strategic plans. Four major initiatives have been identified, for:

- discovery and access: end-user issues
- shared collection development and exchange
- a business model for the global library
- partnership development.

These four initiatives and related activities will form the basis of a project charter, which, at the time of writing, is under development. The global library is an important initiative as it will help to ensure visually impaired people have access to whatever is available, anywhere in the world.

Access to the digital library

The W3C and WAI provide an important framework for ensuring accessible web design, development and assessment, accessible authoring tools, and guidance for creating accessible web browsers, but this framework has often been criticized for being difficult to implement and for not looking at the wider picture in terms of the diverse needs and requirements of different people (Kelly, Phipps and Swift, 2004). Instead of relying solely on guidelines, an alternative is to take a more 'holistic' approach to accessibility, which takes into consideration a number of issues to help create websites that are accessible to as many people as possible. The approach draws on guidelines and best practice (such as the WCAG), as well as usability guidelines, interoperability standards, and engagement with users through feedback, focus groups and accessibility working groups. The aim of this approach is to provide 'a solution which maximises the usefulness to the end user, as opposed to the current WAI approach which encourages mandatory application of a limited set of guidelines' (Kelly et al., 2007).

Challenges facing libraries in their provision of services to all users include increased choice in devices to access the web (for example personal digital assistants or PDAs, smart phones, games, music players, digital TV), further development to mobile phone technologies, and the use of social networking sites such as Facebook and MySpace, and online virtual reality environments such as Second Life. These technologies (often referred to as Web 2.0) present accessibility challenges. A recent study of social networking tools revealed a number of accessibility problems (AbilityNet, 2008). For example, the use of CAPTCHA (Completely Automated Public Test to tell Computers and Humans Apart), which is a type of security question or test often used at login to determine that the 'person' is not a computer, can lock out anyone with a visual impairment, as well as people with dyslexia and learning difficulties. Many social networking tools allow interactions such as providing reviews, adding friends, watching videos and sharing photos which present problems for people using assistive technologies such as screen reading software.

Assistive technology developers therefore need to take into account the new and emerging technologies, and to develop assistive technology software that can better handle the new features, interactions and opportunities offered by Web 2.0. After all, it wasn't so long ago that screen readers were unable to read logically through tables or move between frames, whereas great improvements to assistive technology navigation have now taken place. Therefore, with a combination of good design principles and added navigational features, together with appropriate training, assistive technology software should be able to offer users a more efficient and flexible way to access and interact with websites, and for creating and sharing web content. Issues of affordability of assistive technology are of course another consideration, although there are a number of free assistive technology applications available, (for example Thunder screenreader (www.screenreader.net) and Natural Reader speech output (www.naturalreaders. com/download.htm) (see also Draffan, 2008).

The increase in user created content, with the creation of blogs, wikis, photo sharing sites such as Flickr, and social networking sites such as MySpace, has allowed web users to 'be web developers without any understanding of web code' (Howell, 2008, 64). Therefore authoring tools need to be provided that will create accessible code as standard, not as an optional extra, and should also be usable by people with disabilities. A working group at the W3C is currently working on version 2.0 of the ATAG guidelines and the latest working draft was published in March 2008 (www.w3.org/TR/ATAG20/). Guidelines for accessible authoring tools (such as the WAI Authoring Tool Accessibility Guidelines; www.w3.org/ TR/WAI-AUTOOLS/) are becoming just as important as recommendations, standards and advice linked to creating accessible websites, and should be developed accordingly.

In the UK, the British Standards Institution is in the process of establishing a standard that organizations will be able to follow in procuring or developing an accessible website. A technical standards committee will oversee the development of the standard, which will be based on the PAS 78 guide to good practice in commissioning accessible websites (mentioned earlier in the paper). The aim is to also take into account some of the new types of web service that were not available when the PAS 78 was first developed. It is hoped that the new standard will be published in 2009.

Education and training

When developing any library service, staff training is vitally important and should include training in how to work and interact with visually impaired people (etiquette, use of language, guiding and so on), recognition of the different types of visual impairments people experience, and training in the use of assistive equipment and how to demonstrate it and train users.

Education and training can also help create a culture where accessibility and inclusive design (in the design of buildings, services, websites and so on) is the norm rather than an add-on or afterthought. Taking web accessibility as an example, education and training in this field can influence the current and future generation of web managers, designers and developers, and policy-makers. The UK Cabinet Office study (2005) looked at web accessibility training initiatives in the European public sector and made the following recommendations:

- Web managers and developers in all public sector organizations should make sure that all content commissioners and authors are fully trained in the importance of accessible content, and in the means that are made available for them to achieve this.
- Web designers in the software industry should train all web designers in the requirement for, and techniques to achieve, fully accessible websites. They should also develop a competence framework for web designers that includes web accessibility and use it for personal development schemes and recruitment campaigns.
- Public policy-makers at EU level should carry out a feasibility study . . . into the development of an appropriate qualification in accessible websites for developers, managers and content providers (perhaps aligned with the European Computer Driving Licence).

The MeAC (Measuring Progress of eAccessibility in Europe) study identified ICTs in education as a policy option: 'eAccessibility in the educational context needs a high visibility and attention in future EU-level policy on eAccessibility' (European Commission, 2007). Evidence can be found of web accessibility issues and design being taught to students in various disciplines. Taking LIS as an example, a short review by Eskins and Craven (2008) found that web accessibility is taught within modules and courses such as basic web design (Manchester Metropolitan University, UK), designing usable websites (Sheffield University, UK), electronic publishing (University of Wales, Aberystwyth) and multimedia (Ionian University, Greece). An online course in barrier-free web design developed and provided by the Johannes Kepler University in Linz, Austria, is now in the process of being developed into an international online joint study programme through the Web Access Project (www.bfwd.at/webaccess). This project is funded by the European Commission Lifelong Learning Programme and involves six partner institutions. The overall aim of the project is to provide an accredited study programme, which will lead to a recognized academic award, giving recognition to and enhancing the status of anyone involved in the field of accessible web design.

Conclusions

The provision of library services to visually impaired people is clearly an evolving one. Increased awareness of the importance of equal access to services and resources, influenced in part through appropriate disability equality legislation, but also as a result of cross sector collaboration, has encouraged mainstream libraries to consider the needs and requirements of all their users, and to actively promote those services and resources that help to widen access for all. The introduction of new technologies has helped increase access to and interaction with the resources and services offered by libraries, whether they are delivered through mainstream libraries or specialist 'libraries for the blind'.

As Director of CERLIM, Peter Brophy has influenced improvements to library services for visually impaired people. Of particular importance is the work of the REVIEL project and the recommendation for a NALS, which was taken forward in the work commissioned by STV in 1998 and encouraged co-operation, and ultimately the merger, between the NLB and the RNIB to create the RNIB NLS in 2007. Under Peter's direction, the work of the REVIEL, NoVA and EIAO projects has helped to raise awareness and understanding of the problems experienced by visually impaired people when accessing and interacting with web-based resources. As a result of these studies, the reports, journal articles, and presentations and training events have provided practical advice on how to widen access for visually impaired users of the electronic library and have helped service providers and developers to look beyond the guidelines to a more pragmatic approach to the design, delivery and assessment of electronic library services in the 21st century and beyond.

Acknowledgements

The author would like to thank everyone who provided input to this chapter, in particular Helen Brazier and David Owen whose special issue of *Library Trends: Library and Information Services for Visually Impaired People* informed sections of this chapter. Any errors or misrepresentations presented in the paper are the sole responsibility of the author.

References

AbilityNet (2008) Social Networking Sites Lock Out Disabled Users, *State of the eNation Report*, 18 January.

Brazier, H. (2007) The Role and Activities of the IFLA Libraries for the Blind Section, *Library Trends*, **55** (4), Spring, 864–78.

British Standards Institution (2006) *Guide to Good Practice in Commissioning Accessible Websites*, Publicly Available Specification 78, www.equalityhumanrights.com/en/publicationsandresources/Disability/Pages/ Websiteaccessibilityguidance.aspx.

Brophy, P. (2004) *The People's Network: moving forward,* Museums, Libraries and Archives Council, www.mla.gov.uk/resources/assets//I/id1414rep_pdf_4287.pdf.

Brophy, P. (2008) Issues for Library and Information Services. In Craven, J. (ed.), *Web Accessibility: practical advice for the library and information professional*, Facet Publishing, 97–112.

Brophy, P. and Craven, J. (1999) *The Integrated Accessible Library: a model of service development for the 21st century: the Final Report of the REVIEL (Resources for Visually Impaired Users of the Electronic Library) Project*, British Library Research and Innovation Report 168, CERLIM, Manchester Metropolitan University.

Cabinet Office (2005) eAccessibility of Public Sector Services in the European Union, http://archive.cabinetoffice.gov.uk/e-government/resources/eaccessibility/ content.asp.

Ciber (2008) *Information Behaviour of the Researcher of the Future*, Ciber Briefing Paper, www.jisc.ac.uk/media/documents/programmes/reppres/gg_final_keynote_110 12008.pdf.

Craven, J. (2003) Access to Electronic Resources by Visually Impaired People, *Information Research*, **8** (4), http://informationr.net/ir/8-4/paper156.html.

Craven, J. and Brophy, P. (2003) *Non-visual Access to the Digital Library: the use of digital library interfaces by blind and visually impaired people*, Library and Information Commission Report 145, Manchester, Centre for Research in Library and Information Management.

DDA (1995) Disability Discrimination Act 1995 (c. 50), The Stationery Office.

DDA (2005) Disability Discrimination Act 2005 (c. 13), The Stationery Office.

Draffan, E. A. (2008) Tools Used for Widening Access to the Web. In Craven, J. (ed.), *Web Accessibility: practical advice for the library and information professional*, Facet Publishing, 7–23.

Eskins, R. and Craven, J. (2008) Design for All in the Library and Information Science Curriculum. In Craven, J. (ed.), *Web Accessibility: practical advice for the library and information professional*, Facet Publishing, 113–26.

European Commission (2005) *Standardisation Mandate to CEN, CENELEC and ETSI in Support of European Accessibility Requirements for Public Procurement of Products and Services in the ICT Domain*, M 376-EN, Brussels, 7 December 2005.

European Commission (2007) MeAC Report: assessment of the status of eAccessibility in Europe, http://ec.europa.eu/information_society/activities/einclusion/library/studies/meac_study/index_en.htm.

Hopkins, L. (ed.) (2000) *Library Services for Visually Impaired People: a manual of best practice*, Resource.

Howell, J. (2008) Accessibility Advice and Guidance. In Craven, J. (ed.), *Web Accessibility: practical advice for the library and information professional*, Facet Publishing, 57–72.

Kelly, B., Phipps, L. and Swift, E. (2004) Developing a Holistic Approach for E-learning Accessibility, *Canadian Journal of Learning and Technology*, **30** (3), Autumn, www.ukoln.ac.uk/web-focus/papers/cjtl-2004.

Kelly, B., Sloan, D., Brown, S., Seale, J., Petrie, H., Lauke, P. and Ball, S. (2007) Accessibility 2.0: people, policies and processes, *WWW 2007 Banff, Canada, 7–8 May 2007*, www.ukoln.ac.uk/web-focus/papers/w4a-2007.

Kinnell, M., Liangzhi, Y. and Creaser, C. (2000) *Public Library Services for Visually Impaired People*, LISU Occasional Paper No. 20, Loughborough University Library and Information Statistics Unit.

Machell, J. (1996) *Library and Information Services for Visually Impaired People: national guidelines*, Library Association.

Nomensa (2006) *FTSE 100 Websites Fail Accessibility Requirements*,
www.nomensa.com/news/at-nomensa/2006/4/ftse-100-websites-fail-
accessibility-requirements.html.

Owen, D. (2007) Sharing a Vision to Improve Library Services for Visually Impaired
People in the United Kingdom, *Library Trends*, **55** (4), Spring, 809–29.

Rights.com (2007) *Funding and Governance of Library and Information Services for
Visually Impaired People. International Case Studies, Part I: summary report*,
Rights.com Ltd.

Tank, E. and Frederiksen, C. (2007) The DAISY Standard: entering the global
virtual library, *Library Trends*, **55** (4), Spring, 932–49.

6

Public libraries, an enduring freedom: widening access to learning, information and culture

JOHN DOLAN

Introduction

The career of Peter Brophy spans some of the most interesting decades in the history of public libraries. Peter himself has been an advocate of change and innovation and a keen observer of what is and is not working. In his early career the emergence of new librarians wanting a library to be an active participant in community life met with a mixture of enthusiasm and apprehension. The spirit of community librarianship emerges in the first decade of the 21st century as a mix of user-oriented provision, partnership working, devolution and community engagement with a performance focus on impact beyond outputs.

The library evolves to meet a challenge

Under sometimes negative pressure the library changes slowly to meet new needs. The negative pressure is the easily voiced fear that the library has become outdated by social change, rendered redundant by new communications technologies; or it is the financial pressure of the parent institution: school, college, university or local authority. With the best motivation the library changes also in response to a community expectation, perceived or stated, or to an anticipated need or aspiration.

Increasingly it is not passive but proactive but this is a requirement of a service that is interventionist not reactive, that originates rather than supports initiative, and that leads rather than waits.

Conventionally, the library is a resource that underpins initiative. Collections, information, space to read and study, staff assistance form the main elements of library provision. Ranganathan's five laws of library science (Ranganathan, 1931) are about the collection, organization and delivery of resources to inform and support an initiative, a learning venture or research:

1   Books are for use.
2   Every reader his or her book.
3   Every book its reader.
4   Save the time of the reader.
5   The library is a growing organism.

Underpinning the five laws is a sense of philanthropy, an espousal of liberty and freedom of thought and an inherent desire to support the learner that is not immediately evident. Essentially the five laws determine the critical criteria that make an efficient and effective library. Ranganathan's five laws have proved to be so powerful that they have spawned generations of variations and extrapolations translating them into new sets of principles to meet different settings and periods. For example see Application of Ranganathan's Law to the Web Webology (www.webology.ir/2004/v1n2/a8.html#18).

From the 1960s there emerged a movement that sought to give public libraries a more substantive role in community life. 'Community Librarianship' grew up in poor inner cities finding their way in an increasingly liberal post-war society. Investment in slum demolition and new housing almost invariably dislodged people from their historic physical roots creating communities of new neighbours, which began to unite in community action when the idyll of the newly designed homes and tower block estates turned out to be physically unsatisfactory. In rural areas a growing sense of isolation was spurred by shifting patterns of agriculture, migration to cities and the Beeching cuts to the railway infrastructure, threatening a historic sense of community and security.

Librarians sought to support such communities with information on personal and citizens' rights, work and money, literacy programmes and community cultural activities. For some such a library was 'more like a community centre'; to the community librarian it fulfilled a modern library role as a place for learning, information and a sense of local identity; it was 'more like a library'. Such change was driven by a new perspective on libraries, an outward looking role that began a shift away from the guardianship of collections to the exploitation of information, ideas and knowledge.

In *Whose Problem?* (Coleman, 1981) Patricia Coleman tasked the public librarians of Britain with the responsibility to deliver not just resources but solutions to the excluded minority communities of the larger cities, to the poor, socially and economically disadvantaged and to disabled people. Importantly, and not without controversy, the report of her study highlighted the inconsistency of provision and the widespread reluctance to see the library as an agent for change.

Some wanted it both ways: the library is an essential but passive resource; it is not an active player in community politics and social life. This was a sensitive dilemma for public servants whose employer, the local authority, was often itself in the eye of the storm. It was a new kind of test of the oft lauded 'neutrality' of the public library.

The context today

Leaping forward from the heady days of the 1980s, the world has changed yet some themes are enduring in a post–Thatcher society. In her famous speech Margaret Thatcher said:

> I think we've been through a period where too many people have been given to understand that if they have a problem, it's the government's job to cope with it. . . . They're casting their problem on society. And, you know, there is no such thing as society. There are individual men and women, and there are families. And no government can do anything except through people, and people must look to themselves first.
>
> (Prime Minister Margaret Thatcher, talking to
> *Women's Own* magazine, 31 October, 1987)

The intervening period has seen the emergence and disappearance of the 'no society' society, an *everyone-for-himself* culture, the shift of industry and productivity away from manufacturing to service and latterly to the creative industries serving the knowledge economy.

Migration has become more elaborate and the post-colonial movement to Britain is now intertwined with east European and African migration. Digital technology has changed how we live, communicate and trade while climate change promises unimagined shifts in the balance between poverty and wealth accompanied by the emergence (or re-emergence) of China and India as global powers.

Alongside this is an emerging debate about Britishness that will enrich national identity and self-esteem and has the potential to inform national perspectives and either dispel or reinforce xenophobia. As a G8 economy, Britain performs on a European and global stage facing the challenge to build the capacity to remain an international economic power. Britain aims to sustain its economic position for the wellbeing of its own citizens and to influence world affairs.

Anticipating such need, Tony Blair's mantra 'Education, education, education' has led to disputed success and has not resolved the outstanding skills deficit of 20% functional illiteracy among adults and a workforce under-qualified for the future.

The public library service is lodged within the local government infrastructure. Its funding and accountability are directly connected to the priorities of the local authority, its partners and the voters' perception of importance measured against value and results. It may well have an intrinsic value but its funding, development and partnerships will be evaluated in relation to its contribution to key policy priorities and targets.

Is this scenario an opportunity or a threat to the future of the library? It is a real opportunity for the public library that it can penetrate communities, effect change in people's lives, support identity and cohesion, engage with people and enable people to renew their prospects.

National strategic direction

In the mid-1990s there was an unprecedented boost to the morale, stature and funding of public libraries. Commissioned from the Library and Information Commission by the Department for Culture, Media and Sport (DCMS), a strategy was published for the introduction of internet access in all public libraries. *New Library: the People's Network* (www.ukoln.ac.uk/services/lic/newlibrary/) set out a vision that was not only about technology but about what libraries could achieve with investment in ICT.

Following a further year's work on strategy and planning the funding was subsequently provided from the New Opportunities (national lottery) fund. Not only was there funding for infrastructure (£100m) but, as the original report proposed, this had to be accompanied by training (£20m) and content (£50m). Such spending on libraries transformed the service, drawing new users in significant numbers from younger and more diverse groups. Libraries moved through one project into the 21st century. Subsequently People's Network services brought new facilities and online content such as Enquire, the 24/7 live e-mail access to a librarian; and Reference Online, a national contract, negotiated by MLA, for the supply to public libraries of major electronic reference works.

The enduring value of the People's Network was in the exciting and reassuring future vision it offered as much as in what it physically and technically delivered. The proposal set out the essentials of the approach with mutually dependent strands of infrastructure, content and staff upskilling. It also set out the purposes of the library in terms of what the People's Network should deliver:

- access to knowledge, imagination and learning
- education and lifelong learning
- citizens' information and involvement in society
- business and the economy, training and employment
- community history and community identity
- the National Digital Library.

However, by the end of the 20th century while many libraries were working creatively, and in spite of the People's Network, there was still no consistent national agenda. The Department for Culture Media and Sport (DCMS) launched a ten-year plan to modernize public libraries. It recognized the prevailing mix of strengths:

- local community spaces
- rich and diverse collections
- services which reach out to people
- staff skills.

And weaknesses:

- falling traditional use; a large and continuous fall in borrowing
- fragmented and disparate services and standards of provision
- innovation unevenly spread and not often sustained
- weak leadership; workforce development needs; a recruitment time bomb in the aging workforce; a poor image of prospects among young people
- libraries not seen as central to key local or national agendas
- poor advocacy at all levels.

Through a modest financial investment it commissioned a change programme based on three development strands:

- books, reading and learning
- digital citizenship
- community and civic values.

Action plans arising from the Framework addressed the perceived weaknesses with, among others:

- a leadership programme for senior managers
- peer review and support for the weaker library authorities
- a significant investment in reader and reading development commissioned largely from The Reading Agency
- community engagement
- the People's Network Services.

The programme continues but with a widespread view that transformation of the public library sector in the national mindset is yet to be realized and the library is yet to reach its full, and considerable, potential.

Still, these two intertwined strategies (Framework and the People's Network) have had a modernizing impact on libraries bringing new and different users to libraries. The current challenge is to maintain the momentum of change.

The changing nature of the library

The proactive library that began to emerge in the 1980s should have a new lease of life as the passive role of repository and resource ceases to be seen as its core purpose. Such a library would fail to attract an audience that learns interactively, exchanges information freely and globally and can access physical resources from competing global corporations that are constantly re-inventing the delivery of books, audio and visual media to the user at home in a matter of hours and eventually electronically in moments.

The public library will develop this facility within the decade; if the political and funding constraints that separate library authorities can be bridged to capture the inestimable advantage of a single national catalogue, collection, request facility and speedy supply service a modern version of the traditional library will have emerged. However, that is not the totality of a modern library. Actively delivering content, services and experiences will begin to meet people's expectations of informal learning, discovery and leisure.

Research study of 14 to 35 year olds

The library as a destination is not a new concept; the case has been put more than once for the social model of a library, serving family, community and society. It was again, and richly, put in a study of 14 to 35 year olds for the future development of public libraries (MLA, DCMS, LASER Foundation, 2006). The study looked at the attitudes of 14 to 35 year olds to understand the lifestyles and attitudes to what libraries offer, to understand the rational, psychological and emotional barriers to library use and to explore how libraries could be developed, the services they could offer and other potential roles they could fulfil.

There is potential for growth among Students, Family Activity Seekers, Functional Dabblers ('I think/thought of the library as a place where I can have a look for specific information to help in a task or decision') and Teen Space Seekers. The report comments, 'Taking the needs and requirements of the range of current and potential users into consideration, it is clear that there are six areas in which changes and improvements can be made to public libraries to make them more compelling and a real option for the 14 to 35 age group.' Broadly, in order of priority, these are:

- modernization of style
- enhanced environment
- stock
- electronic access
- location and access
- assistance and support.

For these to have real impact, however, 'the specific needs of the different audiences must be accounted for within the development' (MLA, DCMS, LASER Foundation, 2006).

DCMS survey

The DCMS survey of people aged over 16 years in 28,000 households, Taking Part (DCMS, 2007), indicated that the public library has an above average reach into disadvantaged communities compared with other culture and sport services, including to lone parents, low income groups, and black, minority and ethnic (BME) communities. However, a closer look at the results will indicate that there are overarching influences including childhood use, led by parents and carers, and educational achievement.

Public libraries are already in a position to fulfil significant social and economic needs in the interests of British society but to do so need to develop targeted strategies for designated groups. This is a form of 'marketing', matching services to researched need followed by close monitoring, user evaluation and the assessment of outcomes.

This will generate the evidence that libraries make a positive and effective contribution to national prosperity and wellbeing. However, it requires an investment in research and a consensus around common directions and agreed strategies. Such approaches are not unprecedented but are like most library development, intermittent with little accumulated knowledge on which to build new approaches.

When it works it's brilliant: transferable experiences

There are several national success stories that illustrate potential, including those described below:

- Bookstart, the national books for babies scheme, combines a book for a baby with information and motivational material for parents and carers. Research in the 1990s on a pilot scheme in Birmingham indicated that parents reading to children in early years had a material effect later on the child's motivation to read and literacy attainment. Extended into Bookstart Plus, with packages for toddlers, this is a political winner as well as an effective library role.
- The Summer Reading Challenge is a national programme managed by The Reading Agency offering a co-ordinated, themed and publicized library scheme to keep young people reading. It had some 700,000 participants in 2007.
- The Paul Hamlyn Foundation funded as part of its Right to Read programme a range of work with looked after children. Thousands of young people in public care have few possessions, low educational attainment and uncertain prospects. Through the scheme such young people are now engaged in reading and creative writing and are actively involved in the library – something which the public care system, such as it is, has failed to achieve. It opens up unimagined resources, a supportive environment and opportunities for the future which they would have otherwise missed.
- Untold stories include the service to people who are housebound, which is a unique achievement. It is, however, largely unheard of in wider society and is delivered on too small a scale. The Museums, Libraries and Archives Council (MLA) informally surveyed local authorities in 2006 to find that

there are only 99,000 recipients. In addition to delivering books and information the service is a lifeline for people who have few resources and very little company. For these people the uplifting impact of a trusted visitor combined with days of reading pleasure and useful information make a unique stimulant. With an ageing population this is a service worthy of growth and modernization.

Such services are at the heart of what libraries are good at: reaching people, bringing inspiration, changing lives; such provision is highly regarded among those close to it yet, typical of library provision, largely unknown among political, media and funding stakeholders.

The welcoming library

The nature of such work and its true potential are exemplified in a recent innovative development. In 2008 accommodating refugees and asylum seekers still arouses controversy as Britain looks for a mid-point between the duty and commitment of a wealthy global power (the 1951 Refugee Convention) and the cost to the taxpayer disturbed by media hype (see the interim findings of the Independent Asylum Commission, www.independentasylumcommission.org.uk, and associated media coverage at http://news.bbc.co.uk/1/shared/bsp/hi/pdfs/ 27_03_08asyluminterimfindings.pdf, and, for example, www.independent.co.uk/ news/uk/home-news/asylumseekers-are-left-to-starve-in-britain-397576.html). Although for some, new migrant communities represent a burden on public services, the investment libraries can offer is both humanitarian and in keeping with conventional obligations. It is also in keeping with the library ethos of free and non-judgemental access to information, learning and culture. Libraries are a resource for refugees and asylum seekers. Moreover, library services offset the cost to other services by giving refugees and asylum seekers direct access to self-help opportunities.

Welcome To Your Library (WTYL; www.welcometoyourlibrary. org.uk) is a national project connecting public libraries with refugees and asylum seekers. This was also funded by the Paul Hamlyn Foundation and co-ordinated through London Libraries Development Agency. By increasing opportunities for participation, WTYL aims to improve the accessibility and quality of public library services for everyone. The report of the external evaluation reached several conclusions about what was important in working with refugees and asylum seekers. Some of the learning is proposed as a 'benchmark for public libraries in carrying out activities that enhance social inclusion' and therefore transferable to other settings. The main learning points are that there should be:

- effective planning and evaluation based on the mapping of need
- effective ownership and leadership and willingness to change
- partnership development at all strategic levels; a phased approach to partnership development to enable cross-sector skills sharing, innovation and opportunities to apply with partners for funding to test and develop new ways of working.

Lessons learnt from the WTYL project must be recorded and transferred to avoid the common failure to embed innovation in mainstream provision. Some of the following recommendations are straightforwardly good leadership and management. They are concerned with how learning from the project can be applied more widely across library services with different audiences. Creating an infrastructure for sharing information is key, and learning has to be centralized so that the overall library sector has access to resources that will assist them in planning and delivering community engagement activities. It is important that the development of such an information hub is not left as the responsibility of the WTYL project and The Network alone. This work needs to be nationally co-ordinated, set within the overall context of the development of public libraries, and led by the MLA, Society of Chief Librarians (SCL) and other strategic bodies. This should be set within a long-term strategy that provides for:

- clear performance indicators relating to social inclusion, community cohesion and community engagement targets, including guidance on how to evidence outputs and outcomes
- support for chief librarians to engage with national policy and cross-sectoral agendas
- structural changes such as workforce development to ensure a diverse workforce
- establishing 'critical friends' in positions of authority in other sectors with no direct connection to library service delivery in order to increase the interaction with cross-sector initiatives.

The WTYL development illustrates the changing expectations placed on public library services at the start of the 21st century reflecting not a library mission but a wider mission for public services within local government and with other public, private and voluntary sector partnerships. The themes are indicators of future direction:

- a modern response to a contemporary challenge
- national leadership and co-ordination
- prioritization and targeting of resources
- with identifiable outputs *and* outcomes
- community engagement delivering social justice
- partnership across different sectors.

Planning a sustainable future

The history of libraries is strewn with anecdotal evidence of how the library has supported people undertaking formal education or has been the resource for the self-taught and the independent learner, those who made it in spite of the circumstances and barriers to progress. The challenge has been and still is to demonstrate the value of self-learning at the library to the audience of stakeholders and decision-makers who fund education or reward progression.

There are two major opportunities for public libraries that will span the next decade: skills and learning; and community, or building social capital. Significantly they are also areas where public and academic libraries can and should work together.

Skills and learning

Addressing the national skills deficit, the Leitch Review of Skills (2006) asserted that levels of literacy and associated basic skills have to be raised if Britain is to maintain its economic position in the world. In his foreword, Lord Leitch sums up the need and the opportunity:

> Demographic, technological and global changes present enormous challenges and brilliant opportunities. The population continues to age. Technological developments are occurring faster than we dreamed, dramatically altering the way we work. Competitive pressures on all sectors of the economy are increasing. Manufactured goods, and increasingly services, are traded across the world. Developed nations are relying more and more on their capacity to innovate to drive economic growth. The ability to do this depends upon the skills and knowledge of their people.

Leitch sets clear targets for 2020 for the UK to commit to, including:

- 95% of adults to achieve the basic skills of functional literacy and numeracy, from 85% literacy and 79% numeracy in 2005
- 90% of adults qualified to at least Level 2, from 69% in 2005
- shift the balance of intermediate skills from Level 2 to Level 3, improving the esteem, quantity and quality of intermediate skills; this means 1.9 million additional Level 3 attainments over the period and boosting the number of apprentices to 500,000 a year
- over 40% of adults qualified to Level 4 and above, up from 29% in 2005, with a commitment to continue progression.

There is thus an opportunity for libraries to support the delivery of formal skills training, to be access points to online learning provision and to demonstrate the value of the informal learning that libraries deliver from early years and family learning through to informal learning, mid-career and into older years.

Amid a huge investment in skills, an expansion programme for higher education and a capital investment programme for colleges (all of which ought to include library and information provision), the Department for Innovation, Universities and Skills (DIUS) has issued a consultation on the value and potential of *informal* learning. In *Informal Adult Learning* (DIUS, 2008), the consultation acknowledges different kinds of personal and community development learning that have huge economic and social potential as well as being of value to the individual:

- non course-based activities: talks, presentations, advice and guidance provided by a range of sectors and organizations
- learning outside a dedicated learning environment, arising from the activities and interest of groups.

Such learning is commonplace in public libraries; if it can be evidenced, it is clear that libraries are primary providers of a new and refreshed informal learning programme.

These two government strategies are interlinked and will depend on increased take-up of formal and informal learning. The current capacity of the adult and further education sector is unlikely to achieve the Leitch targets without additional resources. The resources and a potential solution exist in the infrastructure, capacity and help available through the public library network.

Building social capital

Historically, too, public libraries are a community place, a venue, a place of encounter and dialogue. They can also be places of action: performance, presentation, debate. Together with resources teeming with ideas and information they are essentially places of quiet revolution where new ideas and propositions are nurtured and evolve. They are, indeed now more than ever, a unique place in the community in being non-judgemental and freely open to all. Society requires such places that enable social interaction for creative learning and free expression.

Libraries remain, however, a local government service and, in line with other policy trends, community ownership of their purpose and management is an emerging ambition. 'Community engagement' has been stimulated by a national trend to go beyond the conventions of consultation by sharing power and influence with local communities enabling them to make the decisions that are normally in the exclusive gift of councillors and officials. The Big Lottery Community Libraries Programme is an opportunity to rehearse such engagement for the public library sector. In 2007 a fund of £80 million was launched with three aims:

- to invigorate libraries as centres of wider community learning and development and learning based activities
- to create, improve and develop library spaces that meet the needs of the whole community
- to be innovative and promote good practice in the ways libraries are designed and run.

A precondition of eligibility was a community engagement plan and process. The outcome remains unknown as the projects are undertaken from 2008. An evaluation process will assess the extent to which library organizations have changed how they work in order to accommodate the philosophy of community engagement and to measure the outcomes of the change and the impact on local people, families and communities. In spite of (and maybe because of) the 'neutrality' and 'independence' that sit at the core of the library culture, to share with some the decisions that determine what the user can access at the library may seem a threat to its value and relevance to the wider community. Important parameters have to be set both to ensure openness and to protect the needs of the many from the preferences of the few.

Leading solutions

Information, communications and learning technologies

'New technology' has fast become a redundant piece of language as digital technologies are now the norm while innovation and change is a constant. With the People's Network, public libraries became the people's place for accessing global networks and for people with limited personal resources to reach the world of digital information and learning through the internet.

There are barriers, however, to maximizing the information learning technology offer and realizing the full potential of the library offer:

- There is no national standard of provision, making planning, investment and marketing difficult.
- The opportunity to create free content was only partly realized by the focus on the replication of historic collections. The full interactivity of the web to create dynamic services and facilities has not yet been captured.
- Interactive provision and capturing of Web 2.0 is inhibited by a local authority culture of caution and an apprehension about the implications of free access.

In emerging plans for public library development each of these will be tackled. The public library potential is to deliver:

- a national programme of online informal and accredited learning opportunities
- online access to all library collections with permitted self-service interlibrary loans
- free access to electronic publications, resources and interactive communications
- a service that reaches all communities, especially those most excluded from mainstream provision
- information, advice and guidance services with partner agencies
- one-stop-shop access to local government, health and other public services
- a service supported by skilled staff offering support and guidance.

The public library is already a focal point for people in new migrant communities, for people in inner city areas and for those in remote rural communities. Many recent but disparate developments have demonstrated how such provision can be consolidated as integral to the library's role. In a holistic library service the digital dimension of a community building and community learning opportunities will therefore be integral; like the rest of the library it will be designed around local and regional demographic, economic and social needs with communities actively engaged in planning and decisions to be taken.

Workforce

Widening access to learning, information and culture is not solely a matter of technology or resources. Supporting learning, building social capital, reaching excluded communities or working with children and young people will require continued and planned investment in the people who work in libraries. There are serious challenges facing the public library sector, some of which ring true in other library sectors as they all face similar needs in responding to the different user communities they serve. This is not being addressed completely at the present time. The future requires a total workforce solution that addresses:

- diversity in a workforce that reflects the community it serves
- recruitment and retention of a workforce that will promote a changed image and be substantively responsive and innovative
- leadership, advocacy, negotiation, communications and partnership building as a skills set for every part of the organization
- creativity with all technologies, print to digital; understanding change in research, publishing, learning, information and communications
- community engagement, learner support, working with priority groups and a customer-focused service delivery
- multi-agency and partnership working.

A total workforce solution delivers technical prowess fronted by softer skills at every level of the organization so that leadership, communications and innovation are manifest equally in the senior manager working with partner organizations, the community librarian off-site in the community and delivery staff organizing learning and community activities.

The campaign Top Ten New Librarians in 2007 spotlighted librarians demonstrating such an outlook and aspiration, including this entrant, Alexis Dimyan (see Figure 6.1), Luton Library Services, who sees beyond the stereotype into a career that rewards commitment with potential; and who comments: 'I wanted a job that was imaginative, creative, interesting, exciting, challenging, flexible, adventurous, eye-opening, stimulating, dynamic, uplifting, inspiring, heady, captivating, people-centred, laughter-filled and bustling with variety. This is why I have chosen a career in public libraries – what better or more satisfying job could there be?' (see www.lovelibraries.co.uk/librarians.php for all the entrants).

Figure 6.1 Alexis Dimyan at work with young families (with permission)

Partnership

As well as informal ad hoc partnership arrangements, local strategic partnerships (LSPs), especially, are the vehicle for library local authorities to build relationships, plan strategically and pool resources to effect change in the poorest areas. Communities and Local Government (CLG, n.d.) is explicit:

> Lack of joint working at local level has been one of the key reasons why there has been little progress in delivering sustainable economic, social or physical regeneration or improved local services that meet the needs of local communities. A combination of local organisations, and the community, working co-operatively as part of an LSP will have a greater chance of success . . . local authorities and other service providers need to work co-operatively, change the ways they work, reallocate resources and 'bend' their mainstream programmes to tackle issues that really matter to local people.

The future

While libraries may retain an integrity and ethos of their own – free access, information, learning, community and society, knowledge and understanding – they must sit within a relevant policy context. The emerging policy landscape can be seen in an assessment of the future strategic challenges for Britain published by the Cabinet Office Strategy Unit in 2008 (Cabinet Office, 2008). Drawing on an analysis of trends and drivers of change, future projections and scenarios from inside and outside government and a detailed analysis of Britain's strengths and weaknesses, the resulting assessment provides a comprehensive review of the long term challenges and opportunities for Britain, covering nine areas:

1   *Global* Britain; *success* in the world.
2   Economic prosperity: *workers and business* in globalized, competitive world.
3   *Life chances*; reducing inequality, unlock Britain's *talents*.
4   Population; supporting a growing, *ageing, more diverse population*.
5   *Families and communities*: strengthen family life; foster strong communities.
6   *Safe* Britain: safe and secure for all.
7   *Personalized public services*: better tailoring services to *diverse* needs.
8   Climate challenge: making the transition to a *low carbon Britain*.
9   Democratic renewal: *modernizing democracy* for the 21st century.

My emphasis highlights some areas where libraries should be playing a role in delivering the nation's needs. Each represents an opportunity for partnership, investment, research, evaluation and outcomes assessment. In that way the library's contribution can be delivered, monitored and evaluated, informing further future sustainability (see www.cabinetoffice.gov.uk/strategy/work_areas/strategic_challenges0208.aspx).

As libraries of all kinds look ahead into the 21st century there is much common ground between the sectors as learning, research and discovery become a common language. For higher education, SCONUL's vision (see www.sconul.ac.uk/publications/pubs/vision%202010) encompasses strategic features that would sit comfortably in other sectors:

*   personalization of systems and services (to the individual and to communities of users)
*   greater collaboration across sectors and domains and between global communities; resources for lifelong learners will be in increasing demand and will be facilitated by this collaboration

- physical and virtual space will be equally important ... a blended service where the virtual and the actual space are complementary, influenced by the number and diversity of new technologies
- the main trend will be towards the full economic costing of activities, with a requirement for evidence of return on investment. Developments in technology and the shift from the provision of physical items will result in the redirection of staff time and the development or importing of alternative skills. The focus will be on the delivery of personal help, either face-to-face or via web-based services.

LIS developments

These are some of the developments there will be in LIS:

- LIS will increase recruitment of staff with skills in areas such as finance and marketing.
- Greater emphasis will be placed on impact measurement. Impact measures will be developed for the sector and e-measures will be embedded.
- Information fluency will become more important as staff become actively involved in curriculum development and assessment.
- Fund raising will become more central to our activities. The ability to market services and provide a vision will be central to this activity.

The British Library, in turn, looks for renewed statements of vision and mission and lists strategic priorities following consultation with users and reference to national research and economic needs, see British Library, *Redefining the Library* (2005).

Public libraries set out in the 19th century with a radical mission to educate and skill while alleviating social injustice. The public library was not free for nothing; there were social and economic drivers behind the philanthropy and the investment. The map still looks familiar today: personal improvement, lifelong learning, social cohesion, economic prosperity.

Peter Brophy observed (Brophy, 2006) what made projects in the academic sector successful and, more importantly, what ensured that benefits and lessons were embedded as meaningful change:

- a requirement which is recognized as important by a significant part of the target audience

- the potential for cost savings in individual libraries, provided that the directors of those libraries are convinced that the savings will be real
- vision and enthusiasm on the part of those promoting the project or service, coupled with a strong existing profile in the target market
- significant new technological advances
- the final requirement for successful transition is thus the lack of a commercially available alternative capable of delivering the service required.

Despite the barriers, however, it is remarkable how many projects from the last 40 years have made the transition. As a result we have a panorama richly populated with real services delivering information to literally millions of users scattered across the cyberoceans of the world.

Peter Brophy's insight into what will determine future success in the academic library is itself transferable to public libraries in the early 21st century.

References

British Library (2005) *Redefining the Library: the British Library's strategy 2005–2008*, www.bl.uk/aboutus/foi/pubsch/strategy_0508.pdf.

Brophy, P. (2006) Projects into Services: the UK experience, *Ariadne*, February, www.ariadne.ac.uk/issue46/brophy.

Cabinet Office (2008) *Realising Britain's Potential: future strategic challenges for Britain*, The Strategy Unit, February, www.cabinetoffice.gov.uk/strategy/work_areas/~/media/assets/ www.cabinetoffice.gov.uk/strategy/strategic_challenges%20pdf.ashx.

Coleman, P. M. (1981) *Whose Problem? The public library and the disadvantaged*, Association of Assistant Librarians (Group of the Library Association).

CLG (n.d.) Communities and Local Government, www.neighbourhood.gov.uk/page.asp?id=531.

DCMS (2007) *Taking Part Survey: progress report on PSA3: final estimates from year two*, 13 December, www.sportengland.org/071213_progressreportonpsa3finalestimatesfromyeartwo.pdf.

Department for Innovation, Universities and Skills (2008) *Informal Adult Learning – shaping the way ahead*, www.adultlearningconsultation.org.uk.

Leitch Review of Skills (2006) *Prosperity for All in the Global Economy – world class skills*, final report, HMSO,
www.hm-treasury.gov.uk/media/6/4/leitch_finalreport051206.pdf.

MLA, DCMS and Laser Foundation (2006) *A Research Study of 14–35 year olds for the Future Development of Public Libraries: final report*, Museums, Libraries and Archives Council, the Department for Culture, Media and Sport and the Laser Foundation,
www.bl.uk/aboutus/acrossuk/workpub/laser/publications/projreports/publiclibraries.pdf.

Ranganathan, S. R. (1931) *The Five Laws of Library Science*, Madras Library Association.

7

Sceptic 2.0? Social networking technologies in public libraries

JULIET EVE

Introduction (and disclaimer)

Let me start with a story. It seems an appropriate place to start: it is one of the things public libraries do best: Baby Rhyme Time, Storytime for Under 5s, Book Groups, Bibliotherapy etc. Earlier this year I attended an author reading event at a small library in West Sussex. There were about 20 people there, and we listened to a local author who writes crime fiction. She talked, read an extract from her book, answered questions, signed copies and chatted amicably with locals. I have no intention of reading one of her books, but I thoroughly enjoyed myself, and, browsing the display afterwards, came home with a book (which I subsequently read with pleasure) by a different crime writer whom I'd been meaning to read for ages but not quite got round to it. This was a thoroughly, and typically, Library 1.0 experience. However, it struck me that evening that here was a library doing what it does best: serving a local community, making best use of the physical space, using all the library resources (it was a multimedia event; the audience were helped to vote online for this author in a national competition after the reading) and engaging with its users in a thoroughly interactive and meaningful way.

I would like to establish here and now my anti-Luddite credentials. Not only do I have a Facebook profile, I can be found on Linked-In, and I appear on YouTube (see link from February post to the blog InformationMatters at www.informationmatters.net). I also spent two happy years at the Centre for Research in Library and Information Management (CERLIM) researching into the value and impact of ICT in public libraries, collecting evidence to support the case for implementation of what became the People's Network (Eve and Brophy, 2000).

Why is that relevant? It will serve, I hope, to set the discussion below firmly in the context of a reflective and appropriate use of and engagement with technologies, rather than to accept a prevailing 'if it's got 2.0 on the end it must be good' dash to blog, twitter and MySpace our energies away, with no evidence to prove that these activities are actually providing a useful service.

So, to begin at the beginning . . .

What is Web 2.0?

The term Web 2.0 was coined by Dale Dougherty, Vice-President of O'Reilly Media Inc., in reference to technologies 'which facilitate a more socially connected Web where everyone is able to add to and edit the information space' (Anderson, 2007a, 4). O'Reilly outlines seven principles behind the Web 2.0 concept (O'Reilly, 2005a), summarizing the 'core competencies of Web 2.0 companies' as:

- services, not packaged software, with cost-effective scalability
- control over unique, hard-to-recreate data sources that get richer as more people use them
- trusting users as co-developers
- harnessing collective intelligence
- leveraging the long tail through customer self-service
- software above the level of a single device
- lightweight user interfaces, development models and business models.

His 'compact definition' refers to Web 2.0 as:

> the network as platform, spanning all connected devices; Web 2.0 applications are those that make the most of the intrinsic advantages of that platform: delivering software as a continually-updated service that gets better the more people use it, consuming and remixing data from multiple sources, including individual users, while providing their own data and services in a form that allows remixing by others, creating network effects through an 'architecture of participation', and going beyond the page metaphor of Web 1.0 to deliver rich user experiences. (O'Reilly, 2005b)

Anderson (2007a, 13) summarizes the 'big ideas behind Web 2.0' as: individual production and user generated content, harnessing the power of the crowd, data on an epic scale, the architecture of participation, network effects and openness. 'Collaboration, contribution and community are the order of the day' is his nicely succinct phrase, which emphasizes the core principles of Web 2.0. He is more measured in his understanding of what this may mean than many other commentators, suggesting for example, that although 'there is a sense . . . that a new "social fabric" is being constructed . . . it is important to acknowledge that these ideas are not necessarily the preserve of "Web 2.0" but may in fact merely reflect the strange effects and topologies at the micro and macro level that a billion Internet users produce' (Anderson, 2007a).

The idea of collaboration and contribution provides one of the key assumptions behind Web 2.0, namely that 'the service automatically gets better the more people use it' (O'Reilly, 2005a), the 'wisdom of the crowds' effect that has been most famously championed by James Surowiecki (2005).

The ideas behind Web 2.0 were an attempt to understand how some businesses had not only survived the dotcom crash, but were continuing to harness new applications to improve their competitiveness. Thus, much of what O'Reilly describes as Web 2.0 (the 'long tail', the 'wisdom of crowds') refers to how companies like Google and Amazon have 'made a science of user engagement' (O'Reilly, 2005a) to maintain their position as leading brands.

In wider practice, the term tends to refer not only to a new generation of social networking technologies (Facebook, MySpace, Flickr, del.icio.us, to name a few) but to the fundamental attribute supposedly unique to these technologies, user-driven (and 'mashed' and re-mixed) content.

Despite its swift incorporation into the language, not to mention the exponential growth of blogs, Facebook profiles and Flickr sets, the whole idea of Web 2.0 is not without its critics. Tim Berners-Lee, for example, as far back as 1999, said: 'I have always imagined the information space as something to which everyone has immediate and intuitive access, and not just to browse, but to *create*' (quoted in Anderson, 2007a, 13).

He suggests that far from being new, Web 2.0 is 'a piece of jargon, nobody even knows what it means' and that people-to-people connections are 'what the Web was supposed to be all along' (Berners-Lee, 2006). Others, such as Shaw (2005), also criticize Web 2.0 as merely a marketing slogan, maintaining that the applications brought together under the term are 'forward lurches of various standards and technologies, some compatible, some not. Some revolutionary, some evolutionary, some impractical. Some are collaborative, others are highly competitive with each other.' Scholz (2008), uncovering what he terms a 'sea change' from O'Reilly's admission he 'got it wrong', notes, however, that this is 'unlikely to take away from the popular appeal of the phrase that, by now, is dyed into the fabric of the mass media'. Scholz's article proceeds to: 'deflate the claims of revolutionary technical innovation and social empowerment held dear by many Web 2.0 evangelists' (Zimmer, 2008), noting that, as Berners-Lee hinted, many of these technologies have existed long before the term came into use.

Whatever the arguments about the technologically revolutionary aspects of Web 2.0, there is no doubt that Web 2.0 has fast become shorthand for a new set of virtual spaces to engage in, as well as potentially new ways for businesses (or any other kind of institutions, such as universities, libraries and so on) to engage with customers, and for those customers to create content as much as they consume it. What is key about the whole Web 2.0 phenomenon is not whether it is significantly different from Web 1.0, but whether it is *perceived* as such, and therefore becomes the latest 'revolution' that libraries and others are obliged to keep up with and respond to. As Beer and Burrows put it, Web 2.0 is: 'a cluster of contemporary technologies which, *popular rhetoric suggests*, are reworking hierarchies, changing social divisions, creating possibilities and opportunities, informing us, and reconfiguring our relations with objects, spaces, and each other' (Beer and Burrows, 2007) [emphasis added].

The very fact that Web 2.0 is perceived and discussed in this way makes it a vital topic for libraries to engage with: what is the public library for, if not 'changing social divisions, creating possibilities and opportunities, informing us, and reconfiguring our relations with objects, spaces, and each other'?

Library 2.0: definitions

Michael Casey is attributed with the first use of the term Library 2.0, in his LibraryCrunch blog (Casey, 2005; Miller, 2005); a posting on 29 September 2005 certainly refers to 'a Library 2.0 world'.

The term is the expression used to indicate how some of the Web 2.0 features discussed above can be used in library contexts. However, many commentators have defined the phrase to suggest ways of working that go far beyond this. For example, Bradley (2007, 5) refers to the ways in which libraries, by harnessing the 'wisdom of crowds' and the power of these social networking tools, can reposition themselves vis-à-vis their users, and provide a 'richer user experience'. Miller (2006, 1) suggests that: ' "Library 2.0" is a term that provides focus to a number of ongoing conversations around the changing ways that libraries should make themselves and their services visible to end users and to one another.'

This is in line with some of the most popular definitions circulating – appropriately enough – around the blogosphere. Library bloggers who champion Library 2.0 (Sarah Houghton, Michael Stephens, John Blyberg, to name a few) see this as a radically different approach to conceiving of, and delivering, public library services. Thus Houghton's definition (which, as Blyberg (2006) points out, 'has been used as the de facto standard since Michael Stephens simply said he liked it') contends that:

> Library 2.0 simply means making your library's space (virtual and physical) more interactive, collaborative, and driven by community needs. Examples of where to start include blogs, gaming nights for teens, and collaborative photo sites. The basic drive is to get people back into the library by making the library relevant to what they want and need in their daily lives . . . to make the library a destination and not an afterthought.
>
> (Houghton, 2005)

This 'call to arms' can be seen as an answer to the 'question of relevance' which, according to Chad and Miller (2005, 5), is 'perhaps the biggest challenge facing libraries today'. This concern is also articulated by Brindley (2006, 486) who asks: 'How can we serve the needs of the digitally savvy, impatient Google generation for whom the web – a global information commons – has primacy of place for information and knowledge seeking?'

These concerns also resonate with much current debate in library spheres about what the role of the public library is. These definitions are, however, a little misleading in a number of ways. First, the use of the word 'simply' in Houghton's definition is disingenuous to say the least; to make a library service genuinely *interactive, collaborative and driven by user needs* is not in fact a simple task. This requires a shift in the way services have traditionally been delivered (I am not necessarily arguing against this, but merely pointing out that the culture shift required to do so is anything but simple). Moreover, it rides over the trickier issues of defining who your community is – and the answer to this is likely to reveal many different user communities, with potentially conflicting wishes and needs. Second, and perhaps more importantly, it also assumes a technologically driven solution to a complex social and political need – the provision of relevant public library services. If commentators like Houghton are not advocating Web 2.0 as the answer to addressing this issue, then use of the term Library 2.0, echoing as it does its parent term Web 2.0, is perhaps misguided.

Chad and Miller (2005, 11) maintain that: 'The concept of Library 2.0 builds upon all that has been best about libraries to date, harnesses technological potential and community capability in order to deliver valuable, valued and world-class services directly to those who stand to benefit from them, whether or not they (ever) physically enter a library building.'

If the authors are suggesting that this is *already* what Library 2.0 is doing, the first and most obvious question is: where is the evidence? None is offered in their white paper – it is written in a tone and tense which both suggests this is what libraries are doing, and what they could do in future, if Library 2.0 is adopted. It also fails to define exactly what it is that libraries have done best to date and ignores one of the major assets the public library service has at its disposal: its buildings.

Bradley (2007, 8) too is convinced that Library 2.0 is a new concept, 'and something that is entirely different and quite radical' as it 'puts the technical control and development of resources right in the hands of the librarian in an unprecedented way'. This seems a very limited reason for suggesting Library 2.0 is new; while the idea that librarians could get on with the job of creating and managing digital resources, free from the constraints of their IT department, may for many be something indeed quite liberating (and long battled for) in the day to day hierarchies and bureaucracy of local government, it hardly suggests a radical approach to librarianship. Moreover, the key focus of many Web 2.0 enthusiasts is the notion (and this is the 'new' aspect) that end-users (rather than librarians) are creating content.

What is also interesting about some of the Library 2.0 rhetoric is the assumption of new activity taking place merely by virtue of new technologies being invoked. Thus Hayward and Rooney (2008, 2) can report as a 'top tip' that one benefit of blogs is 'you can go to your users rather than expect your customers to come to you'. Aside from the casual slippage from user to customer, which raises a whole set of other questions about how libraries are positioning themselves, this fundamentally disregards the issue that users still have to (want to) find, access and read a library blog. Signing up to an RSS feed may be the only extent to which librarians could realistically suggest that information is going to the user unrequested.

Among all the enthusiasm for Library 2.0, there are a few voices offering a more cautious approach. Maness (2006), for example, provides a more focused definition, suggesting we conceive of Library 2.0 as: 'the application of interactive, collaborative, and multi-media web-based technologies to web-based library services and collections' (Maness, 2006, 3).

He sensibly restricts his definition to web-based services, rather than library services generally, suggesting this 'avoids potential confusion' and 'renders [the term] more useful in professional discourse'.

Anderson (2007b, 196) also draws attention to the fact that the concept has spawned the same debate as its parent term: 'the discussions associated with it, much of which has taken place in the blogosphere, have proved to be controversial at times' (Anderson, 2007b, 196).

He summarizes this debate as follows:

> Proponents argue that new technologies will allow libraries to serve their users in better ways, emphasize user participation and creativity, and allow them to reach out to new audiences and to make more efficient use of existing resources. Perhaps the library can also become a place for the production of knowledge, allowing users to produce as well as consume? Others worry that the label is a diversion from the age-old task of librarianship.
>
> (Anderson, 2007a, 35)

More significantly, Anderson highlights the issue that 'there has been very little theoretical, peer-reviewed work related to Library 2.0'.

Library 2.0: is it really something new?

Part of the problem with Library 2.0 seems then to be that in reality it refers to Web 2.0 technologies as used in libraries, yet the rhetoric surrounding it suggests a completely new approach to delivering (all) library services, and something of a revolution. In a sense, of course, this should not come as a surprise; very similar rhetorical flourishes were made over five years ago, when information and communication technologies (in particular the People's Network) were first introduced into the public library service. That also produced an enthusiastic response from those in the library world who saw it as the answer to the question: how do public libraries remain relevant to users in the 21st century? The Tavistock Institute's evaluation of the People's Network suggested that the introduction of the technology could (and should) facilitate a 'paradigm change' from the library role as 'enabling the citizen to consume and receive' to a role in 'enabling the citizen to produce and distribute', namely the shift from 'the transmission of information' to 'the co-creation of knowledge' (Sommerlad et al., 2004, 134). Yet their own research also noted that 'By far the most dominant uses of the PN [People's Network] were for the internet and email' (Sommerlad et al., 2004, 77), and their study provides little evidence of the 'co-creation of knowledge'.

The Library 2.0 phenomenon appears to be heading down the same path – it is perceived by some as the answer to all our problems, and the way to facilitate a 'more participative approach' (Chad and Miller, 2005, 10) to service provision, but there is little evidence to suggest that there is either a desire for this, or that it is likely to happen. Moreover, research indicates that active participation and content generation in Web 2.0 environments generally is very low. A report by Hitwise in 2007 suggested that the vast majority (between 80 and 90%) of users are indeed users, rather than creators. Roughly 10–15% make some contribution in the form of editing, adding comments and so on, but only a tiny 1–5% of users actually create and add new content. For example, only 0.18% of YouTube users use the site to upload videos (Tancer, 2007). Nielsen has previously maintained that: 'In most online communities, 90% of users are lurkers who never contribute, 9% of users contribute a little, and 1% of users account for almost all the action' (Nielsen, 2006).

How are libraries currently using Web 2.0 technologies?

What then, are public libraries doing with these new technologies, and are they transforming the delivery of services?

The City of Burbank public library, in California, has made much use of Web 2.0 facilities, hosting not only a website, but a range of services. These include their Ask the Librarian service, which proclaims itself 'available 24 hours a day, 7 days a week' despite the disclaimer that 'Requests received Saturdays, Sundays or holidays will be handled as if submitted on Mondays' (City of Burbank, 2001a). It also hosts a general blog (http://burbanklibrary.blogspot.com/), a blog devoted to its Burbank Reads initiative, championed as 'Building Community, Page by Page' (http://burbankreads.blogspot.com/). Also available are two wikis: the AskWiki (http://burbank.wikidot.com/) and the LittleWiki for children (http://littlewiki.wikidot.com/). Contrary to custom, both their wikis have the following disclaimer: 'Unlike most wikis, our public cannot freely edit its contents. However, suggestions for websites and resources to include on this website are welcome' (City of Burbank, 2001b).

This restriction on public participation seems to undermine much of the rhetoric found in the Library 2.0 literature. It also highlights perhaps one of the fundamental issues behind libraries' (and indeed other institutions') uptake of these so-called democratic technologies: allowing unrestricted access is in competition with the existing culture of *delivery* of services which are most familiar and comfortable. The Burbank wikis differ from their blogs to the extent that a range of librarians (and chosen others) can edit existing pages, rather than hosting a series of individual posts in the way blogs allow.

This approach seems to fit into Bradley's (2007, 8) conception of Library 2.0 discussed above, namely that the tools free *librarians* from the constraints of the technical restrictions in their institutions. They have not, however, managed to break free from their cultural habits as librarians. They certainly have not 'harnessed community capability' (Chad and Miller, 2005, 11) – they seem, in fact, to have deliberately excluded it. I do not mean here to disparage what the Burbank team have done, all their pages are very well put together, full of useful information, and indicate that the library is indeed engaged in a number of highly imaginative community activities designed to attract users and make the most of the library's assets. What struck me is the extent to which these sites promote and celebrate what the library does in its *physical* space: the 27 posts on Burbank Reads blog, for example, include details of six film screenings in the Central Library, and a number of activities (ranging from a 'Mad Science' Family Day to a rock and roll concert, to guest talks, to an advertisement for merchandise), all around the theme of their current read, *Rocket Boys*.

It is hard to conceive how all of this is actually something new – it is a harnessing of new technologies to promote and support the library and its activities, yes, but not a fundamental shift in the delivery of services.

Similarly, the UK's Bournemouth Book talk blog, established in July 2007, supports an existing service for reader development; in February 2008 there were nine posts, all by the reader development librarian, which generated nine comments.

Cheshire Public Library, in Connecticut, also has a wide range of technologically based user services. The Online Book Club will e-mail you a five-minute selection of a book every day (www.supportlibrary.com/su/su.cfm?x= 478864); library users can download audiobooks, receive monthly book reviews by e-mail and browse photos of library events on Flickr (http://flickr.com/ photos/11115952@N05/sets/). Their services to teenagers include a podcast, a 'teen-driven cultural magazine featuring teen writers, musicians, reviewers, commentators, and more' (Cheshire Public Library, 2008). This innovation does 'accept club news/local announcements, original creative writing, music, music/book/event reviews' from teenagers in the area (which need to be submitted to the teen librarian), and also has a linked-in Facebook profile and group, which has 21 members (at 6 April 2008).

A search for public library Facebook profiles (most of them based in the USA) reveals that there are 175; many of these have fans, and indeed the pages appear to be ranked by number of fans. Seattle public libraries have the most fans (361 on 13 April, 2008), and eight of the others on this first page of 'hits' have 100 or more. These numbers soon drop to numbers in the twenties. As a measure of 'interactivity' between libraries and their users, then, Facebook profiles may not be attracting huge numbers (although these figures do not reflect the number of people looking at the profiles, of course). The activity in other parts of Web-world 2.0 does also not suggest a surge of enthusiasm: Burbank Library's blog hosted 21 posts in March 2008 (one of its highest counts), and attracted only two comments – one from another regular blogger (presumably one of the librarians) and the other from 'Tim' wishing he could have been present at Friends of the Burbank Public Library amateur photography event – to see the photos necessitated a physical trip to the Central Library. Again, hardly evidence of a thriving web-based engagement between library service and its community.

Public libraries and young people: the 'Google generation'

Members of the 'Google generation' (Brindley, 2006, 486) are widely perceived to be the heaviest users of Web 2.0 technologies. A recent report found that social networking sites were most popular with teenagers and young adults:

> Ofcom research shows that just over one fifth (22%) of adult internet users aged 16+ and almost half (49%) of children aged 8–17 who use the internet have set up their own profile on a social networking site. For adults, the likelihood of setting up a profile is highest among 16–24 year olds (54%) and decreases with age.
> (Ofcom, 2008, 5)

Other research, however, points to the decline in uptake of sites by younger users. For example, during August 2006, 18 to 24 year olds were responsible for over 80% of page views in Facebook, and under 1% of page views was from those aged 25 to 34. A year later, the 18–24 year old group was responsible for just 24% of page views, whilst usage by 25 to 34 year olds had risen to 52% of page views. Use by these 'early adopters' fell by 43% between March and September 2007, suggesting a 'life cycle' of use which becomes increasingly functional as the initial novelty wears off (Human Capital, 2007). Other figures indicate that the over 55s are 'close to becoming the largest demographic age group online' (Charlton, 2007).

Young people, then, are more likely to engage with social networking sites currently, which may mean they are an appropriate space for libraries to promote their services. However, it may also be the case that libraries jump on this particular bandwagon just as it is rolling out of town, if the usage patterns for other social networking sites follow those of Facebook discussed above. Moreover, other research into use of social networking sites by young people points to the fact that 'communicating with known contacts is the primary reason that most people use social networking sites' (Ofcom, 2008, 42). The report further suggests that these sites are used as 'an entertainment tool but also as a way of creating and giving oneself identity. Importantly, the identities and profiles presented are generally constrained by social expectations' (Ofcom, 2008, 60). Whether young people are likely, then, to add public library pages to their friends, or want to be seen participating in web-based library activities, is an issue that needs researching.

The findings of a report into public library provision for 14 to 35 year olds (MLA et al., 2006), often known as the Destination Unknown report after the seminar that launched it, do not indicate that public libraries are high on the list in the image management of teenagers. The report found that the profile of current library users is 'older' and that usage of library services drops after the age of 14, with the lightest use to be found among the 14–35-year age group (MLA et al., 2006, 9). Among non-users, 'negative perceptions of libraries are fairly deeply entrenched' (MLA et al., 2006, 5).

The research suggests that to improve the value of the public library as a destination, services need to be 'adjusted' (rather than radically altered) to better match the needs of this age group. A number of 'universal' requirements are suggested, including the modernization of the style or ambience of the library, improved stock, electronic access, and improved assistance and support from technical facilities and staff.

What is interesting about the report is that it does not seek to put libraries in competition with those able to provide a better consumer experience (for example bookshops or music stores), but to capitalize on their existing collections to make the most of them. For example, in the area of music and CDs, the perception about libraries is that they would not have the latest stock, and copies would be few. The report therefore suggests that libraries capitalize on their ability to bring collections together, and draw on their supporting learning and developing skills remit by offering guidance and support for aspiring musicians (MLA et al., 2006, 20).

Where libraries continue to be seen as relevant, even among this age group, is in supporting learning: 'The idea of a source outside school, however, was often very compelling and an incentive to work' (MLA et al., 2006, 24). Improving this aspect of library work, by developing staff support beyond the traditional role of the librarian (for example, by using external staff to provide dedicated sessions), was seen as an opportunity to give the service 'real value'.

Section 4.3 of the report concentrates on 'Teen Space Seekers'. What is clear from the report, is that, despite emotional barriers to library use (they are 'boring', you have to be quiet), teenagers *do*, and could certainly be encouraged to, see libraries as a place to go: 'With very few options in terms of places to socialize, the library, if offering permission to be there and dedicated space, was somewhere to go. If offering activities and material which matched with their interests, this was compelling, as with little disposable income, it was again something to do independently of adults and family' (MLA et al., 2006, 52).

The key barrier to usage here was 'the perception that they offer nothing relevant to this age group' (MLA et al., 2006, 52). The research suggested that if their needs could be met, 'marketing messages that will be meaningful to Teen Space Seekers include . . . core sentiments' – covering issues such as a place to socialize, access state of the art technology, get help with homework and advice about future aspirations, develop and share interests (for example in music). A number of issues seem of particular relevance here: the importance of avoiding 'overt . . . teen language' and attempting to be 'cool' rather than just relevant; references to 'community' (seen as an adult concept), and, significantly, overt responsibility or getting involved: 'Overt messaging regarding "involvement" is also likely to be problematic. The teenagers in this sample, while wanting access to library services, did not want to have to take overt responsibility for them' (MLA et al., 2006, 54).

Findings like these do not encourage the idea that establishing a presence on social networking sites, or encouraging young people to generate content within a public library context, are likely to succeed in attracting those who already feel excluded from them. Moreover, they specifically undermine some of the key aspects of the Web 2.0 rhetoric – the emphasis on communities of use, collaboration and so on.

How, then, should public libraries seek to improve what they offer young people? Success stories like that of Sighthill Library in Edinburgh indicate that it is indeed possible to create a library which is the destination of choice: 'When people from other agencies come down here looking for all the young people, and get told you'll find them down the library, they don't believe it,' laughs Milne. 'It's the last place they'd expect them to be!' (Hirst, 2006).

Sighthill managed this by a combination of involving young people in a range of activities, from a 'Computer Crazies' club to a 'Yoothboox' scheme and even a football team. They did, in fact, exactly what Houghton above suggests – but not by creating virtual spaces and hoping teenagers would find them, but by engaging in the much messier and complex business of consultation (with young people and their carers) and partnership working (with other local agencies). The results have been highly successful, not just in increasing library usage, but in challenging anti-social behaviour, and, most importantly, by making the library a place young people want to go; a physical place to go where they can experience interaction of the kind they don't have elsewhere.

It is hard to imagine that Web 2.0 tools would be able to have the same impact; would teenagers used to relating to the library as a place to vandalize really have behaved differently if they had come across library blogs, MySpace pages and RSS feeds?

The Museums, Libraries and Archives Council (MLA), as part of the Framework for the Future programme and in consultation with the National Youth Libraries Board, identified at the beginning of 2008 the library services young people could expect, including 'Free, safe and welcoming spaces in the local community where they can have their personal space, to meet together and widen their horizons' (MLA, 2008). This is in keeping with other initiatives, such as the Department for Children, Schools and Families' 'myplace' programme, which is seeking to fund partnerships that will deliver 'ambitious, world class places that will offer young people co-located support services and the widest possible range of high quality activities' (Big Lottery Fund, 2008). Providing young people with an alternative to the virtual spaces they already inhabit, rather than trying to compete (poorly) with these, seems a far better use of the time and energy of public librarians than a reactive, potentially too tardy, response to what may be yet another passing technological fad.

Conclusions

To return to my Library 1.0 experience: what I am arguing for in this chapter is a more reflective and thoughtful approach to the appropriate use of Web 2.0 technologies in public libraries. It is not that Web 2.0 technologies have no place in the library world; they have the potential to contribute to publicizing and celebrating library services and activities; namely, they can be useful as a marketing tool. We should not see them at the moment as anything more than that, although future developments may begin to reshape the extent to which communities actively participate in and create value-added services. Some of the current rhetoric surrounding their adoption is unhelpful; at worst it is technological determinism at its crudest, and at best it is an overstatement of what technologies *may* facilitate, if that is what public library users call for and begin to develop.

References

Anderson, P. (2007a) *What is Web 2.0? Ideas, technologies and implications for education*, Joint Information Systems Committee, www.jisc.ac.uk/media/documents/techwatch/tsw0701b.pdf.

Anderson, P. (2007b) 'All that Glisters is not Gold': Web 2.0 and the librarian [editorial], *Journal of Librarianship and Information Science*, **39** (4), 195–8.

Beer, D. and Burrows, R. (2007) Sociology and, of and in Web 2.0: some initial considerations, *Sociological Research Online*, **12** (5), www.socresonline.org.uk/12/5/17.html.

Berners-Lee, T. (2006) *developerWorks Interviews: Tim Berners-Lee*, www.ibm.com/developerworks/podcast/dwi/cm-int082206txt.html.

Big Lottery Fund (2008) *myplace Information leaflet*, www.biglotteryfund.org.uk/prog_myplace_leaflet.pdf.

Blyberg, J. F. (2006) *11 Reasons Why Library 2.0 Exists and Matters*, www.blyberg.net/2006/01/09/11-reasons-why-library-20-exists-and-matters/.

Bradley, P. (2007) *How to Use Web 2.0 in Your Library*, Facet Publishing.

Brindley, L. (2006) Re-defining the Library, *Library Hi-Tech*, **24** (4), 484–95.

Casey, M. (2005) *Librarians Without Borders* (blogpost 26 September 2005), www.librarycrunch.com/2005/09/.

Chad, K. and Miller, P. (2005) *Do Libraries Matter? The rise of Library 2.0*, white paper, Talis.

Charlton, G. (2007) *Silver Surfers Expand Their Online Presence*, e-consultancy blog, 17 May, www.e-consultancy.com/news-blog/363351/silver-surfers-expand-their-online-presence.html.

Cheshire Public Library (2008) *The Cheshire Public Library Podcast*, www.cheshirelib.org/teens/cplpodcast.htm.

City of Burbank (2001a) *Ask the Librarian*, www.burbank.lib.ca.us/ask.cfm.

City of Burbank (2001b) *LittleWiki: Burbank children's wiki*, http://littlewiki.wikidot.com/start.

Eve, J. and Brophy, P. (2000) VITAL Issues: the perception, and use, of ICT services in UK public libraries, *LIBRES: Library and Information Science Research*, **10** (2), http://libres.curtin.edu.au/libres10n2/vital.htm.

Hayward, A. and Rooney, E. (2008) Blogs and Wikis in Libraries: our new best friends?, *Refer*, **24** (1), 1–4.

Hirst, J. (2006) *Lending a Hand – Sighthill Library, Edinburgh – Winner: outstanding team of the year; local government award*,
www.publicfinance.co.uk/features_details.cfm?News_id=27617.

Houghton, S. (2005) *Library 2.0 Discussion: Michael squared*,
http://librarianinblack.typepad.com/librarianinblack/2005/12/library_20_disc.html.

Human Capital (2007) *Facebook: an empirical analysis*, presentation at Poke 1.0 – a Facebook social science research symposium, organized by the London Knowledge Lab, University of London, 15 November 2007.

Maness, J. (2006) Library 2.0 Theory: Web 2.0 and its implications for libraries, *Webology*, **3** (2), Article 25,
www.webology.ir/2006/v3n2/a25.html.

Miller, P. (2005) Web 2.0: Building the New Library, *Ariadne*, **45**,
www.ariadne.ac.uk/issue45/miller/intro.html.

Miller, P. (2006) *Library 2.0: the challenge of disruptive innovation*, a Talis white paper,
www.talis.com/resources/documents/447_Library_2_prf1.pdf.

MLA (2008) *Libraries and Young People*,
www.mla.gov.uk/website/programmes/framework/framework_programmes/libs_and_young_people.

MLA, DCMS and Laser Foundation (2006) *A Research Study of 14–35 Year Olds for the Future Development of Public Libraries*,
www.mla.gov.uk/resources/assets//R/Research_study_of_14_35_year_olds_for_the_future_development_of_public_libraries_9841.pdf.

Nielsen, J. (2006) *Participation Inequality: encouraging more users to contribute*, (Alertbox column, 9 October, 2006),
www.useit.com/alertbox/participation_inequality.html.

Ofcom (2008) *Social Networking: a quantitative and qualitative research report into attitudes, behaviours and use*, Ofcom,
www.ofcom.org.uk/advice/media_literacy/medlitpub/medlitpubrss/socialnetworking/.

O'Reilly, T. (2005a) *What Is Web 2.0: design patterns and business models for the next generation of software*,
www.oreilly.com/pub/a/oreilly/tim/news/2005/09/30/what-is-web-20.html?page=1.

O'Reilly, T. (2005b) Web 2.0: compact definition?,
http://radar.oreilly.com/archives/2005/10/web-20-compact-definition.html.

Scholz, T. (2008) Market Ideology and the Myths of Web 2.0, *First Monday*, **13** (3), www.uic.edu/htbin/cgiwrap/bin/ojs/index.php/fm/article/view/2138/1945.

Shaw, R. (2005) *Web 2.0? It doesn't exist*, http://blogs.zdnet.com/ip-telephony/?p=805.

Sommerlad et al. (2004) *Books and Bytes: new service paradigms for the 21st century library*, Big Lottery Fund.

Surowiecki, J. (2005) *The Wisdom of Crowds: why the many are smarter than the few and how collective wisdom shapes business, economies, societies and nations*, Abacus.

Tancer, B. (2007) *Hitwise US Research Note: measuring Web 2.0 consumer participation*, Hitwise, available on request at www.hitwise.com/registration-page/us-social-networking-report.php.

Zimmer, M. (2008) Preface: critical perspectives on Web 2.0, *First Monday*, **13** (3), www.uic.edu/htbin/cgiwrap/bin/ojs/index.php/fm/article/view/2137/1943.

Theme 3
Changing directions of information delivery

8

Institutional repositories in tertiary institutions: access, delivery and performance

ROWENA CULLEN AND BRENDA CHAWNER

Introduction

Academic libraries have played a key role in the scholarly communication process for the past 150 years. They have experienced major changes in the creation, dissemination and preservation of knowledge, through changing social, philosophical and educational paradigms, and taken advantage of new technologies to fulfil their mission. Academic librarians have shown themselves to be adept at adjusting to these changes, and been proactive in advancing research, scholarship and knowledge. With the advent of institutional repositories, they are being asked to adopt another new technology, one that brings with it the potential for a further paradigm shift in scholarly communication. Roosendaal and Geurts (1997) identified four key functions of scientific/scholarly communication:

- registration: identifying the 'owner' of the intellectual property
- certification: establishing the quality of the research
- awareness: making the research available to others
- archiving: long-term preservation to make the results available to future researchers.

The first two have traditionally been carried out by hard copy scholarly journals, particularly registration (by tracking the date an article was submitted for publication) and certification (via the review process). Physical collections in libraries distributed the archiving function, and awareness was largely the responsibility of secondary sources, in particular abstracting and indexing services. Institutional repositories have the potential to change the way all four functions are carried out.

This chapter covers key concerns that led to the development of institutional repositories (IRs). This includes selected national and international initiatives, issues related to the creation, maintenance and use of repositories, and discussion of the extent to which IRs can meet the high expectations their promoters place on them.

History

In the late 20th century, existing channels for scholarly communication, particularly in the sciences and medicine, suffered from time lags in refereeing and publishing journal articles. Systems for distributing paper pre-prints by mail or facsimile were clumsy and slow, and researchers found it difficult to keep up with new developments in their fields. In the early 1990s, the rise of the internet and the web made other communication and publishing options possible, starting with e-mail distribution, then moving to the web. The first web-based pre-print server, arXiv, was started at Los Alamos National Laboratory in 1991. It initially accepted physics pre-prints, and has been extended to include aspects of mathematics, computational linguistics and neuroscience. Its goal was to capture pre-prints in electronic form, to make them available to the widest possible audience. Other disciplines have adopted the arXiv model, for example, economics, which has EconPapers, and cognitive psychology, with CogPrints, covering psychology, neuroscience and linguistics.

At the same time, journal subscription costs were increasing significantly, particularly in science and medicine (White and Creaser, 2004). Many libraries responded by cancelling subscriptions, and, as a result, researchers lost access to key material. In 2001 the Budapest Open Access Initiative published a manifesto calling for open access to peer-reviewed journal literature (Open Society Institute, 2002). This recommended two strategies: self-archiving of refereed journal articles in open electronic archives, and publishing in open access journals, which publish their content freely on the web (but may impose author charges).

Jones, Andrew and MacColl cite the Open Archives Initiative in 1999 as a major factor in the rise of institution-based repositories (Jones, Andrew and MacColl, 2006, 7). The first academic IR projects were the EPrints archive at Southampton and the DSpace initiative at MIT. Rather than having a subject or discipline focus, these projects collect the publications of staff from an individual institution. Academic librarians, who were often the initiators of these projects, shared the ideals of the Budapest initiative, and promoted the IR as an institution-based tool for self-archiving. Clifford Lynch, an early promoter of the repository concept, defines an IR as a 'set of services that a university offers to the members of its community for the management and dissemination of digital materials created by the institution and its community members' (Lynch, 2003, 328). While this definition places no limits on the scope of a repository, to date most IRs have focused on theses, pre-prints or post-prints, or authorized copies of journal articles, rather than datasets or teaching material.

Jones, Andrew and MacColl (2006) suggest that IRs were developed partly because some academics were reluctant to deposit their work in discipline-based repositories, or were concerned about the longevity of external repositories. An institutional repository, by contrast, could be deemed more credible and trustworthy. However, for some, this creates the dilemma of whether an author should deposit their research in their institutional repository or in a discipline-specific repository. Heath, Jubb and Robey (2008) make a case for subject repositories as the prime destination for research data, despite the greater challenges of curation and preservation. They argue that researchers are not interested so much in the research outputs of a particular institution, but rather what is available in a particular field.

IRs have now become a global phenomenon – they have been established in over 50 countries, including four in Africa. The majority, though, are in North America, Europe and Australasia. Interest in establishing and promoting IRs is likely to continue, particularly as academic staff increase their online presence and adapt their work patterns. With growing interest in using Web 2.0 tools such as blogs, RSS, wikis and virtual communities, universities will need to provide future scholars with appropriate tools for promoting their work and discovering the work of others. As Lynch (2003, 328) noted, 'the intellectual life and scholarship of our universities will increasingly be represented, documented, and shared in digital form'. IRs are one of the tools that make this possible.

Projected benefits of institutional repositories

Reasons for setting up IRs vary, and a range of projected benefits has been suggested in the literature. These include benefits to the researcher, to the institution and to individual disciplines. Academic libraries also benefit from being involved in IR initiatives, and there are implications for scholarly communication overall.

Pinfield (2002) suggests that the primary benefit to researchers is exposure – by having their research and publications openly available on the web, not just in fee-based databases, scholarly journals or books, their work is likely to be used and cited more. As a result, their reputation will be enhanced over the long term, due to the recognition they gain from this. Other benefits to researchers include stewardship and preservation of their publications in digital form, which frees them from the need to maintain this content on a personal computer or website (Lynch, 2003, 330).

Many of the benefits identified, though, are at the institutional level. In a survey of academic library directors and senior administrators carried out in 2006, Rieh et al. identified 'capturing the intellectual capital of [the] institution' as the most important benefit of an IR (Rieh et al., 2007). Other benefits at the institutional level include increasing the institution's prestige by exposing research carried out by its staff and students. Crow suggests that this will be a much more effective way of highlighting an institution's total academic outputs, which are otherwise spread among many publications (Crow, 2002, 6). A further benefit will be increased differentiation between institutions, because of the unique content in individual repositories. Anecdotal evidence suggests that potential students with an interest in a discipline may be attracted to an institution that makes its research in the field widely available through a repository. Improved long term preservation of the institution's digital assets is another benefit, through centralizing content in known, standardized formats (Crow, 2002, 12).

Benefits to individual disciplines result from streamlining the scholarly communication process. By encouraging their staff and students to lodge pre- and/or post-prints of their publications in the repository, institutions decrease the time needed for other researchers in the field to become aware of new findings, which should result in less duplication of research (Pinfield, 2002, 262). Similarly, research results become available to people in developing countries, who otherwise have limited access to traditional publications. IRs have the potential to facilitate new modes of scholarly publication – because their scope is defined by the institution, the content can be tailored to the needs of participating researchers and disciplines. The scope of the IR will thus evolve over time as these needs change.

Benefits to the academic library are improved relationships with contributors and a better awareness of staff and student research interests. Buehler and Boateng (2005) suggest that reference staff will be able to make more use of their knowledge of library content. This is likely to result in improved staff confidence in dealing with enquiries about research, and will also allow them to better identify resources that may be of interest to researchers, providing a form of current awareness service.

In summary, compelling arguments suggest that IRs will be successful, because of the opportunities they provide staff and students to make their work widely accessible, and because they give institutions a new channel for promoting the work of their staff.

IR technologies, standards and metadata

All IRs require technology to fulfil their objectives. The main hardware requirement is a web server with sufficient capacity for the projected repository content, and software that supports the repository core functions of ingest, metadata creation, access control, resource discovery and display, and preservation (Gibbons, 2004). There is some interest in extending the functionality of IR software to incorporate social networking functions, such as commenting, tagging and bookmarking (Davis, 2008). A majority of current IRs use open source software, with the most popular being EPrints and DSpace. Other open source options are Greenstone and Fedora/Fez. The main commercial software used for IRs is Digital Commons, originally developed for the Berkeley Electronic Press (bepress). VITAL, available from VTLS, is a commercial package that uses the Fedora open source project as a backend. Unlike the open source options, which require institutions to manage their own servers, Digital Commons offers a hosted solution, in which the content is located on remote servers managed by bepress.

IR projects may involve other technologies, depending on the type and format of content being accepted for deposit. If the content is not already in electronic form, it will need to be converted using a scanner followed by optical character recognition. Multimedia files, such as sound, image or video files, may need to be converted into a standard format to facilitate display, or for long-term preservation.

Persistent URLs, or 'handles', are another feature of repository software. These provide a long-term solution to the problem of URLs changing when systems or institutions change, and are an important enabler of the preservation function of an IR.

While a stand-alone institutional repository can be useful for people who already have an interest in a specific institution, the true benefit of an IR comes from the ability to expose metadata about the repository content to search engines so that it can be found by a wider community. A key standard for this type of interoperability is the Open Archives Initiative Protocol for Metadata Harvesting (OAI-PMH), which allows metadata for items in a repository to be extracted and indexed separately. This allows people to search multiple repositories on a single site, and is important for exposing an institution's data to users anywhere in the world. OAI-PMH-compliant harvesting software operates as a 'robot', crawling a known set of repositories on a scheduled basis to capture their metadata and index it. A key feature of the OAI-PMH protocol is its support for incremental harvesting, which allows harvester software to operate more efficiently. There are a number of harvester projects that capture OAI-PMH data; one of the most popular is the PKP Harvester, initially developed by the Public Knowledge Project at Simon Fraser University.

Much of the software used in this area, for both individual repositories and for harvesters, has been developed under an open source model. To ensure ongoing development, these projects will need continued support from their community members. The predominance of open source software may result in commercial IR software being discontinued, and therefore the limited number of companies offering commercial IR software is a concern.

Metadata

The type of metadata used to describe resources stored in an IR is important in successful metadata harvesting, interoperability, access and discovery. Unqualified Dublin Core (DC) metadata is the minimum standard to comply with OAI-PMH requirements; this is the basic descriptive metadata needed to describe an item and identify its originator, and is supported by most repository software. This does not necessarily provide enough detail for some types of content, and most repository software will support extensions to the metadata being collected, particularly for journals, rights, version control and preservation. The Australian RUBRIC project, which was set up to provide a toolkit to help institutions choose repository software, noted that Dublin Core is adequate for most repositories, but that it has limitations where detailed searching is needed (RUBRIC, 2007).

The process used to ingest material into an IR will determine who creates the metadata. Initial advocates for IRs saw them as being used for 'self-archiving', in which authors submit documents themselves; this model is particularly common in IRs that collect theses. The advantage of this approach is that it minimizes the number of steps in the process, but it may result in metadata of variable quality, or in the submission of material that does not comply with institutional policy or with a journal publisher's copyright restrictions. Many IRs are now using mediated submission, in which authorized library staff are responsible for creating all new records. Mediated submission is more likely to result in high-quality metadata, and allows staff to convert formats if necessary and check the copyright status of the work.

If the IR allows metadata to be harvested, its quality is particularly important to ensure useful and relevant search results. This is where it is helpful for institutions who contribute to a central hub to agree on standards for element content, as well as structure. The New Zealand harvesting project, KRIS (Kiwi Research Information Series), has agreed on extensive metadata standards, which specify which elements are mandatory, important, medium and low priority, and also specifies standards for the content of the elements. For example, the subject fields use the 'Marsden' Fields of Research codes, which were developed to classify applications for research funding. One benefit of this standardization is that the metadata can be checked, and error reports produced when problems are found in the harvesting process.

Key issues in creating and managing a repository

There are many other basic considerations that institutions need to take into account when setting up and managing a repository to ensure it is a sustainable and effective information management system. Despite clear guidance from experts in the field, such as the Research Libraries Group (now part of OCLC), and Jones, Andrew and MacColl's excellent monograph (Jones, Andrew and MacColl, 2006), examination of even a small sample of repositories suggests that their parent institutions have adopted a range of policies, especially in relation to scope and content. It is possible, given that IR technology is still on the brink of what we could term its mature phase, that there will be greater uniformity appearing as the systems mature. On the other hand, it could be argued that most IRs have adopted technical standards that facilitate enhanced access and interoperability, such as software and metadata standards, while issues of scope and content reflect more local priorities. For most tertiary institutions, strength in specific disciplines, reflected in both their library collections and their research outputs, creates their point of difference, and it may be appropriate to reflect these differences in their IR content.

The process of establishing an institutional repository begins with business analysis, the creation of a business case, and consideration of business issues (Jones, Andrew and MacColl, 2006). Key decisions include whether to 'go it alone' or collaborate with other institutions, what software will be used, which unit in the institution will manage the repository, what will be included (scope), and how the repository will be funded. The organization must decide to what extent it can comply with emerging standards, based on available resources. Individual accounts of how repositories have been established, many of which are reported in the online journal D-Lib, and some of which are described in Cullen and Chawner (2008), suggest that not all institutions focus initially on developing the business case or exploring best practice, and some fail to take into account issues of scalability, sustainability and quality or trustworthiness, key elements of the scholarly publishing process that has dominated the past century of academic research output.

The Research Libraries Group (RLG), addressing the issue of trustworthiness, has done invaluable work identifying the attributes of a 'Trusted Digital Repository', defined as 'one whose mission is to provide reliable, long-term access to managed digital resources to its designated community, now and in the future' (Research Libraries Group, 2002). The report's authors argue that this definition, and the attributes they define, are critical to gaining the trust of the academic community, and acceptance of the concept.

The attributes of a trusted repository, as defined by the RLG/OCLC working party, include:

- compliance with the reference model for an Open Archival Information System (OAIS)
- administrative responsibility
- organizational viability
- financial sustainability
- technological and procedural suitability
- system security
- procedural accountability.

This detailed report, which is now used for audit procedures (Research Libraries Group, 2007) also defines the level at which the criteria should be applied (for example management level, collection level, or item/record level).

The OAIS reference model defines the critical functions of a repository, as submission and 'pre-ingest' activities, ingest, archival storage, data management, preservation planning, archive administration and access/dissemination, assigning standards to each (Consultative Committee on Space Data Systems, 2002). The RLG report defines these as they would apply to a trusted repository, as for example:

Before a repository can accept responsibility as a reliable archiving service, management tools must be in place, covered by a well-documented and agreed-on collections policy document. For most libraries and archives, this will be in the form of a collections management/development policy. Many of the same criteria apply to both digital and traditional. However, for digital materials these elements are the most critical:

- evaluation criteria for assessing potential submissions; that is, selection criteria for digital preservation
- collections development strategies and technical strategies for continuing access
- collections development procedures, including review procedures pertaining to retaining and de-accessioning materials.

(Research Libraries Group, 2002, 44)

Scope

Defining scope is a major task in establishing a repository. Scope decisions determine whether the repository will contain research outputs alone or other items of interest in the institution, such as historical items being digitized for preservation or access, audiovisual media, institutional records and reports, learning objects and pictorial records. The RLG/OCLC report notes that 'The sheer variety of digital materials and the role that they play in the collection make development and application of collection policies very challenging. The existence or lack of a physical equivalent influences decisions about whether and how the digital resource is preserved' (Research Libraries Group, 2002, 17). Genoni (2004) notes that content-related issues will be crucial to the success of institutional repositories, but that they remain largely unresolved. It is not surprising therefore that, in his study of 25 UK repositories, Allen (2005) noted a great variety in scope and content, several small and under-utilized repositories, and that the contents were dominated by science and technology. This unevenness in content, he noted, can lead to loss of trust or reputation, and make it more difficult to persuade contributors of the value of the repository. The same pattern was observed in the repositories by the Numbers Project (McDowell, 2007; Thomas and McDonald, 2007), which also found a wide range in the number of items deposited. The largest proportion of items deposited (41.5%) was student work (primarily PhD and other theses), followed by faculty scholarly output (37%), of which only 13% was peer reviewed (the remaining items were considered to be scholarly, but not peer reviewed, or in report format). The remaining content was made up of pictures, presentation slides, institutional material (brochures, newsletters, minutes and reports), and digitized historical material (McDowell, 2007). The typical pattern of deposit was one item per depositing author (even when thesis deposit was excluded); over 70%, and up to 75% of authors in some key repositories, had contributed only one paper. Unless well-reasoned decisions are made early, and the rules on scope are clear, the value of the repository, its purpose and focus may be compromised by a lack of support from academic staff.

A key issue here is whether articles and conference papers should be deposited and retained only after peer review and acceptance, or at the time of submission, and whether they should be updated if changes were made before formal publication. There is as yet little agreement in either the scholarly or library communities about these issues, which will have a significant impact on the use, reputation and value of the repository. Probets and Jenkins (2006) suggest, therefore, that clear and effective policies should be established addressing the *attributes* of items for deposit, including: type of document, status (peer-reviewed, accepted, published and so on), format, who may contribute (only employers, or co-researchers, affiliates), and whether related output (presentations, workshops, work in the same series) should be accepted. The Scholarly Publishing and Academic Resources Coalition (SPARC) Institutional Repository Checklist and Resource Guide (SPARC, 2002) argues that a repository *should* include post-print, grey literature, and, in particular, pre-prints, (as well as theses), as long as this material is carefully handled, and properly managed. The SPARC paper suggests that each institution will want to make its own decision on these matters, and take into account the changing nature of scholarly publishing and open access. In this case, careful attention to assignment of categories, content management systems and version control will be required. This view is supported by Lynch (2003), who argues that repositories should 'reflect campus life, symposia, performances, lectures'. A subsequent SPARC position paper (Crow, 2002) also encourages a broader view of scope, including work in progress, grant applications and reports, as well as student reports (not confined to research degrees), classroom and teaching materials, computer programs, audiovisual material, creative works, institutional documents and reports.

Certainly, the greater the variety of content, and the broader the policy, the greater the need for high-quality processes to manage version identification and control. The potential number of versions created as part of a research project, and the potential number of relationships between iterations, versions and manifestations, further complicated by projects with co-authorship and collaborative work, create problems for repositories, which need to define relations between items (Puplett, 2008). This is similar to the issues being addressed by the Functional Requirements for Bibliographic Records (FRBR) standard (IFLA, 1998), and FRBR could offer a possible solution to the problem. The RIVER study (Rumsey, 2006), VERSIONS (2008) and the subsequent Version Identification Framework (VIF) project (VIF, 2008), all funded by the Joint Information Systems Committee (JISC), have also focused on guidelines to alleviate end-user confusion over the status of and relationships between content they find in a repository. A key decision for repository managers, then, is which version(s) should be ingested, how to organize multiple versions effectively, and how to describe them so they can be found, identified and related.

Sustainability

In the early stages of establishing a repository, securing staff with appropriate skills is critical (Cullen and Chawner, 2008). Longer term issues involve ongoing cost, of which staffing is likely to be a major component, scalability and sustainability. Jones, Andrew and MacColl (2006) argue that the development and maintenance of an institutional repository may even require organizational restructuring. Staff with high level cataloguing and metadata skills are required just when many institutions have decided to outsource cataloguing or purchase their cataloguing records with metadata already in place.

Rieh et al. (2007) suggest that staffing costs account for nearly 40% of a repository's total budget. By contrast, the Auseaccess website wiki, written largely by enthusiasts for the Open Access philosophy, states:

> Creating an institutional repository is cheap, convenient, and takes little effort. It takes about $A3000 to $A10000 for hardware, nothing for the software since it is open-source, and say two to three weeks' work to get the repository up and running. For the next two years, it may require say a half-time commitment by a librarian to manage and promote the repository, but thereafter the time requirement should be easily absorbable into the university's budget.

This optimism is not borne out by recent studies, such as the LIFE project (www.life.ac.uk/), which should produce more reliable data on the true costs of repositories.

The LIFE project, a venture supported by the Ligue des Bibliothèques Européennes de Recherche (LIBER), is led by the British Library and University

College London (UCL) Library Services in the UK with funding from the JISC. The remit of the LIFE project is to investigate:

- what the long-term lifecycle and preservation costs for a library in higher and further education may be to carry out long-term digital preservation
- what the comparative long-term lifecycle and preservation costs of a paper and digital copy of the same publication may be
- at what point there may be sufficient confidence in the stability and maturity of digital preservation to switch from paper to digital (for preservation purposes)
- what the relative risks of digital versus paper archiving may be (McLeod, Wheatley and Ayris, 2006).

The project has developed a methodology to calculate the long-term costs and future requirements of the preservation of digital objects, by analysing and comparing a number of different types of digital assets and applying a life-cycle approach to each. The cost heads comprise: acquisition, ingest, metadata, access, storage and preservation. More detailed work on the lifecycle and preservation costs of an item in an institutional repository will be released in Summer 2008 (Ayris, P. et al., 2008). These findings will, among other things, try to establish whether digital preservation is the cheapest and most cost-effective option for the long-term preservation of a library's assets.

Long-term preservation has been used as a powerful justification for the creation of repositories, although not all the issues related to preservation of content have been resolved, and now are not likely to be resolved for some time. The OAIS reference model (Consultative Committee for Space Data Systems, 2002) provides detailed recommendations about best practice and appropriate work flows for each stage of the preservation process. The Australian Partnership for Sustainable Resources (APSR) has extended this endeavour, advocating the use of 'preservation metadata' to enable long-term discovery and access once technology formats become obsolete (Lee, Clifton and Langley, 2006).

An alternative solution for the preservation of text is proposed by the 'Digital Scholar's Workbench' project developed at the Australian National University (Barnes, 2007). Observing that most scholars write in Microsoft Word™, and deposit their outputs as pdf files, Barnes advocates that repositories avoid reliance on proprietary software, by using (and encouraging scholars to create) documents in structured rather than visual formats, such as DocBook, TEI or XHTML. 'Digital Scholar's Workbench' offers a range of file format conversion and publishing services that re-format documents for long-term preservation. While initiatives of this kind will be urgently needed for the long-term sustainability of the majority of repositories which are heavily text-based repositories, the solution Barnes proposes adds another barrier that will increase the reluctance of researchers to incorporate deposit into their research workflow.

Copyright, intellectual property and third-party copyright

Intellectual property and copyright legislation are major issues confronting any institution that takes on the role of publisher in hosting and making available the research output of its staff. As Jones, Andrew and MacColl note, the early adopter group of 'liberal-thinking, technologically savvy academics, with a great enthusiasm for participating in new endeavours' (Jones, Andrew and MacColl, 2006, 117) who populated the initial repositories paid little heed to intellectual property rights. As librarians took over the initiative the risks inherent in running a repository began to be examined, and a number of guidelines now exist to help institutions work their way through the legislative minefield of copyright across varying jurisdictions. The Australian-based Open Access to Knowledge (OAK) Law Project's Guide (Pappalardo and Fitzgerald, 2007), for example, clarifies Australian law on matters such as pre-prints, post-prints and conference papers, and the responsibilities of repositories and depositors (noting that pre-prints are normally included in the publisher's copyright over post-prints). Much of their advice would apply to other jurisdictions.

Once a repository is established with either pre- or post-prints, the institution needs to understand its new responsibilities. Jones, Andrew and MacColl suggest that when an institution seeks to establish an IR, it changes its role in the dissemination of knowledge from managing collections of material from external sources to that of publisher (Jones, Andrew and MacColl, 2006). It must therefore be aware of the rights and interests of all stakeholders, from authors, funders and the institution itself, through to users and the general public. It also needs to manage the risks inherent in this new role. These include the risk of copyright infringement, defamation, the provision of inaccurate information, and disclosure of confidential information (Jones, Andrew and MacColl, 2006, 145). Even in the comparatively straightforward area of intellectual property, however, not all institutions developing IRs show awareness of their liability. Kelley et al. (2002) found that only 52% of surveyed institutions had developed an intellectual property policy.

Third-party copyright issues are equally overlooked by many institutions. Jones, Andrew and MacColl argue that material embedded within a thesis (such as text or images) created by a third party who holds copyright cannot be covered by the defence of 'fair use' since this only extends to examination and research, and that publishing the thesis in an IR will breach copyright (Jones, Andrew and MacColl, 2006, 200). This issue has not been raised in the past in relation to hard copy theses deposited in libraries. Gadd, Oppenheim and Probets found only 25% of self-archiving authors wishing to self-archive previously published research sought the necessary clearance from the original copyright holder of any material cited in their research paper (2003, 259). Although to our knowledge there has not been any case law covering material in repositories for breach of third-party copyright, it is surely not long before the first of such cases arise. As with breaches of intellectual property, many institutions cover themselves by stating that, should such a challenge arise, they will immediately withdraw the offending publication (Cullen and Chawner, 2008).

A related issue arises as institutions seek to add recent theses to their IRs, and digitize earlier ones. Social science research methods commonly involve surveys, interviews or focus groups with individual participants. In the past two decades this kind of research has been recognized as raising personal privacy issues, and most institutions require researchers to seek informed consent from participants for the use of information provided. This usually involves explaining to participants how confidentiality of the research data will be maintained, where any report containing the research results will be published, and what protections individuals are guaranteed in the use of their personal data, opinions, habits and preferences. Publication of a research report in an academic journal, or deposit of a thesis in closed access stacks in a library, available only on request, is a very different matter from its deposit in an institutional repository, accessible via the internet. Not only are participants and organizations at greater risk of being identified in this 'open access' environment, they almost certainly did not give their 'consent' to this level of exposure.

This is an even more crucial issue in countries where indigenous peoples have alternative paradigms of knowledge ownership. In collectivist societies, for example, knowledge is not owned by the individual but by the family or tribal group. One individual (whether they are a member of an indigenous community, or a researcher working with an indigenous community) may not be able to assign rights to an institutional repository to make research results available in an 'open access' environment. While some academics might decline to deposit their research publications for these reasons, others may not give due consideration to such issues. This is a further risk to be added to those noted by Jones, Andrew and MacColl (2006).

Content recruitment

Statistics from registries such as the Registry of Open Access Resources (ROAR) and OpenDOAR show that growth in the number of items in repositories has not reached early expectations. As Peter Brophy comments 'it is . . . noticeable that generally few academics have deposited significant numbers of their publications'. He continues: 'The reason for the slow development of repositories appears to be that the deposit of publications does not fit well within academics' workflows – it requires separate actions which have to be prioritized within busy schedules. Since the incentives are yet unclear or at best unproven, it is not surprising that this activity fails to reach the top of the "to do" list' (Brophy, 2008, 10).

The willingness of academics to contribute to a repository depends on a number of factors. Historically, as noted above, particularly in the sciences, groups of researchers keen to share their research findings, and with an element of competitiveness, have led the way. Other early adopters are those from more recently developed academic disciplines, or who are seeking to build an academic community across a dispersed workforce, such as Nursing Studies (Cullen and Chawner, 2008). In contrast, academics accustomed to the well established routines of publication in academic journals of known prestige, with effective systems of peer review and dissemination, see little benefit in alternative methods of access to the same material. As Hendler (2007) notes, prestige of publication venue plays the single largest role in faculty decisions about the destination of their research.

A University of California Office of Scholarly Communication (2007) report indicated that academics have little awareness of opportunities for open access publishing, continue to publish in traditional venues, and identify a major obstacle to change as 'the existing reward systems of tenure/promotion (and even grant making) which favour traditional publishing forms and venues' (University of California Office of Scholarly Communication, 2007, 3). This well established reward system is currently being reinforced by an international focus to use research outputs to measure tertiary institutions, which emphasizes publication in the most prestigious journals and conference proceedings in a discipline.

Arts and humanities researchers differ in a number of ways in their use of library services from their colleagues in the sciences and social sciences, and these differences continue to be evident in the digital world. Allen's survey (Allen,

2005) highlights the importance of peer review for British as well as US academics. He found that humanities scholars have low awareness of repositories and their value to the research community, perceive the value of repositories to be to the reader, rather than the scholar depositing, and have ongoing concerns about repositories, such as peer review, plagiarism and intellectual property ownership. More recent research in the UK about the impact of e-publishing and open access for researchers in the arts and humanities suggests that they are much less aware and make significantly less use of e-publications and open access services (Heath, Jubb and Robey, 2008). This may be partly because the advance of knowledge in the arts and humanities is typically slower than in other disciplines, and researchers are more likely to be interested in the final versions of articles, or post-prints, rather than pre-prints. Because of the very long half-life of journals in the humanities, publishers may be less willing to allow open-access posting of e-prints even after an embargo period (Heath, Jubb and Robey, 2008). However, the authors also note that although many journals let authors make their material available through repositories, their willingness in some cases outruns the inclination of their authors to self-archive.

Content recruitment therefore continues to be a major problem with institutional repositories. All respondents in the Census of Institutional Repositories in the US reported having difficulty recruiting content from faculty and graduate students, and that study found that the more mature the repository is, the more sceptical respondents (that is staff responsible for administering the repository) have become about the success of any given recruitment strategy (McDowell, 2007). These findings, echoed in many other reports of individual repositories, challenge the fundamental open access philosophy that posits institutional repositories as an alternative tool for the current scholarly publishing model (McDowell, 2007), and it appears that members of the academic and research community do not see IRs as part of the publication process. It is possible that more active recruitment of content, with library or repository staff managing the process, rather than leaving it to academics themselves, will be more successful. The issue of mediated deposit therefore has wider ramifications than quality control in the area of metadata, and may affect uptake and the perceived value of the repository.

It is clear that tertiary institutions wanting to increase their rate of deposit (and use) need to actively market the concept of the institutional repository within their institution. Advocacy is an ongoing task to ensure that new depositors are being recruited, and that previous depositors continue to contribute updates of their research output, and remain committed to the overall success of the repository. Barton and Waters (2004) suggested that academics may need to be exposed to information about the repository service seven times before they are fully aware of it. This would be done through reports and policy papers presented at Academic Boards, presentations at faculty and departmental meetings, library newsletters, meetings with individual staff members, and personal exchanges between academics. Securing high level support within the institution for the establishment of the repository, and finding a high profile 'champion' within the institution, who will deposit a substantial body of research, and be seen to benefit from doing so, is a strategy adopted by many institutions. But even institutions that have secured such a champion find that the rate of deposits tails off after an initial flurry of interest.

In response to this situation, many, along with Brophy (2008), have suggested that repository use must be embedded in research and research publication processes. However, the mechanisms necessary to achieve this are cumbersome, and run counter to the prevailing ethos of academic life, with its claims of academic freedom, and the right of researchers to make their own decisions about the use of their research output. Embedding repository deposit in the research process itself is likely to be more acceptable in independent research institutes, which employ full-time researchers, whose loyalty to the institution may be stronger than that of academics in the tertiary education sector, whose loyalty is to their discipline, rather than their employer. But, as Foster and Gibbons (2005) found in their in-depth study of 25 academics at the University of Rochester, it is relatively easy to determine what academics want, but another matter to deliver it. Trialling a 'work-practice methodology', they have developed a Researcher Page/Research Tools enhancement of DSpace, providing workspace for work in progress, supporting shared authorship, and links to other research materials, which they hope will significantly increase repository use in their academic community, leading to a higher rate of deposit.

The most effective (and the most controversial) means used to maximize rates of deposit is mandatory deposit, a requirement that researchers employed by an institution deposit the outcome of their research in the institution's repository. Tertiary institutions that have adopted this policy, while allowing some exceptions, and rarely being aggressive in pursuit of those who do not deposit, have indeed had high rates of deposit. Henty (2007) cites the Queensland University of Technology as one such example. There are also downsides to this approach – not the least of which is the high workload involved in managing the process (modifying metadata, employing version control, checking intellectual property rights have been observed and overseeing quality control), whether self-deposit or mediated deposit is employed. A more widely adopted solution is to mandate deposit of theses from any research degree awarded by the institution, and encourage the deposit of other staff publications. However, some academics are taking the initiative for themselves. Members of the Faculty of Arts and Sciences at Harvard University voted recently to require all staff to allow the university to deposit their peer-reviewed publications in the Harvard repository. In proposing this policy, Stuart Shieber, professor of computer science at Harvard, commented that the decision 'should be a very powerful message to the academic community that we want and should have more control over how our work is used and disseminated' (Guterman, 2008).

Growth of institutional repositories

Recent IR literature indicates that repositories are being implemented at a growing rate. A 2005 survey of American institutions found that 40% had established institutional repositories (Lynch and Lippincott, 2005) and Van Westrienen and Lynch's 2005 study of European countries showed some approaching similar levels, although there was considerable variation in their results. Suber (2008) reports that the number of repositories grew by over 20% in 2007. By April 2008, OpenDOAR listed over 1100 repositories, indicating the popularity they have gained in a decade.

OpenDOAR defines four categories of repository – aggregating (aggregating data from several subsidiary repositories), governmental, disciplinary and institutional (which now represents over 75% of the repositories listed) (OpenDOAR, 2008). IRs listed by OpenDOAR include small research institutes, universities, other tertiary institutions (e.g. polytechnics and institutes of technology), publishing houses and museums. IR consortia have been established, within which software and technical support are provided collaboratively, but individual members set their own policies concerning content and promote access to their repository through their web pages. There are a number of repository consortia listed on OpenDOAR, such as the US-based LASR (Liberal Arts Scholarly Repository), NZ-based Coda (An Institutional Repository for the New Zealand ITP Sector) and Brazil's Projeto Maxwell. In the UK, SHERPA-LEAP (London E-Prints Access Project), a University of London partnership led by UCL, has created open access institutional repositories at 13 University of London institutions, including Birkbeck College, the Royal Holloway and SOAS.

National and international initiatives

While most repositories have been established for individual institutions, a number of national and international initiatives have been set up to help organizations planning a repository project, or provide central services, such as metadata harvesters. National initiatives are evident in countries where a high proportion of institutions have established an IR. This section describes selected national and international initiatives, to illustrate the range of activities that have been undertaken. It is by no means a comprehensive discussion of all such initiatives.

The Netherlands

The Netherlands was one of the first countries to undertake a national project to support the development of institutional repositories in its universities. The Digital Academic REpositories (DARE) project, begun in 2003 and ending in 2006, involved 13 Dutch universities, the National Library of the Netherlands, the Royal Netherlands Academy of Arts and Science, and the Netherlands Organization for Scientific Research. Its main objectives were to help institutions set up individual repositories, provide central services based on repository content, and initiate and promote the submission and use of content. In April 2008 the central harvester listed over 150,000 items in the Dutch repositories. A unique feature of the DARE project is the identification of some records as belonging to the 'Cream of Science' – from the top Dutch scientists, and the 'Promise of Science' – doctoral theses from all Dutch universities. In June 2008 the DareNet site will be integrated into the National Academic Research and Collaborations Information System (NARCIS) site (www.narcis.info/index).

The United Kingdom

In the UK, the Joint Information Systems Committee (JISC) has undertaken a number of projects to promote the development of IRs. The SHERPA and SHERPA Plus projects led to the establishment of over 20 repositories using the EPrints software, and also produced a number of 'good practice' documents, which are available on the Repositories Support Project website (www.rsp.ac.uk/). Electronic Theses Online Service (EThOS) is a national project to provide a single database for all UK theses, which will be based in the British Library (Russell, 2007). UKOLN, based at the University of Bath, maintains a wiki for participants in JISC repository projects. The most recent JISC project, funded to March 2009, focuses on cross-searching facilities across repositories; helping institutions develop a critical mass of content, identifying preservation solutions; and providing advice for the development of repositories.

In April 2008 the UK had 121 repositories; the largest is DSpace at Cambridge, which has approximately 187,000 records, and includes heritage materials such as broadcasts, images and lectures, as well as research outputs. The typical UK repository is considerably smaller, though, with a median of 366 records, and a mean of 3491. EPrints is used in 48.8% of UK repositories, and DSpace in 19.8% (ROAR, 2008). The Depot, housed by the EDINA national data centre at the University of Edinburgh, is a repository for UK researchers who do not have access to a repository at their employing institution.

Australia

The first Australian initiative to set up repositories involved theses, and the Council of Australian University Librarians (CAUL), in association with seven Australian universities, began preliminary work on what became the Australasian Digital Theses (ADT) project in 1998/99. Participating institutions host digital versions of their theses on local servers, and standardized metadata is harvested to a central server. In April 2008 the project had 40 participants, seven of which were New Zealand universities.

The Australian Commonwealth Department of Education, Science and Training (DEST) funded a number of projects to establish and support institutional repositories in Australian universities, starting with Federated Repositories of Digital Objects (FRODO) in 2003. Other DEST-funded projects include the Australian Research Repositories Online to the World (ARROW), Australian Partnership for Sustainable Repositories (APSR), Managed Environment for Research Repository Infrastructure (MERRI) and Regional Universities Building Research Infrastructure Collaboratively (RUBRIC). By spreading the funding across a range of projects, different universities took on the 'lead' role, and universities of all sizes have benefited from the results.

The RUBRIC project has developed an extensive toolkit that contains documents and tools for institutions that are implementing an IR. The topics covered include system options, publicity and marketing, populating the repository, managing the repository, metadata and access management. The toolkit also includes scripts for migrating data to a repository. The National Library of Australia national metadata harvester, the ARROW Discovery Service, provides access to records from 24 Australian university IRs, plus other research collections such as open access journals.

New Zealand

New Zealand lagged behind other countries in establishing institutional repositories. In 2005 the National Library sponsored the feasibility study *Institutional Repositories for the Research Sector* (Rankin, 2005), and a follow up workshop. New Zealand's first IR was established in late 2005, at the University of Otago Business School. Progress in implementing repositories continued in 2006, when a number of library consortia successfully applied to the Tertiary Education Commission for start-up funding for repository projects. The projects were:

- Institutional Repositories Aotearoa (IRA), which involved the University of Auckland, Victoria University of Wellington and the University of Canterbury; all IRA project participants use the DSpace software, and each runs its own server
- Coda, An Institutional Repository for the New Zealand ITP Sector, a DigitalCommons project for institutes of technology and polytechnics
- OARiNZ, Open Access Repositories in New Zealand, led by the Christchurch Polytechnic Institute of Technology, which involved universities and polytechnics; it provided its members with a range of repository implementation options, and also sponsored the development of a wiki-based knowledge base for members of the New Zealand IR community
- A national metadata harvester known as KRIS (Kiwi Research Information Service), based at the National Library of New Zealand; all institutions with IRs participated in developing national metadata guidelines to facilitate retrieval through this centralized utility.

In addition, LCONZ, an existing consortium of four university libraries, began an investigation of repository options, and has chosen DSpace as its preferred software. By April 2008 all New Zealand universities, as well as seven of its polytechnics, had established IRs. There was considerable variation in the size of the repositories, with those in universities being larger than those in polytechnics. The University of Auckland's IR, with over 1900 records, was the largest.

Japan

The Ministry of Education, Culture, Sports, Science and Technology (MEXT) has encouraged Japanese university libraries to develop institutional repositories to promote sharing of knowledge throughout Japan and internationally. Approximately two-thirds of the national universities, and some research institutes, have already taken up this initiative. In mid-April 2008, there were 81 IRs listed on the National Institute of Informatics (NII) website (www.nii.ac.jp/irp/en/list/), including two 'associated repositories', where several universities have joined to establish an IR system. One of these, the Yamagata University repository, includes around 100 items from nearby local public universities and colleges, which enhance the 950 items deposited by Yamagata University researchers. The Hiroshima Associated Repository Project (HARP) is also building a repository that will include items from nearby local public universities. The largest repositories are those of the Nagoya University, Kyoto University, Hokkaido University, University of Tsukuba and Chiba University, which each contain many thousands of items, including theses, books, articles, pre-prints and research reports, and research databases. DSpace is the most commonly used software, but Fedora is also used.

International initiatives

A number of national initiatives have become useful on an international scale, particularly those that capture information across borders. These include directories of open access repositories, harvesters that provide access to the content of a range of repositories, and information resources for repository managers.

ROAR, referred to earlier, is based at the University of Southampton in the UK. It listed 1048 publicly accessible repositories in April 2008, 550 of which are categorized as 'institutional or departmental'. Thirty-six countries are represented in ROAR, with the US responsible for 23% (128). DSpace and EPrints are used in the majority of these repositories – 35% (198) and 27% (151) respectively.

OpenDOAR (Directory of Open Access Repositories) was begun as part of the SHERPA project in the UK, and is housed at the University of Nottingham. It provides a searchable list of repositories and allows people to search repository contents and view repository statistics. In April 2008 it included 907 institutional repositories from 54 countries; 21% (146) are based in the US. Unlike ROAR, which lets anyone register a repository, OpenDOAR mediates applications, and has a list of criteria used to decide whether a repository will be included or excluded. These stem from its commitment to the concept of open access to full text resources, and sites that contain metadata only, or restrict access in some way, are excluded.

OAIster, based at the University of Michigan, began in 2001 as a project to develop a broad, generic, information retrieval resource. It has become an international 'union catalogue' of digital resources, providing access to over 15.5 million records from 950 repositories in April 2008.

Rights MEtadata for Open archiving (RoMEO) is also associated with the SHERPA project. It began in 2001 with JISC funding, and is a database of standard publisher permissions in their copyright transfer documents. It categorizes publishers by colour, based on the 'openness' of their agreements. Green publishers allow the archiving of either pre- or post-prints, while blue and yellow indicate more restrictive agreements. 'White' publishers do not support any form of author archiving.

A complementary project, JULIET, lists organizations that fund research and their policies concerning access to research results, in particular whether they support open access publishing, open access archiving and data archiving. The list is still growing (approximately 30 in April 2008), and most of those listed are in the UK or Europe.

These examples show that national initiatives are particularly useful in helping institutions get their repositories started, and that there is a strong commitment to sharing information about good practice, particularly within countries. The various international initiatives, particularly the RoMEO and JULIET services, provide useful resources to facilitate the growth of repository content, and the harvester services assist in making the content more visible, and increase use of the material. An unanswered question is the extent to which these initiatives are sustainable. At the moment, many rely on project-based funding, and their long term future will depend on having an institutional sponsor, as is the case with OAIster, or developing a business model to generate the revenue needed to continue operating.

Evaluating institutional repositories

Given that the goals of institutional repositories are to provide a long term archive to preserve the scholarly output of an institution, to make the research outputs of its staff more accessible, and to enhance the reputation of the institution through access to and use of this research, the most obvious metrics for measuring the success of institutional repositories are number of deposits, number of downloads, and number of citations. Services such as ROAR and OpenDOAR currently collect and publish information about the number of deposits in each IR, and these indirectly relate to the more important issues of preservation, increased citation rates, and institutional reputation. However, an apparently respectable rate of growth may be due to occasional large imports of a batch of materials from one source (such as a conference hosted by the institution) rather than acceptance and uptake across the academic community (Davis and Connolly, 2007).

Evaluation of the 'success' of a repository must also take into account the user interface (ease of use, ease of deposit, availability across networks, and so on); measures related to interoperability; quality of the metadata, and links to metadata harvesting systems; quality and scope of content, and relevance of this to institutional goals; and measures related to long-term sustainability and preservation (Carr and Brody, 2007). Overall, there is consensus emerging on high-level criteria that institutional repositories should meet. Jones, Andrew and MacColl (2006) summarize these, and add criteria as follows:

- institutionally defined (no extra-institutional issues to be resolved, as in subject repositories, easily integrated into existing system, in terms of style, semantics and technology)
- scholarly (not necessarily publishable but of value to academics)
- cumulative and perpetual (the collection is expanding, and items are preserved in perpetuity)
- open and interoperable (access to the collection, and its content freely available)
- digitally capture and preserve many aspects of campus life (dependent on decisions made by the institution on scope)
- search without constraints (software employed able to answer queries from human and automated users, effective user and web interface).

Based on the model of the Trusted Repository developed by RLG/OCLC, the RLG/NARA Audit Checklist for Certifying Trustworthy Digital Repositories is the most comprehensive system currently being advocated for the evaluation of a repository, and covers both technical and management issues in considerable detail. It is rapidly becoming a de facto standard (an ISO standard has been applied for) and it is itself based on ISO 9000 and ISO 17799 covering data security and information management systems. Some institutions have already used the checklist to evaluate their own repositories and explore inter-institutional comparisons (Kaczmarek et al., 2006). Work on the checklist itself is ongoing, and other institutions that have trialled it as a measurement tool have been invited to contribute experiences (Moore and Smith, 2007).

However, use of the repository by the scholarly/research community to share their work in an open access environment and the flow-on impacts of this, *must* be the over-riding criteria for success. Most IR software tracks download counts per item, and many institutions use counts of item downloads to market their IR within the institution. It is also clear that making theses available through deposit in an IR has greatly enhanced access to this type of research output, although anecdotal evidence suggests that some theses are embargoed or withheld when their authors want to publish their work as a monograph. However, there is no research available demonstrating that downloads of an author's work equate to an increased citation rate, reputation or likelihood of publication in a high-ranked journal – still the primary measure of academic success. These measures are needed to ensure the long-term viability of IRs as a core element in the research processes of tertiary institutions. At present, as Salo (2008) notes, IRs 'are parasitic on existing research and scholarly-publishing processes. They do not facilitate prior peer review, or colleague feedback, and the many interesting ideas surrounding open review, post-publication review, and overlay journals have yet to come to fruition.'

Academic success is still dependent on the traditional systems of scholarly communication.

Conclusion

In the few years since the first institutional repositories were established, the initiative has made rapid progress, and gained considerable support in the academic library community, if not the wider academic community. There is a substantial body of literature available outlining individual experiences, lessons learned, and recommended best practice. Proprietary and open source software is available, standards are being developed and agreed, the first monographs on the subject are appearing, and a body of published research is emerging. The initiative has clearly reached a stage of early maturity. Looking back, it is possible to categorize the development of repositories in general as having three stages: an early historical phase, the current phase of emerging maturity, and a future phase which could become a new era of cyberscholarship. Throughout the mature stage, we are likely to see technology consolidate, greater interoperability and migration between IRs, increased adoption of standards, and activity focused around well managed consortia, which offer lasting value to their members.

If the future phase, the predicted new era of cyberscholarship, eventuates, it is likely to be characterized by new workflows for scholars and researchers, and the introduction of Web 2.0 technologies into the scholarly communication process to facilitate commentary and interaction between researchers. The incorporation of new research into current work, the linking of e-research databases (containing accessible datasets) with the findings being published from them, and more collaborative interdisciplinary research may mean there is often no final authoritative version of the research output. At the same time, topic-based sub-communities may form within an institutional repository, which will need to allow researchers not formally associated with the institution to work and publish within it. This vision tends to support Blaise Cronin's view that cultural differences among disciplines will persist and combine with technological innovation to discourage the emergence of a unified model of scholarly communication, and eventually encourage 'a much more heterogeneous and dynamic publishing ecosystem'. At this point, multiple paradigms of scholarly communication may be forced to co-exist, and judgements of research reputation to take all of them into account.

Even if the current model succeeds, many of the benefits promoted in the early phase of repositories, such as the value of easier discovery, leading to greater exposure and therefore citation of the individual scholar's outputs, and the enhancement of the reputation of the institution, may be short-lived gains as the number of repositories and the number of items they hold increase. The task of capturing the intellectual output of the institution, and preserving it in perpetuity is in jeopardy unless tertiary institutions can make better progress in bringing academics and researchers onside, increasing their deposit rates substantially, and ensuring they have adequate policies in place for financial and technological sustainability.

As Jones, Andrew and MacColl note, the main drive to establish institutional repositories has come from the academic library community (2006, 139). As libraries pursue this new role as 'publisher' they have many hurdles to overcome, and a considerably greater investment to make, in terms of commitment and resources, if they are to succeed in inserting themselves into the scientific/scholarly communication process. Libraries must ensure they can fulfil all four functions of registration, archiving, awareness and certification (Roosendaal and Geurts, 1997). While it could be argued that, in time and with appropriate resourcing, IRs may be able to take over the first three functions, Prosser (2005) argues that open access journals are the best solution for certification in this environment. Certainly individual institutions have little expertise in managing certification, and place increasing reliance on external measures of the quality of the output of their own researchers, by using established rankings of journals and publishers. Given the size of the current world of scholarly publishing, the increasing number of monographs published each year, the numbers of new journals, and exponentially increasing number of published articles and conference proceedings, the academic library community has set itself a larger task than it has realized. It may be time to revisit the initial benefits promulgated for institutional repositories, and redefine the value they can bring to an institution in terms of return on investment. If they are to contribute in a meaningful way to the process of scholarly/scientific information creation, they will need to demonstrate how they can adequately fulfil the functions of scholarly/scientific communications systems, that is, meet the highest performance criteria as well as enhancing access and delivery.

References

Allen, J. (2005) *Interdisciplinary Differences in Attitudes Towards Deposit in Institutional Repositories*, unpublished Master's thesis, Department of Information and Communication, Manchester Metropolitan University, http://eprints.rclis.org/archive/00005180/.

Australian Partnership for Sustainable Repositories (2007) *2007 Initiatives*.

Ayris, P., Davies, R., McLeod, R., Miao, R., Shenton, H. and Wheatley, P. (2008) Lifecycle Information for E-literature: an introduction to the second phase of the LIFE project. In *LIFE2 Conference*, 23 June 2008, British Library, London, (unpublished), http://eprints.ucl.ac.uk/8608/.

Barnes, I. (2007) *The Digital Scholar's Workbench*, The Australian National University.

Barton, M. and Waters, M. (2004) *Creating an Institutional Repository: LEADIRS Workbook*, Cambridge, MA: MIT Libraries, www.dspace.org/implement/leadirs.pdf.

Brophy, P. (2008) Telling the Story: qualitative approaches to measuring the performance of emerging library services, *Performance Measurement and Metrics*, **9** (1), 7–17.

Buehler, M. A. and Boateng, A. (2005) The Evolving Impact of Institutional Repositories on Reference Librarians, *Reference Services Review*, **33** (3), 291–300.

Carr, L. and Brody, T. (2007) Size Isn't Everything: sustainable repositories as evidenced by sustainable deposit profiles, *D-Lib Magazine*, **13** (7/8), www.dlib.org/dlib/july07/carr/07carr.html.

Consultative Committee for Space Data Systems (2002) *Reference Model for an Open Archival Information System (OAIS): recommendation for space data system standards*, CCSDS 650.0-B-1, Blue Book, http://public.ccsds.org/publications/archive/650x0b1.pdf.

Cronin, B. (2003) *Scholarly Communication and Epistemic Cultures*, Association of Research Libraries, www.arl.org/scomm/disciplines/Cronin.pdf.

Crow, R. (2002) *The Case for Institutional Repositories: a SPARC position paper*, www.arl.org/sparc/bm~doc/ir_final_release_102.pdf.

Cullen, R. and Chawner, B. (2008) *Institutional Repositories in New Zealand: comparing institutional strategies for digital preservation and discovery*, paper presented at *Digital Discovery: Strategies and Solutions*, IATUL 2008, 20–24 April 2008, Auckland, NZ.

Davis, P. M. and Connolly, M. J. L. (2007) Institutional Repositories: evaluating the reasons for non-use of Cornell University's installation of DSpace, *D-Lib Magazine*, **13** (3/4), www.dlib.org/dlib/march07/davis/03davis.html.

Davis, R. H. (2008) *The Margins of Scholarship: repositories, web 2.0 and scholarly practice*, paper presented at *OR08: Open Repositories 2008*, 1–4 April 2008, Southampton, http://pubs.or08.ecs.soton.ac.uk/2/1/submission_99.pdf.

Feijen, M., Horstmann, W., Manghi, P., Robinson, M. and Russell, R. (2007) DRIVER: building the network for accessing digital repositories across Europe, *Ariadne*, **53**, www.ariadne.ac.uk/issue53/feijen-et-al/.

Foster, N. F. and Gibbons, S. (2005) Understanding Faculty to Improve Content Recruitment for Institutional Repositories, *D-Lib Magazine*, **11** (1), www.dlib.org/dlib/january05/foster/01foster.html.

Gadd, E., Oppenheim, C. and Probets, S. (2003) RoMEO Studies 1: the impact of copyright ownership on academic author self-archiving, *Journal of Documentation*, **59** (3), 243–77.

Genoni, P. (2004) Content in Institutional Repositories: a collection management issue, *Library Management*, **25** (6/7), 300–6.

Gibbons, S. (2004) Establishing an Institutional Repository, *Library Technology Reports*, **40** (4), 5–67.

Guterman, L. (2008) Harvard Faculty Adopts Open-Access Requirement, news blog, *Chronicle of Higher Education*, 12 February, http://chronicle.com/news/article/3943/harvard-faculty-adopts-open-access-re.

Heath, M., Jubb, M. and Robey, D. (2008) E-Publication and Open Access in the Arts and Humanities in the UK, *Ariadne*, **54**, www.ariadne.ac.uk/issue54/heath-et-al/.

Hendler, J. (2007) Reinventing Academic Publishing – part 1, *IEEE Intelligent Systems*, **22** (5), 2–3.

Henty, M. (2007) Ten Major Issues in Providing a Repository Service in Australian Universities, *D-Lib Magazine*, **13** (5/6), www.dlib.org/dlib/may07/henty/05henty.html.

IFLA (1998) *Functional Requirements for Bibliographic Records*, final report, Saur.

Johnson, R. K. (2002) Institutional Repositories: partnering with faculty to enhance scholarly communication, *D-Lib Magazine*, **8** (11), www.dlib.org/dlib/november02/johnson/11johnson.html.

Jones, R. and Andrew, T. (2005) Open Access, Open Source and E-theses: the development of the Edinburgh Research Archive, *Program*, **39** (3), 198–212.

Jones, R., Andrew, T. and MacColl, J. (2006) *The Institutional Repository*, Chandos.

Kaczmarek, J., Hswe, P., Eke, J. and Habing, T. G. (2006) Using the Audit Checklist for the Certification of a Trusted Digital Repository as a Framework for Evaluating Repository Software Applications: a progress report, *D-Lib Magazine*, **12** (12), www.dlib.org/dlib/december06/kaczmarek/12kaczmarek.html.

Kelley, K. B., Bonner, K., McMichael, J. S. and Pomea, N. (2002) Intellectual Property, Ownership and Digital Course Materials: a study of intellectual property policies at two- and four-year colleges and universities, *Portal: Libraries and the Academy*, **2** (2), 255–66.

Lee, B., Clifton, G. and Langley, S. (2006) *PREMIS Requirement Statement Project Report*, Australian Partnership for Sustainable Repositories.

Lynch, C. (2003) Institutional Repositories: essential infrastructure for scholarship in the digital age, *Portal: Libraries and the Academy*, **3** (2), 327–36.

Lynch, C. and Lippincott, J. (2005) Institutional Repository Deployment in the United States as of Early 2005, *D-Lib Magazine*, **11** (9), www.dlib.org/dlib/september05/lynch/09lynch.html.

McDowell, C. (2007) Evaluating Institutional Repository Deployment in American Academe Since Early 2005: repositories by the numbers, part 2, *D-Lib Magazine*, **13** (9), www.dlib.org/dlib/september07/mcdowell/09mcdowell.html.

McLeod, R., Wheatley, P. and Ayris, P. (2006) *Lifecycle Information for E-literature: full report from the LIFE project*, research report, LIFE Project, http://eprints.ucl.ac.uk/1854/; http://eprints.ucl.ac.uk/1855/.

Moore, R. W. and Smith, M. (2007) Automated Validation of Trusted Digital Repository Assessment Criteria, *Journal of Digital Information*, **8** (2), http://journals.tdl.org/jodi/article/view/198/181.

OCLC (2003) *OCLC Environmental Scan 2003: research and learning landscape*, www.oclc.org/reports/escan/.

Open Society Institute (2002) Budapest Open Access Initiative, www.soros.org/openaccess/read.shtml.

OpenDOAR (2008) Open Access Repository Types – worldwide, statistical chart, www.opendoar.org/about.html#scope.

Pappalardo, K. and Fitzgerald, A. (2007) *A Guide to Developing Open Access Through Your Digital Repository*, The OAK Law Project, Queensland University of Technology, http://eprints.qut.edu.au/archive/00009671/01/9671.pdf.

Pinfield, S. (2002) Creating Institutional Repositories, *Serials*, **15** (3), 261–4.

Probets, S. and Jenkins, C. (2006) Documentation for Institutional Repositories, *Learned Publishing*, **19** (1), 57–71.

Prosser, D. (2005) Fulfilling the Promise of Scholarly Publishing: can open access deliver? Paper presented at *Open Access: the option for the future!?*, IFLA satellite meeting No. 17, Oslo, Norway, www.ub.uio.no/konferanser/ifla/IFLA_open_access/SPARC%20IFLA2.pps.

Puplett, D. (2008) Version Identification: a growing problem, *Ariadne*, **54**, www.ariadne.ac.uk/issue54/puplett/.

Rankin, J. (2005) *Institutional Repositories for the Research Sector: feasibility study*, Affinity Limited, http://wiki.tertiary.govt.nz/tertiary/wikifarm/InstitutionalRepositories/uploads/Main/IR_report.pdf.

Registry of Open Access Repositories (2008) http://roar.eprints.org/.

Research Libraries Group (2002) *Trusted Digital Repositories: attributes and responsibilities*, an RLG-OCLC report, www.oclc.org/programs/ourwork/past/trustedrep/repositories.pdf.

Research Libraries Group (2007) *Trustworthy Repositories Audit and Certification: criteria and checklist (TRAC)*, www.crl.edu/PDF/trac.pdf.

Rieh, S. Y., Markey, K., St Jean, B., Yakel, E. and Kim, J. (2007) Census of Institutional Repositories in the US, *D-Lib Magazine*, **13** (11/12), www.dlib.org/dlib/november07/rieh/11rieh.html.

Roosendaal, H. E. and Geurts, P. A. T. M. (1997) *Forces and Functions in Scientific Communication: an analysis of their interplay*, paper presented at CRISP 97 Cooperative Research Information Systems in Physics, University of Oldenburg, Germany, www.physik.uni-oldenburg.de/conferences/crisp97/roosendaal.pdf.

RUBRIC (2007) Repository Software, www.rubric.edu.au/repositories/choosing_a_repository.htm.

Rumsey, S. (2006) The Purpose of Institutional Repositories in UK Higher Education: a repository manager's view, *International Journal of Information Management*, **26** (3), 181–6.

Russell, J. (2007) EThOSnet: building a UK e-theses community, *Ariadne*, **52**, www.ariadne.ac.uk/issue52/russell/.

Salo, D. (2008) Innkeeper at the Roach Motel, *Library Trends*, **57** (2), Fall.

Scholarly Publishing and Academic Resources Coalition (2002) *SPARC Institutional Repository Checklist and Resource Guide*, www.arl.org/sparc/bm~doc/IR_Guide_&_Checklist_v1.pdf.

Suber, P. (2008) Open Access in 2007, *Journal of Electronic Publishing*, **11** (1), http://quod.lib.umich.edu/cgi/t/text/text-idx?c=jep;cc=jep;rgn= main;view=text;idno=3336451.0011.110.

Thomas, C. and McDonald, R. (2007) Measuring and Comparing Participation Patterns in Digital Repositories: repositories by numbers, part 1, *D-Lib Magazine*, **13** (9/10), www.dlib.org/dlib/september07/mcdonald/09mcdonald.html.

University of California Office of Scholarly Communication (2007) *Faculty Attitudes and Behaviours Regarding Scholarly Communication: survey findings from the University of California*, http://osc.universityofcalifornia.edu/responses/activities.html.

van der Kuil, A. and Feijen, M. (2004) The Dawning of the Dutch Network of Digital Academic REpositories (DARE): a shared experience, *Ariadne*, **41**, www.ariadne.ac.uk/issue41/vanderkuil.

Van Westrienen, G. and Lynch, C. A. (2005) Academic Institutional Repositories: deployment status in 13 nations as of mid 2005, *D-Lib Magazine*, **11** (9).

VERSIONS Project (2008) www.lse.ac.uk/library/versions/.

VIF (2008) Version Identification Framework, www.lse.ac.uk/library/vif/index.html.

Walters, T. O. (2007) Reinventing the Library: how repositories are causing librarians to rethink their roles, *Portal: Libraries and the Academy*, **7** (2), 213–25.

White, S. and Creaser, C. (2004) *Scholarly Journal Prices: selected trends and comparisons*, Library and Information Statistics Unit, Loughborough University, www.lboro.ac.uk/departments/dils/lisu/downloads/op34.pdf.

9

Folksonomies to ontologies: the changing nature of controlled vocabularies

RICHARD J. HARTLEY

Introduction

Throughout a distinguished career as both practitioner and researcher, Peter Brophy has been concerned with the effective delivery of information resources to users and potential users. As both practitioner and researcher, he has been interested in the development of new services to users. There have been a number of recurrent themes throughout his work, among which are novel service delivery from academic libraries and the exploration of the possibilities of exploiting new information technologies in service delivery. Examples include BIBDEL Libraries Without Walls: the delivery of library services to distant users (www.cerlim.ac.uk/ projects/bibdel/index.php), and Franchise: Library Support for Franchised Courses in Higher Education (www.cerlim.ac.uk/projects/franchis/index.php). He explored the concept of the hybrid library in the HyLife project (www.ukoln.ac.uk/services/elib/projects/hylife/) and more recently the eMapps.com (www.eMapps.com) project has explored the use of mobile technologies to motivate active learning among primary school children across Europe. It is many years since Ranganathan first advocated 'every reader his book'. Brophy has been a dedicated proponent of an updated version of this mantra, as evidenced by his work as practitioner and researcher and explored more widely in the conference series 'Libraries without Walls' of which he was a creator.

Although his concern has been with what might be termed the macro level of service delivery and exploration of the possibilities for new service development, those services have often been underpinned by matters of vocabulary and vocabulary control in its many guises. His emphasis has been on exploring technology, but I will argue that though technology offers new possibilities for service delivery, language is and will remain at the heart of effective information resource discovery and access. This is particularly the case in the English language with its vast vocabulary. Bryson (1990) has pointed out that this has been caused by its propensity to absorb words from many different languages and offers some fascinating examples of Anglo-Saxon nouns for which the relevant adjective has been imported from elsewhere: mouth/oral, book/literary, water/aquatic, town/urban. Examples such as these demonstrate the complexity of effective retrieval and explain why automated means may require forms of vocabulary control for many years to come; or more likely that there will remain a need for human involvement in the retrieval process and totally automated retrieval will remain an elusive 'holy grail'.

After a period of time in which it has appeared that controlled vocabularies were in decline, there has been a resurgence of interest in vocabularies spurred by the emergence of the world wide web. In a report in *Library and Information Gazette*, Penny Bailey sums up the situation by noting 'Controlled vocabularies, thesauri and structured indexing are more important than ever' (quoted in Buckley Owen, 2008). As a result, new forms of vocabulary control, and new applications of vocabulary control, are emerging as service delivery becomes ever more automated. In this chapter, I explore the extended nature of controlled vocabularies and research and development which is underway to explore and extend their use in electronic service delivery.

The next section of the chapter will briefly review the traditional notion of controlled vocabularies. It is followed by suggested reasons for their decline. This is succeeded by an attempt to explain the resurgence of interest in controlled vocabularies. Then a brief exploration of the extended range of approaches to vocabulary control will be addressed. Finally there will be a consideration of new and emerging applications of vocabularies with various degrees of control in providing access to electronic information resources.

Controlled vocabularies: the traditional approach reviewed

Curiously, although controlled vocabularies are often written and spoken about they are rarely if ever formally defined. My working definition follows. Controlled vocabularies are lists of selected or approved words which are used to represent subject matter to promote retrieval. There are a range of different types of controlled vocabulary which have different degrees of structure and, it is assumed, effectiveness in retrieval. Those controlled vocabularies which originated in libraries and were intended both for the physical organization of books as well as content representation tended towards the summarization of document content in one or two headings or classification numbers, while those used in bibliographic databases representing the content of journal papers and research reports have tended towards in-depth representation by many terms.

Traditionally controlled vocabularies have existed in several forms, namely enumerative classification schemes of which the best known is the widely used Dewey Decimal Classification Scheme, more recently faceted classification schemes such as London Education Classification scheme, subject headings such as Library of Congress Subject Headings (LCSH) and thesauri such as the well established ERIC thesaurus or the INSPEC thesaurus.

Enumerative classification schemes are used to represent the subject content of an information object through the attribution of one or more classification numbers to the object and in the case of physical objects such as books in libraries, to provide a means of subject organization such that objects with similar subject matter are filed together. Supposedly enumerative classification schemes are ones in which all the possible classification numbers are enumerated in a schedule and these are the numbers available to be assigned to information objects. However, matters are not that simple and the presence of the word 'supposedly' was not accidental. Largely as a result of the work of the Classification Research Group in the 1960s on the development of faceted classification schemes (see below), large scale enumerative classification schemes such as Dewey have increasingly incorporated rules for the synthesis of classification numbers rather than simply enumerating all the possibilities. Recent editions of the schedules have included tables of auxiliary numbers and rules for their synthesis appear within the schedules; an obvious example is the addition of numbers to represent geographical areas. In addition there are many examples in the Dewey schedules where there is guidance on permitted synthesis of the form 'Add to the base number XXX, the number YYY'. For example:

659.2	Public relations
659.28	Public relations in specific kinds of organization

Add to base number 659.28 the numbers following 658.04 in 658.041–658.049 e.g. corporations 659.285.

Faceted classification schemes were developed in an attempt to overcome the perceived shortcomings of the more traditional enumerative schemes, which were seen to be inflexible in the ways in which different subjects could be combined. The consequence of this inflexibility was that classifiers often had to make unsatisfactory compromises in the application of classification numbers to information objects. Arguably this was not too serious if the classification scheme was perceived as principally a device with which to 'mark and park' books on library shelves, but if it was to be used as a serious and effective tool for information representation and subsequent retrieval then the inflexibility was a significant disadvantage. The approach developed in a faceted scheme was to avoid a single hierarchical structure but to provide a series of terms in hierarchies with an associated notation and rules for the flexible combination of terms from the various hierarchies. Typical examples of facets that are applicable in many situations are things, parts or components, materials, properties or behaviours, operations and operating agents. Further information can be found from the relevant Wikipedia entry and its links (http://en.wikipedia.org/wiki/Faceted_classification) and guidance on the creation of a faceted scheme is provided by Vickery (1960).

Generally it is accurate to note that enumerative classification schemes cover all fields of knowledge whereas a faceted scheme covers a restricted subject field. It is also fair to argue that the major impact of the development of faceted classification schemes to date has been in the increased use of synthesis in so-called enumerative schemes, though as is noted later in this chapter this situation may be changing. Although faceted classification was developed as an answer to the shortcomings of enumerative classification schemes, their use in libraries has been relatively limited and it is only in the digital world that they have come into their own, where objects might be approached by different users and for different tasks in many different ways; such diversity of unpredictable approaches can be catered for with faceted classification schemes (Morville, 2005).

Subject headings are another device developed essentially in the field of library cataloguing and intended principally for the representation of the information content of books in libraries. They can be characterized as having broad subject coverage but very limited hierarchical structure. The best known examples of subject headings are the LCSH and its simplified version Sears List of Subject Headings. Like enumerative classification schemes, subject headings developed as practical tools prior to any theoretical considerations. Although LCSH has been subjected to a makeover such that it now more closely resembles structured thesauri (see below), it will always suffer from the legacy of inconsistency of term structure, which has been noted by many authors. A fuller description of LCSH and its structures and weaknesses can be found in Rowley and Hartley (2008).

In the context of indexing and information retrieval a thesaurus is an approved list of terms, which can be used in indexing a range of information objects to enable their subsequent retrieval. Although this is the basic minimum for a thesaurus, most pundits would argue that a properly structured thesaurus is more than simply a list of terms used in indexing but should include clearly defined relationships between the terms. Conventionally relationships can be equivalence, hierarchical or associative. Equivalence relationships are used to specify that one term is an approved term and should be used in preference to terms with the same or similar meanings. Hierarchical relationships are used to show the permanent relationship between entities, for example whole–part relationships, while associative relationships are context specific term relationships, an example of which in some contexts might be that between 'aluminium' and 'pipes'. In addition to use in indexing, it is expected that thesauri might be used in the searching of databases. Some attempts have been made to provide thesauri as drop down menus from which terms can be selected to construct a search statement; see for example the pioneering work of the late Stephen Pollitt (Pollitt, Ellis and Smith, 1994). More recently thesauri have become readily searchable as a part of online databases.

Although not always regarded within the context of a controlled vocabulary, the standardization of names, or name authority control, is increasingly complex and important. Variations of this author's name are:

R. J. Hartley
Richard J Hartley
Richard John Hartley
Dick Hartley

This readily demonstrates the need for some means of providing a name in a consistent form. Clearly there are more complex examples including name changes brought about through marriage and divorce. Further complexity is added when names are translated and transliterated between languages and scripts, for example the well known Greek poet Constantine Cavafy might appear as any of:

Cavafy, C.P. (Constantine P.)
Kabaphes, Konstantinos Petros
Cavafy, Constantine P.
Kavafis Konstantin
Cavafis, Constantinos
Kavaphes, Konstantinos Petrou
Kavafis, Konstantinos Petrou
Kavafis, Constantino
Kavafis, Konstandinos

The importance of name authority control has long been recognized in cataloguing quarters and so unsurprisingly the best developed personal name authority file is the Library of Congress Name Authority File (http://authorities.loc.gov/). However, there are other well known authorities such as those provided by the Getty, which offers a union list of artist names (www.getty.edu/research/conducting_research/vocabularies/ulan/). One extreme example of the need for controlling the forms in which names may appear is provided by the artist El Greco for whom the Getty vocabulary lists more than 50 name variations. Although the need to control name variations has long been recognized in cataloguing circles, it has become apparent in other circles more recently. The emerging era of open access has brought the importance of the consistent naming of individuals to the attention of a wider community. For example the Cascading Citations Analysis Project (CCAP) of Dervos and colleagues recognized the need for a universal author identification system and developed a working system in 2006 (Dervos et al., 2006). More recently the UK Joint Information Systems Committee has commissioned research into the requirements for a service that will reliably and consistently record the names of individual researchers. This has led to the Names project at MIMAS, which is ongoing in summer 2008 (http://names.mimas.ac.uk/).

Human beings are not the only entities the consistent naming of which has been the subject of attention. Geographical names can cause problems, for example in the change of names of countries (Ceylon, Sri Lanka) and cities (Bombay, Mumbai). Again the Getty has made a major contribution to name control with its thesaurus of geographical names (www.getty.edu/research/conducting_research/vocabularies/tgn/). Other areas where consistent naming of entities is both important and complex are corporate names and also the naming of chemicals.

The declining role of controlled vocabularies

Although vocabulary control extends beyond the arena of subject vocabulary control, it is in this area that there has been and remains greatest interest. Since the early days of librarianship there had been an assumption of the importance of controlled vocabularies, particularly in the form of enumerative classification schemes or subject headings as a means of providing subject access to books and other materials in libraries. Probably the first challenge to this assumption came with the results of the Cranfield Index Language tests in the 1960s. These tests represented the first attempt to test the efficacy of controlled vocabularies in a controlled manner. They are chiefly noted for the creation of the measures recall and precision and for demonstrating that some form of relatively objective testing was possible, and the second Cranfield test in particular cast doubt on the value of controlled languages by demonstrating that in retrieval terms simple keywords appeared to perform at least as effectively as any controlled vocabulary.

Although the Cranfield tests cast doubt on the value of controlled vocabularies, arguably it was the widespread appearance of initially remote search services such as Dialog in the 1970s followed by bibliographic databases on CD-ROMs and OPACs in the 1980s which presented a challenge to the importance of controlled vocabularies. The appearance of these technologies initiated the move away from searching by intermediaries who understand record structures and controlled vocabulary structures and their exploitation to searching by end users who did not have the same level of system knowledge and so tended to search simply through the use of keywords.

The significance of services such as Dialog in the move from controlled vocabularies can be challenged, but what cannot be argued against is the impact of search engines in general, in particular Alta Vista and, more recently, Google. As a result of these tools information retrieval is no longer the province of the minority but it has become an everyday activity of the majority. In the words of Morville (2005), 'the humble keyword has become surprisingly important in recent years . . . keywords have become part of our everyday experience'. In addition to the emergence of the 'humble keyword' as a dominating factor in retrieval, it has to be remembered that the controlled vocabularies are expensive beasts. There is the significant cost of their initial creation, the cost of their maintenance and the cost of their application in the indexing of information objects. The importance of a means of maintaining the controlled vocabulary is readily demonstrated by examination of those controlled vocabularies that have remained in use over extensive periods. Whether we consider classification schemes such as Dewey or Library of Congress Classification Scheme or thesauri such as the ERIC thesaurus or subject headings such as Medical Subject Headings (MeSH), they have a common feature in being maintained by a strong organization, which more or less guarantees their continued existence. Given the cost and effort of using controlled vocabularies and the misleadingly simple application of keywords as used in search engines, it is scarcely surprising that through the 1980s and 1990s there was a steady decline in their use for both indexing and searching.

The resurgence of controlled vocabularies

In the previous section of this chapter, it was argued that developments in technology and widespread uptake of the technology, most particularly search engines, was the cause of the decline in the perceived relevance of controlled vocabularies. In this paragraph, perhaps perversely, it is argued that it is developments in technology and the use of technology that is making possible a resurgence of interest in controlled vocabularies. The argument has three strands. The first strand is the consequence of the very success of search engines. Search engines crawl through huge volumes of data on the web to create their vast databases, with the result that when a searcher combines keywords, the result is often an unmanageably large number of 'hits' from a large number of sources the quality of which has not been verified. Included in that number of 'hits' will be any number of 'false drops' – items retrieved because they contain the search terms but with different meanings or in different combinations from that desired by the searcher.

Although any attempt to replicate this example will result in a different answer it will serve to illustrate the point. Suppose that a searcher is interested in the use of information technology in secondary schools. A search of Google using the search statement:

+ 'information technology' + 'secondary schools'

resulted in about 779,000 items. Even accepting that the output is ranked in terms of relevance, a return of this size is of limited value. What does the searcher do with it? In practice, look at the first two or three screens and ignore the rest. Initially one can be highly impressed by such a return typically generated in less than half a second. On reflection, the downside of such a huge retrieved set becomes more apparent. Contrast this with a search on the educational database ERIC. A search for those items in which the terms 'information technology' and 'secondary schools' appeared only in the controlled vocabulary (descriptor) field yielded just 14 items only minutes after the Google search. Obviously an important part of the reason for the much lower number of retrieved items is the fact that the database searched is far more restricted. However, although the retrieval solely of items to which human indexers have assigned the two thesaurus terms has produced a much more manageable set, it is a set containing items that are much more likely to be relevant than the crude combination of keywords. So although Morville (2005) has argued that 'the humble keyword has become surprisingly important in recent years . . . keywords have become part of our everyday experience', I would counter by saying that increasingly the unsophisticated reliance on the 'humble keyword' has now become a part of the problem. The recognition that unfettered use of keywords leads to retrieval problems is one reason for the renewed interest in controlled vocabularies.

Nevertheless it is probable that the second strand of the argument is currently the more significant. That strand relates to attempts to develop the web into the so-called semantic web. The semantic web is the vision of Tim Berners-Lee, the inventor of the current world wide web, which he envisions as an extension of the web such that the information is 'understandable' by computers. The vision was eloquently portrayed by Berners-Lee as follows:

> I have a dream for the Web [in which computers] become capable of analyzing all the data on the Web – the content, links, and transactions between people and computers. A 'Semantic Web', which should make this possible, has yet to emerge, but when it does, the day-to-day mechanisms of trade, bureaucracy and our daily lives will be handled by machines talking to machines. The 'intelligent agents' people have touted for ages will finally materialize.
>
> (Berners-Lee, 1999)

Given the sheer scale of the web, the desirability of developing a situation in which an increasing amount of information processing is undertaken automatically between computers without human intervention seems inescapable. However, although the desirability may be inescapable, the complexity should not be underestimated. A whole series of working groups under the aegis of the World Wide Web Consortium (W3C) are beavering away to help realize the dream. In order to do so it is necessary to develop and more crucially implement means of consistently tagging information on the web with its information type and develop consistent means to representing its meaning. Although it is clear that computers can distinguish between say London as author, place and subject as long as the data is appropriately tagged, the problem of ensuring there is consistent subject representation across the whole of the web is much more daunting. Nevertheless, as will be explored below, progress in developing the building blocks is being made.

The final strand is the possibilities created by numerous of the social networking facilities of which a prime example is the photo sharing service offered by Flickr (www.flickr.com). Other examples are the social bookmarking sites such as del.icio.us (http://del.icio.us/) and Connotea (www.connotea.org/). Collaborative tools such as these have led to the widespread application of social tagging or folksonomies as they have become known. Although the requirements of the semantic web are leading to extensions of controlled vocabularies through the development of increasingly structured approaches, social tagging is offering new approaches, which are less structured than the traditional view of controlled vocabularies in the bibliographical world.

Controlled vocabularies: an extended view

The resurgence of interest in controlled vocabularies has produced more varieties of controlled language than those that emanated from the bibliographical world. Following the example of Tudhope and colleagues, I will briefly review the extended range of controlled vocabularies in an order of increasing structure (Tudhope, Koch and Heery, 2006).

The concept of social tagging, or collaborative assignment of keywords, has emerged with the development of social networking tools on the web. In essence they are nothing new; it has long been the practice of journals to require authors of academic papers to add a series of keywords to a paper. These words are natural language terms chosen by the author to represent the content; they are not terms chosen from a predetermined list. It is simply that in the guise of social tagging this practice has become widespread. In some circles the terms are listed as a folksonomy: a term derived from the combination of the terms folk and taxonomy and intended to refer to the language of the people in a specific community. In the language of old information retrieval systems they would be referred to as 'identifiers' or 'uncontrolled terms'. Like 'identifiers', it may turn out that the major role of terms in a folksonomy is the identification of potential terms that need to be added to a controlled vocabulary. In the context of which, it is interesting to note the emergence of 'tag clouds'. A tag cloud is a visual display of the relationship between a set of terms in which the use of typeface size and physical proximity can be used to show the relationship between terms.

The simplest forms of controlled vocabularies are simply term lists in which there is no hierarchical relationship, but which simply control synonyms. As was noted earlier in the chapter, the use of lists of terms extends well beyond subjects into areas such as names of people, places, organizations and chemicals; that is so-called authority files. In terms of subjects a term list might simply be an alphabetical list from which indexers or searchers can choose terms. For this reason, on occasions they are referred to as 'pick lists'. Authors such as Tudhope and colleagues, presumably for the sake of completeness, include glossaries, dictionaries and gazetteers as forms of term lists.

A term that has emerged recently is 'synonym ring'. A synonym ring is nothing more than a set of terms that are deemed to be synonymous in a given retrieval context. A ring brings together the set of terms deemed to be equivalent for retrieval purposes. So for example spelling variants, common and scientific names, abbreviations and the full term, or name variations of an individual could be treated as equivalent within a synonym ring. A search term would initially be processed against the synonym rings to check for synonyms; if found then the search would be broadened to include all the terms in the ring. This brings searching a step closer to concept searching rather than simply being searching for the character entered character string. This may sound useful, but there are of course problems: just what does constitute an exact synonym? The answer is likely to be context dependent. For example in some contexts 'wood' and 'forest' might be deemed to be synonyms yet in other contexts 'wood' is a material used by carpenters and as it happens the name of my in-laws! Unfortunately as soon as context dependency is introduced, universal applicability and transferability disappear.

The forms of controlled vocabulary mentioned so far in this section of the chapter are simply lists of approved terms or equivalent terms. As was noted earlier there are several forms of controlled vocabulary which define the relationship between terms. In a very limited way this is done by subject headings. However, it is achieved more effectively and more consistently in thesauri, enumerative classification schemes and faceted classification schemes. Although it is rarely mentioned, it is worth noting that thesauri and faceted classification schemes are closely related. The former indicates term relationships through the standardized use of BT, NT, RT, use and UF; the latter does so through its notation. Faceted schemes of course have the additional feature of rules for the combination of terms from different facets.

A relatively recent addition to the panoply of controlled vocabularies is that of ontologies. An ontology can be defined as the agreed definition of a set of terms within a subject or domain area and the relationship between those terms. So far this definition is not different from that of other controlled vocabularies like thesauri and classification schemes. However, the difference is that because of the way that ontologies are created within specific tools, such as OWL (web ontology language), they can be used to reason within the domain.

Another tool which is developing under the auspices of the W3C is that of Simple Knowledge Organisation System (SKOS). SKOS is intended to be a framework within which existing controlled vocabularies can be represented more simply than within ontologies, such that they can be used in the development of the semantic web.

Finally, the word taxonomy has become widely used in recent years. I have left it until last in this consideration of vocabularies because it has become a word used in different ways by different people. Until recently it was essentially used in the context of the organization of biological organisms into hierarchies. However, with the development of the web and of knowledge management, its use has broadened. Different authors refer to a taxonomy in different ways: as a means of structuring a website, as a means of organizing a directory, as a structure created through the application of some automated categorization process or as a means of reflecting the structure of a corporation on an organization portal. Given the diversity of meaning it is arguably best not used and when seen in the literature it is important to understand precisely to what the author refers.

Controlled vocabularies: new uses

Controlled vocabularies continue to be used in the traditional way for organizing documents in libraries, and for describing the content of information objects to enable their retrieval, but their use is now being extended through new applications such as social bookmarking and the tagging of images on a photo sharing websites into the creation of languages with much less control than has historically been the case. Whether these lists of terms can truly be referred to as controlled languages is open to debate, and whether their application has a role to play in effective retrieval must remain highly doubtful. The need for more structured languages such as those developed with ontology software, such as OWL, or with SKOS, is much clearer. Effective computer-to-computer processing of information can only occur if that information is unambiguously tagged for both its structure and its content. Consistent content representation can only occur through the widespread use of readily available controlled vocabularies.

What remains in considerable doubt is whether such applications will bring about the perceived effects hoped for in the vision of the semantic web. Personally, I have considerable doubts. It was noted earlier that the cost of developing and maintaining a controlled language such as a thesaurus or a classification scheme is significant. Therefore a reasonable prediction is that ontologies will be even more expensive to create. So it follows that they are only likely to be created in those circumstances where there are considerable financial or other benefits to be gained from their application. Furthermore, the Cranfield tests and their successors cast doubt on the efficacy of controlled languages as effective retrieval tools. There is a huge literature criticizing the tests on grounds ranging from the relevance of laboratory tests to real-world searching to methodological arguments about their execution, but the one thing which remains conspicuous by its absence is evidence contradicting the Cranfield findings. Therefore I suspect that what will emerge is a web which is semantic in parts.

Summary

This chapter has briefly reviewed the range of controlled vocabularies which were at the heart of much bibliographic work for many years. It has sought to explain why there was a decline in interest in controlled vocabularies and more recently why technological developments have enabled and in some cases required a resurgence of interest in controlled vocabularies, albeit of an extended variety. The effectiveness, economics and hence importance of specific types of controlled vocabularies will remain an open question for the foreseeable future. What will not remain an open question will be the incontrovertible fact that, whatever the developments in technology, it is language which will remain at the heart of information retrieval and information services for many years to come.

References

Berners-Lee, T. with Fischetti, M. (1999) *Weaving the Web: the original design and ultimate destiny of the world wide web by its inventor*, Harper, Chapter 12. Quoted in Wikipedia (http://en.wikipedia.org/wiki/Semantic_Web).

Bryson, B. (1990) *Mother Tongue: the English language*, Penguin Books, 68.

Buckley Owen, T. (2008) Simpler Systems Needed to Suit Future Searchers, *Library and Information Gazette*, 8–21 February, 1–2.

Dervos, A., Samaras, N., Evangelidis, G., Hyvärinen, J. and Asmanidis, Y. (2006) The Universal Author Identifier System (UAI_Sys). In *Proceedings [of the] 1st International Scientific Conference, eRA: The Contribution of Information Technology in Science, Economy, Society and Education*, workshop proceedings on CD, Tripolis, Greece (http://dlist.sir.arizona.edu/1716/).

Morville, P. (2005) *Ambient Findability*, O'Reilly.

Pollitt, S., Ellis, G. P. and Smith, M. P. (1994) HIBROWSE for Bibliographic Databases, *Journal of Information Science*, **20** (6), 413–26.

Rowley, J. and Hartley, R. (2008) *Organizing Knowledge: an introduction to managing access to information*, 4th edn, Ashgate.

Tudhope, D., Koch, T. and Heery, R. (2006) *Terminology Services and Technology: JISC state of the art review*, UKOLN.

Vickery, B. C. (1960) *Faceted Classification*, Aslib.

Theme 4

Performance, quality and leadership

10

An evaluation decision-making system: development and implementation of a web-based evaluation learning and instructional tool

CHARLES R. McCLURE AND JOHN T. SNEAD

... libraries need to develop services that enable and encourage users not simply to be passive receptors of information, but themselves to create new information and other objects that they can share with their worldwide community.

Peter Brophy (2004, 14)

US public libraries received $9.7 billion in operating income in FY 2005 (National Center for Education Statistics, 2008): 81% from local sources, 10% from state sources, 1% from federal sources, and 8% from other sources (gifts, fines, donations, and so on). Regardless of how much each individual library received, public library administrators and librarians are under increasing pressure to articulate the value and impacts of their library services and resources to these sources of funds. The process for determining value, impacts, outcomes, satisfaction and so on increasingly requires more attention and more tools. The project described here is one attempt to assist public library administrators to develop better evaluation tools.

Researchers and library practitioners have developed a number of evaluation strategies and tools to help libraries articulate value, impact, quality and other benefits related to the use of services and resources. Identification of the best evaluation methods to use as part of these strategies, however, and obtaining access to sources of information capable of providing useful service and resource data, presents a formidable task for many libraries. Oftentimes, methods and evaluation tools are not compared against each other nor do they take into consideration local situational factors that may affect the success with which these tools can be implemented.

The project described in this paper, an evaluation decision management system (EDMS) (EDMS, 2008, available at www.libevaluation.com/edms), addresses how public libraries:

- develop evaluation strategies to demonstrate value and impacts
- identify the best evaluation methods for these strategies
- access a range of service and resource data from national library-based databases.

Public libraries can address the above through a centralized online portal that encourages users to share and create a range of information related to evaluation. In addition, this paper identifies issues related to the development and implementation of a web-based instructional system and assesses the effects of technology development on evaluation of networked services and resources. Although the project is currently under development as this paper is written (2008), a number of lessons have been learned that may be of use to others developing such an evaluation tool.

Background

Local community leaders, individuals from government and private funding agencies, and others often ask public libraries questions about the value, quality and impact of services they provide and the use of resources, such as (Bertot and Davis, 2004; Bertot and McClure, 2003a, b; Griffiths et al., 2004; Holt, 2003; Matthews, 2004; McClure and Bertot, 1998; Ryan and McClure, 2003):

- How many users come into the library to use internet workstations?
- In what ways do library resources meet community needs?
- How, and in what ways, do patrons benefit from reading online or print material?
- For every dollar invested in the library, what does the community get in return?
- Does the library need to continue to fund print collections in the same amount or can the library divert more resources to online material?
- How do users of library services rate the quality of the services they receive from the library?

Library practitioners and researchers develop and engage in a number of evaluation strategies to attempt to answer these and other questions regarding library services and resources.

There is little available guidance to libraries from library practitioners and researchers, however, about which specific evaluation strategies and approaches will provide the best data and greatest impact to answer such questions. Because of this lack of guidance, libraries may generically apply pre-developed evaluation strategies with little or no regard for their local situational contexts and needs. For example, at times libraries assess services and resources using applied, systematic evaluation programmes and at other times through ad hoc evaluation efforts (Bertot and Snead, 2004 a, b; Brophy and Coulling, 1996; Durrance and Fisher, 2005; Hernon and Dugan, 2002; Matthews, 2004; Van House et al., 1987).

Consequently, it is essential that researchers and library practitioners have guidance on which evaluation strategies and approaches will provide the best data capable of producing the greatest desired effect based on a local library's situational context and evaluation needs. The type of guidance library administrators need includes:

- what evaluation approaches are available
- which evaluation approaches might best meet their data needs, either library developed or imposed by external funders, organizations and so on
- how to develop an overall evaluation plan that makes effective and efficient use of library resources
- how to implement an evaluation plan using local library resources
- how to analyse and present evaluation findings
- how to create advocacy strategies that promote library value and the use of services and resources to improve library support.

Without an understanding of the above, a public library may not be able to conduct the most useful and informative types of evaluation or successfully demonstrate value and impact of provided services and resources to the communities they serve and to funding organizations (Bertot, 2004; Bertot and Snead, 2004 a, b).

How-to manuals, tool kits, and other forms of assistance are available that provide details on evaluating selected or individual library services and resources. These manuals typically fall largely into four identifiable, selected key evaluation areas:

- outputs assessment and use of performance measures
- outcomes assessment
- quality assessment
- value determination.

No effort to date, however, has provided integrated assistance in determining which evaluation approach to use relative to specific library situational factors, data needs, and a host of other considerations (Bertot and McClure, 2003a, b; Bertot and Snead, 2004 a, b; Griffiths et al., 2004; Matthews, 2004; McClure and Bertot, 2003; Ryan and McClure, 2003).

With so many evaluation options available, there is a substantial need to bridge evaluation approaches to situational factors in order to provide public library managers and librarians with understanding and guidance in the selection of best practice evaluation strategies and methods that meet their needs. The EDMS addresses how best practice evaluation strategies support public libraries' efforts to demonstrate the value of their libraries to the communities they serve.

Evaluation of library services and resources

There are multiple motivations for public library evaluation efforts, such as questions prompted by stakeholders, internal management needs, and/or requirements by funding agencies. A key issue driven by various motivations, however, involves the selection of evaluation methods that provide relevant data capable of informing the decision-making process of library managers. Selection of evaluation methods should answer a range of questions asked by various stakeholder groups (for example library boards, county/city executives, funders, customers, state library agencies) regarding library services and resources; or enhance informed decisions regarding a library's range of services and resources.

Given the differing motivations for evaluation to answer questions and inform the decision-making process, public librarians and managers generally approach meeting an evaluation need from at least three different perspectives (Bertot and Davis, 2004):

- stakeholder type (who is requesting certain data)
- data or information need (what data are necessary/sought)
- evaluation approach (outcomes assessment, service quality and so on).

The EDMS enables public librarians and managers to access the system's contents from these different perspectives to meet specific library evaluation needs.

In addition to the motivational perspective, evaluating library services and resources requires effort, knowledge and an investment of time. Evaluation is a complex process that involves allocation of staff and other library resources; use of various methods (for example surveys, focus groups, log file analysis); and co-ordination of data collection efforts, data analysis, and the presentation of findings to numerous stakeholder groups (for example library board, city council, others).

Among the benefits of evaluation is the ability to describe and understand the impacts, benefits, uses and user satisfaction with library services and resources. The perils of poor evaluation, however, range from wasting library resources to providing useless data that does not demonstrate impacts of services and resources to the public library community.

The EDMS

The EDMS addresses multiple priorities that include evaluating the impact of library services on users or communities; improving knowledge about users' information needs, expectations and behaviour; and providing knowledge that enhances people's ability to use library resources. The EDMS meets these priorities by identifying:

- leading evaluation methods used in a public library setting
- types of data each method provides and how each data type is related to specific library services, resources and programmes
- strengths and weaknesses of each method and the success with which libraries have employed the different methods
- how situational contexts and local factors within library settings affect the successful use of these methods
- ways in which to engage in and use various evaluation strategies, analyse evaluation data, interpret evaluation results, and present evaluation findings.

In terms of these priorities, EDMS module content assists public librarians and managers in selecting evaluation approaches capable of yielding information that describes use of library services and resources. EDMS module content also includes user-based ratings of library services and resources; identifies ways to improve library services and resources based on user feedback; and measures and assesses the value and impacts of library services and resources to the communities that libraries serve. The EDMS provides information related to the management, improvement and advocacy for public libraries' continued provision of services and resources in terms of meeting user needs.

Ultimately, this project provides sustained guidance to public librarians and managers in understanding and selecting appropriate evaluation approaches and access to training modules on the types and uses of evaluation approaches maintained in a centralized, public-access setting. The project promotes customizable strategies for developing evaluation methods specific to a local public library setting and access to a sustainable web-based source of information that includes tools on evaluation to support the strategies. The EDMS builds on existing research supported by grants from the Institute of Museum and Library Services and the State Library and Archives of Florida.

Project design

The overall purpose of the EDMS is to provide a product that will help public librarians and managers match data collection needs with the best evaluation approaches to demonstrate public library value or impact to communities served. The following goals guide this process. Public librarians and managers will successfully:

* capture evaluation information regarding library services and resources that best meets user, community and public librarian or manager information needs
* select and use appropriate, efficient and effective evaluation approaches in order to undertake informative evaluation activities
* understand uses, impacts and benefits, value and other aspects of library services and resources to a library's local community and funders
* advocate at a local level benefits, impacts, and value of library services and resources.

Meeting these goals improves library services that better meet patron needs and will provide practical methods and mechanisms for providing evaluation results to local, state and federal funding agencies. To achieve these goals, the project has the following objectives:

* to compare and contrast types of data provided by each leading evaluation approach
* to determine what such data enables libraries to say about their services and resources
* to compare and contrast the strengths and weaknesses of leading evaluation approaches
* to describe the success with which selected public libraries are currently employing a number of different evaluation approaches

- to better understand how library situational factors (organizational, community, other) affect the successful use of leading evaluation approaches
- to develop guidelines and practical recommendations to assist library managers in selecting appropriate evaluation approaches and determining under what circumstances selected evaluation approaches offer a best fit given their evaluation needs
- to provide assistance in using evaluation data for library advocacy purposes
- to design and create a nationwide and sustainable EDMS to facilitate assessment efforts in public libraries, based on an iterative development process with project partners.

The study team used ongoing, iterative evaluation techniques and input from its advisory committee throughout the course of the project to ensure that development of the EDMS meets project objectives and user needs.

The study team's expectation was that the EDMS best meets the needs of users by designing it so that it addresses the following outcomes:

- Public librarians and managers identify data needs of local community officials and funding agencies.
- Public librarians and managers identify data sources needed to assess services and programmes within specific library situational contexts.
- Public librarians and managers select evaluation approaches appropriate to targeted data needs within specific situational contexts.
- Public librarians and managers disseminate evaluation results in a format appropriate for target audiences.
- EDMS users and project partners more successfully advocate for improved library services and programmes.

The study team worked with members of the project advisory committee and project partners to identify these outcomes in the initial phase of the project.

To facilitate the use and sustainability of the EDMS, the Information Institute, project advisory committee and project partners plan a number of activities to disseminate the results of the project, which include:

- training sessions at major professional conferences, i.e. American Library Association (ALA) annual and winter conferences, Public Library Association (PLA) conferences, annual Federal-State Cooperative System (FSCS) state data co-ordinator meetings, and so on

- presentations at professional conferences, selected professional committees, and membership organizations, i.e. ALA, PLA, state library association meetings, ALA/PLA statistics committees, Urban Libraries Council (ULC) meetings, and so on
- announcements on selected electronic lists, e.g. public library lists, state library agency public library lists, Chief Officers of State Library Agencies (COSLA) lists, appropriate lists maintained by ALA, and so on
- creation of an ALA-supported evaluation website by the ALA Office for Research
- other dissemination efforts as identified.

The purpose of the above efforts includes spreading awareness of the project and informing various stakeholder groups of the potential usefulness of the EDMS to the public library community.

The project currently has four partners, the Baltimore County Public Library (BCPL), the Omaha Public Library (OPL), the Mid-York Library System, New York (MLS) and the ALA Office for Research. The library partners represent a diverse library community along a number of demographics, including library size, service community, geographic region and evaluation needs. In addition, all of the partners have substantial experience and interest in evaluation efforts and provide an important practitioner-based perspective for the project in general and the EDMS in particular.

Evaluation plan

The project relies on three types of evaluation to judge its success — summative, formative and outcomes-based assessment. The combination of these three evaluation strategies affords the study team and the Institute of Museum and Library Services (IMLS) multiple ways to judge the success of the study. At the end of the project, the project team will conduct a summative evaluation to determine the degree to which the project accomplished its objectives.

To conduct the summative evaluation, the project team will engage in two primary efforts. The first is the functionality, usability and accessibility testing of the EDMS. The Information Institute project team conducts usability (system presentation), functionality (system features) and accessibility (access for users with disabilities) testing of the EDMS with public librarians, managers and MLS students.

The second summative evaluation is field analysis. The project team conducts additional assessments of the EDMS with key constituencies such as the state data co-ordinators involved in the FSCS annual public library surveys conducted by the National Center for Education Statistics (NCES) and PLA's Research and Statistics Committee. The purpose of the field analysis is to gain additional feedback on the utility of the EDMS to public libraries, how the EDMS can facilitate decision-making and advocacy efforts, and system features for continued improvement.

Throughout the project, the project team employed a number of formative evaluation techniques to ensure that the study is proceeding appropriately. First, the advisory committee served in an evaluation capacity and provided regular feedback and review of project products, process and issues. Second, a number of activities built into the project enabled the study team to obtain feedback and suggestions from public librarians and managers. Third, project partner public libraries and others field-tested the EDMS. In addition, the study team engaged in functionality, usability and accessibility testing of the EDMS throughout its development process.

The project goals and objectives, as measured through the use and application of the EDMS, inform the outcomes-based assessment of the project. One key strategy for outcomes assessment is the development of surveys and other feedback mechanisms in the EDMS that enable users to inform the study team along several EDMS dimensions that include:

- usefulness of the content
- EDMS design and functionality
- participants' ability to use the EDMS for advocacy purposes.

The findings from these outcomes-based evaluation activities inform the continued development of the EDMS beyond the life of the grant.

EDMS implementation

The current version of the EDMS consists of selected modules, 'commons' and infrastructure areas that include:

- instructional modules that provide guidance for planning, managing and conducting evaluations

- interactive modules that present local library level public access computing statistics based on the Information Institute's 2006 internet national level survey, create templates for NCES related library statistic generation, and develop report generation modules useful for library reporting and advocacy purposes
- a commons area that provides a uniform presentation of references and resources; and the EDMS communication centre (phpBB threaded discussion list, as described on page 174) to improve interaction between participants of the EDMS system
- an About Us section that provides information about the EDMS and the Information Institute
- contact templates for individuals to provide comments, feedback, and to suggest additional resources and references.

In addition, the EDMS includes an infrastructure developed specifically to sustain and update the site, access national level resources and databases, generate reports on-the-fly using data from the national-level databases, and allows for future refinement and expansion of the site.

Refinement of the EDMS includes ongoing development of the support structure for future implementation of modules in the instructional, interactive and commons areas. Refinement also includes the ongoing design to improve interactivity between the project's SQL database and future added databases, i.e. annual NCES databases and Information Institute internet databases.

Figure 10.1 offers an overview of the EDMS. The various EDMS areas of development:

- offer ways in which to think about and engage in evaluation efforts
- stress that different evaluation approaches meet different assessment needs
- provide public librarians and managers with decision tools to facilitate the most appropriate evaluation approach to meet their data needs
- assist public libraries in understanding and using best practices in evaluation to demonstrate the contributions that libraries make to the communities that they serve.

The EDMS as it has evolved provides access to a broad spectrum of information and includes interactive aspects intended to aid libraries with evaluation and advocacy purposes; however, the EDMS does not produce standards or force compliance with a set of evaluation approaches or guidelines.

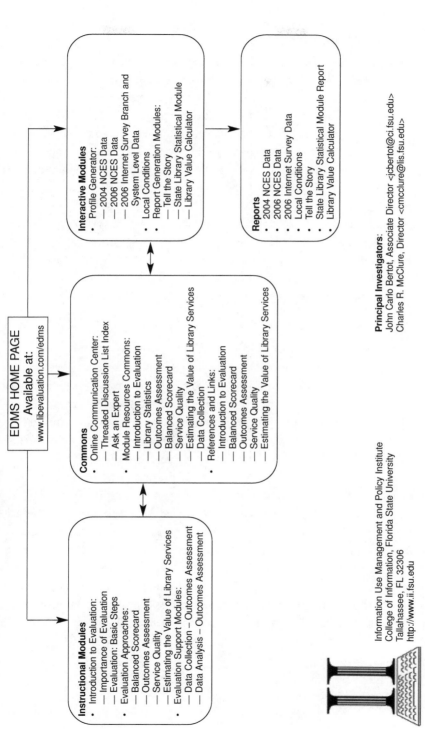

Instructional Modules
- Introduction to Evaluation:
  — Importance of Evaluation
  — Evaluation: Basic Steps
- Evaluation Approaches:
  — Balanced Scorecard
  — Outcomes Assessment
  — Service Quality
  — Estimating the Value of Library Services
- Evaluation Support Modules:
  — Data Collection – Outcomes Assessment
  — Data Analysis – Outcomes Assessment

Commons
- Online Communication Center:
  — Threaded Discussion List Index
  — Ask an Expert
- Module Resources Commons:
  — Introduction to Evaluation
  — Library Statistics
  — Outcomes Assessment
  — Balanced Scorecard
  — Service Quality
  — Estimating the Value of Library Services
  — Data Collection
- References and Links:
  — Introduction to Evaluation
  — Balanced Scorecard
  — Outcomes Assessment
  — Service Quality
  — Estimating the Value of Library Services

Interactive Modules
- Profile Generator:
  — 2004 NCES Data
  — 2006 NCES Data
  — 2006 Internet Survey Branch and System Level Data
  — Local Conditions
- Report Generation Modules:
  — Tell the Story
  — State Library Statistical Module
  — Library Value Calculator

Reports
- 2004 NCES Data
- 2006 NCES Data
- 2006 Internet Survey Data
- Local Conditions
- Tell the Story
- State Library Statistical Module Report
- Library Value Calculator

EDMS HOME PAGE
Available at:
www.libevaluation.com/edms

Information Use Management and Policy Institute
College of Information, Florida State University
Tallahassee, FL 32306
http://www.ii.fsu.edu

Principal Investigators:
John Carlo Bertot, Associate Director <jcbertot@ci.fsu.edu>
Charles R. McClure, Director <cmcclure@lis.fsu.edu>

Figure 10.1 An overview of the EDMS

Selected key issues

The overall purpose of this project is to develop a web-based learning and instructional tool that will help public librarians and managers determine the most appropriate evaluation approach that best fits unique situational needs and factors of a library for the type of information required. EDMS design enables public librarians and managers to use the system's guidance and instruction to identify evaluation methods and match the methods to local library needs and budgetary constraints. In addition, the EDMS will help public librarians and managers use these evaluations to demonstrate the value of library services and resources.

During the development and implementation of the EDMS, however, the study team identified a number of issues that affected the evolution of the EDMS website. A selection of key issues discussed here includes customization of on-the-fly reports, integration of communication features into the site, academic v. real-world perspectives, engaging users with the site, and sustainability of the site.

Customization of on-the-fly reports

The EDMS consists of instructional modules, interactive modules, a commons area and information areas (about the EDMS, the Information Institute, and giving contact information). With the exception of the interactive component of the EDMS, development of each of the other areas occurred with relatively few issues. The interactive components of the EDMS, however, created a number of technology issues related to the customization of on-the-fly reports.

Interactive reports contain data drawn from national level library databases (nationwide-based NCES and Information Institute internet studies). Technology developers of the EDMS incorporated the original Access databases and Excel spreadsheets from NCES and the Information Institute surveys, respectively, into an SQL format. Reports available from the interactive component contain data integrated into report templates, which also contain fields for the addition of descriptive and/or explanatory text. These fields allow users to customize the reports for management, planning, and/or advocacy purposes. The integration of technology and database design, however, created a number of issues related to the development of the EDMS.

Integration of technology

The study team completed the initial development of the infrastructure of the site, integrated national level databases into SQL format, and created report templates designed specifically for the generation of data-driven reports for specific areas of interest. Examples of each type of interactive template are implemented and functional; however, the process of creating queries to fill template fields from the SQL database took longer than anticipated.

In addition, the overall development of interactive modules to auto-generate reports based on specific library situational contexts and needs also proved to be much more challenging than anticipated, requiring significantly more technical expertise and study team time than originally planned. For example, the design team intended that library reports include a problem-solving aspect where libraries could use data from national surveys combined with prescribed questions to identify local situational contexts for problem-solving purposes.

The resultant report would address a specific problem or issue, such as the cost (budgeting issue) of adding public workstations to improve public access to the internet. Data included in the reports from national surveys would provide libraries with the means to compare the number of public workstations to state and national averages and libraries would follow a prescribed process to create a report that specifically addresses a local library problem or issue. Creating a report template capable of identifying local situation contexts and needs useful for all libraries, however, was not feasible or practical.

Based on the advice from the partners and advisory committee, the study team revised the design criteria for the interactive problem-solving modules. The study team revised the library report templates from the problem-solving approach to data and text presentation where libraries could use national level survey data and include descriptive text for the data to tell their own stories based on their local situational contexts. This tell-the-story approach allows libraries to use national data for planning and advocacy purposes based on local library conditions and factors.

By working with the partners and advisory committee, the study team determined (both technically and intellectually) from its previous efforts in designing such modules that programming or anticipating the extent of potential situational factors affecting report development or dissemination for a particular library is unrealistic. Current templates allow participants of the interactive site of the EDMS to identify specific situational contexts and needs and add descriptive and explanatory text to report generated data from the SQL database as needed to tell their own story.

Database design

Interactive components require a login process so users of the system can save reports created by interactive modules for future reference and/or refinement. Initial planning for a login process included an option for users to view and interact with the modules without logging into the system; however, providing this option created presentation and content issues throughout the interactive component. Adjustments to the initial option design led to the requirement of all users to login to view or interact with the interactive modules of the site.

As mentioned in the section on integration of technology, the technology developers of the EDMS site integrated several national databases into the SQL database. The integration process created issues unique to how the SQL system provides users of the EDMS access to data that is specific to a local library, such as the presence of unique identifiers for each library associated with the library's data fields in the system and library personnel knowing the unique identifier to begin the query process. For users of the EDMS to create customized reports, they need to access data specific to that library.

Theoretically, each library has a unique identifier associated with the library, referred to as an FSCS ID. For users of the system who know the FSCS ID for a particular library, they can enter the ID and proceed with the interaction process. EDMS technology developers had to develop a unique FSCS ID location protocol, however, for users who do not know a library's FSCS ID or for libraries with IDs that for a number of reasons do not provide a unique identifier for that library.

Communication features

The Commons area contains a functional threaded discussion area (an open source discussion-forum software called phpBB, available at www.phpbb.com) and a template for users to contact experts for each instructional module of the EDMS (the Ask an Expert templates). The initial design of the communication area of the EDMS included blogs, wikis, list-servs, a threaded discussion list and other similar types of interactive communication features. Each of these types of communication software, however, can require a substantial amount of moderation time for sustainability purposes.

For the first version of the EDMS, the study team focused on the inclusion of a threaded discussion list and selected the phpBB software; however, a number of issues arose related to this type of discussion list. For the EDMS, the study team initially planned for all users of the system to have open access to the discussion list. This led to an influx of multiple spam posts to the list that required a considerable amount of time to clear. In discussions with experts in the field of online communication software, the experts identified spam as a key issue with all open-access discussion lists and none could suggest better alternatives or suggestions other than to limit access to the list and develop an approval protocol to allow entry to the discussion areas.

In addition, the study team planned for a synchronous login process where a participant could login to either the EDMS or the phpBB yet have access to both. The proprietary nature of the phpBB software, however, prohibited full implementation of this login process.

Academic v. real-world perspective

Developers of instructional and information systems, such as the EDMS, often must consider the presentation of the system from a user perspective, particularly when users of the system are in essence volunteers willing to participate. The study team continuously focused on a user perspective, from design to implementation; however, issues related to users' comprehension and understanding of the various component parts of the EDMS continue as ongoing development and testing of the system occurs.

To address this issue, the study team recruited members of the library community to participate on the advisory committee and as project partners. The advisory committee, project partners and other experts from the field who provide insights and contributions to the project are integral to maintaining the academic/real-world perspective through comments and suggestions offered to improve the system. In addition, the study team recruits individuals from library staffs and experts from the library field (academic researchers, library practitioners, state library staff and so on) as participants of usability studies and focus groups. As part of this ongoing evaluation process of the EDMS, these participants provide invaluable insights into the ongoing development and refinement of the EDMS system.

Engaging users with the site

In addition to the inclusion of potential participants as part of the ongoing evaluation process of the EDMS (as described above), the study team plans and implements workshops, seminars and presentations in conjunction with key public library and library conferences to engage users with the EDMS site. Some reasons for the need to engage users with the site include:

- to introduce the library community to the EDMS
- to provide an introduction to available information and resources on how best to use evaluation information and evaluation frameworks, such as the EDMS, for library advocacy in the local community
- to improve assessment and development of public library services and programmes based on library resources and needs of a library's community
- to engage in numerous marketing efforts to increase awareness and use of the EDMS.

Ultimately, the users of any instructional system determine the success or failure of the use and usefulness of the content and presentation of the system; therefore users are integral participants throughout the design and implementation process of any instructional system project.

Sustainability

The Information Institute is committed to keeping the EDMS current and operational after the end of the IMLS project-funding period, and developed a number of approaches to sustain the effort. First, during the project (and also for a planned two-year post-project window), the Institute engaged organizations such as COSLA, the Public Library Data Service (PLDS), PLA, ALA and other organizations for their direct support to ensure continued and ongoing support, development and benefit of the EDMS to public libraries.

Second, the Information Institute continues to work with current support organizations (the advisory committee, project partners, experts in the field and so on) to take ownership for the development and ongoing evolution of the EDMS. The ultimate goal of the project is to establish ongoing support for the EDMS that will promote its continual updating, revision, new module development and system enhancements; however, developers must continue to address actual sustainability of systems such as the EDMS in terms of effort and the availability and allocation of resources.

Third, the EDMS has been designed so that users of the system can update the components and provide additional discussion and information about evaluation approaches. The EDMS will allow participants to post good examples of evaluation reports, new resources and opinions about the strengths and weaknesses of the various evaluation methodologies. To some extent basic social networking applications will be built into the EDMS.

Future developments and moving to Web 2.0 and beyond

Understanding the potential uses and applications of the web for evaluation instruction and other contexts is an ongoing, rapidly developing process, and the approaches and strategies by which public libraries will select and develop various evaluation methods is a rapidly evolving and changing environment as well. The EDMS described in this paper might soon be out of date after the completion of the project because of this changing environment and require wholesale upgrades to stay current with new development in web applications such as Web 2.0 and beyond (Stephens, 2007).

The current trend in the use of social networking applications is likely to have significant impacts on internet-based service roles. A recent report from OCLC (2007, vii–viii) notes:

> Social sites like MySpace, Mixi, Facebook and YouTube have built a new 'social web' connecting communities of hundreds of millions of users across much of the industrialized world. In June 2007, the world's top three social sites (YouTube, MySpace, Facebook) attracted more than 350 million people to their Web sites according to comScore. . . . We know relatively little about what these emerging social Web communities will mean for the future of the Internet or the possibilities they hold for library services on the Internet.

In the future, then, is it possible that public library users will develop their own interactive and participatory evaluation approaches incorporating such techniques? Will the developers of the EDMS be able to enhance the use and impact of this site with such techniques?

As one example, the website Library Thing (www.librarything.com/) provides a means for users to enter and catalogue their personal library or a reading list, connects users to other people reading the same or similar books, offers recommendations of books of interest, gives blogging space, and much more. As of February 2008, members have catalogued some 23 million books. Designers of online information systems can incorporate these types of applications into interactive and social networking instructional modules such as the EDMS.

Other examples of these new types of internet applications include Bibliocommons, which is 'transforming online library catalogues from searchable inventory systems into engaging social discovery environments' (www. bibliocommons.com/). The notion of social networked communal cataloguing, resource discovery among information and people, participatory readers' adviser, and more, has very significant implications for how public library internet-based evaluation may evolve. Indeed, inclusion of such applications could make tools such as the EDMS much more useful.

In a recent paper, Lankes et al. describe library service in terms of participatory networks in which the library is a 'conversation'. They go on to state (2007, 19):

> A core concept of Web 2.0 is that people are the content of sites; that is, a site is not populated with information for users to consume. Instead, services are provided to individual users for them to build networks of friends and other groups (professional, recreational, and so on). The content of a site then comprises user-provided information that attracts new members of an ever-expanding network.

The Lankes et al. paper raises numerous challenges and issues for the future of public library internet-based services for application to web-based evaluation instruction. Of special interest to the topic discussed here, however, is to what degree could these participatory network conversations promote public library evaluation instruction and how can we design such systems? To what degree will developers be able to design exciting and dynamic internet-based instructional sites that are participatory and draw on social networking principles successfully?

At the heart of all of these various social networking applications is a peer-to-peer relationship of community members not well understood in terms of how they will affect instructional modules such as EDMS. Many of the social networking applications 'push' services to users, offer links to other information, much of it directly from other peers, and ultimately allow internet users to define and create information services that are personalized or customized to meet their specific needs. Perhaps more importantly, they encourage the development, content and services to evolve based on participants' needs and creativity, the point made by Brophy in 2004 we quoted at the opening of this chapter.

An underlying notion of these social networking applications is personal trust among participants and a sense of value of receiving the opinions from others. Obtaining access to interactive evaluation modules is not the same as obtaining the opinion, insights and experiences of someone regarding an evaluation topic of special interest (for example assessing the quality of a digital reference service) who is trusted by the user and with whom the community of users has shared values. A major conclusion of the OCLC study *Sharing, Privacy and Trust in Our Networked World* (2007) is that internet users increasingly have less concern about privacy, confidentiality and trustworthiness about these social sites. Thus, they are increasingly likely to participate in providing personal information, views and various library evaluation experiences that develop these sites.

Planning for the future of public library interactive instructional web-based sites such as the EDMS also needs to consider how such websites can be successfully evaluated. Evaluating such sites that are built into a social networked environment would involve consideration of a number of factors:

- Traditional evaluation approaches typically base assessment on an imposed or organizationally accepted set of service goals and objectives. Evaluation based on social networked activities builds on dynamic, personally self-driven goals and objectives, which are constantly evolving and changing.
- Outcome measures (for example) that assess changes in behaviour, skills and/or attitudes may be of less importance in social networking service roles where learning, contacts, quality of life and other individually based measures are most important. Moreover, individually based process measures may have greater validity for measuring user success than system-based outcomes.
- Comparing the 'success' of users across various types of social networking evaluation applications presents numerous challenges given the situational nature of users of these applications.
- The nature and definition of 'community' as it relates to the library's service population changes significantly in a social networking context. Successful social networking applications rely on 'virtual' communities that span the globe and not 'local' communities defined by an artificial geographical or political boundary.
- Separating the evaluation and measurement of the technological infrastructure of the website from the actual use of that application may be impossible. In short, to what degree are evaluators measuring quality of the technology as opposed to the use of that technology?
- Success of an individual's use of an internet based socially networked instructional service is dependent on the skills and knowledge of the user – one person's success versus another's may have little to do with the application itself.

These are but a few of the challenges that the future holds for successful design and evaluation of web-based instructional tools such as the EDMS, which build on social networking applications.

Existing public library evaluation strategies may continue to be of use for many public libraries, but evaluation approaches that incorporate social networked and participatory techniques may be rapidly changing and evolving, dependent on a range of library factors such as staff skills and available information technology infrastructure, and situational factors and skills of individual users. Thus, the public library community may find it useful to move from a static to a dynamic evaluation mentality and incorporate a range of Web 2.0 techniques into library evaluations.

Regardless of how evaluation methods and instruction evolve, public libraries will continue to be asked to justify their budgets; demonstrate the impact, outcomes, benefits, quality, value and so on of the library; and have to consider the reporting of these data in complicated political environments that vary from library to library. To do this successfully, public library administrators will need to have access to the best evaluation tools possible and be able to judge which evaluation methods and tools will best meet their needs. The EDMS is a first effort to assist them in this endeavour.

Acknowledgement

The authors acknowledge the research and development work contributed to the EDMS by project Co-Principal Investigator John Carlo Bertot as well as a number of other staff at the Information Use Management and Policy Institute including Paul Jaeger, Myke Falcon, Mega M. Subramaniam, Wade Bradley Bishop, Na Ding, Joe Ryan, Susan Thomas, Joe Matthews, Beverly Choltco-Devlin and Alan S. Hanstein, President of Paragon, Inc. The authors also gratefully acknowledge the support for the project from the US Institute of Museum and Library Services.

References

Bertot, J. C. (2004) Libraries and Networked Information Services: issues and considerations in measurement, *Performance Measurement and Metrics*, **5** (1), 11–19.

Bertot, J. C. and Davis, D. M. (2004) *Planning and Evaluating Library Networked Services and Resources*, Libraries Unlimited.

Bertot, J. C. and McClure, C. R. (2003a) Outcomes Assessment in the Networked Environment: research questions, issues, considerations, and moving forward, *Library Trends*, **51** (4), 590–613.

Bertot, J. C. and McClure, C. R. (2003b) *Assessing LSTA Project Outcomes: methods and practice*, www.ii.fsu.edu/index.cfm.

Bertot, J. C. and Snead, J. T. (2004a) Selecting Evaluation Approaches for a Networked Environment. In Bertot, J. C. and Davis, D. M. (eds), *Planning and Evaluating Library Networked Services and Resources*, Libraries Unlimited, 22–48.

Bertot, J. C. and Snead, J. T. (2004b) Social Measurement in Libraries. In Kempf-Leonard, K. (ed.), *Encyclopedia of Social Measurement*, Academic Press.

Brophy, P. (2004) Beyond the Mainstream of Library Services. In Brophy, P., Fisher, S. and Craven, J. (eds), *Libraries without Walls 5: the distributed delivery of library and information services*, Facet Publishing, 7–15.

Brophy, P. and Coulling, K. (1996) *Quality Management for Information and Library Managers*, Gower.

Durrance, J. C. and Fisher, K. E. (2005) *How Libraries and Librarians Help*, American Library Association.

EDMS (2008) *Evaluation Decision Management System*, Information Use Management and Policy Institute, www.libevaluation.com/edms.

Griffiths, J. M. et al. (2004) *Taxpayer Return on Investment in Florida Public Libraries: summary report*, Florida State Library.

Hernon, P. and Dugan, R. E. (2002) *An Action Plan for Outcomes Assessment in Your Library*, American Library Association.

Holt, G. E. (2003) *Public Library Partnerships: mission-driven tools for 21st century success*, www.public-libraries.net.

Lankes, R. D., Silverstein, J. and Nicholson, S. (2007) Participatory Networks: the library as conversation, *Information Technology and Libraries*, **26** (4), 17–33.

Matthews, J. R. (2004) *Measuring for Results: the dimensions of public library effectiveness*, Libraries Unlimited.

McClure, C. R. and Bertot, J. C. (1998) Public Library Use in Pennsylvania: identifying uses, benefits, and impacts – final report, http://slis-two.lis.fsu.edu/~cmcclure/.

McClure, C. R. and Bertot, J. C. (2003) Analysis of E-rate Data, www.ii.fsu.edu/index.cfm.

National Center for Education Statistics (2008) *Public Libraries in the United States: fiscal year 2005 [NCES 2008-301]*, US Department of Education, Institute of Education Sciences.

OCLC (2007) *Sharing, Privacy and Trust in our Networked World*, OCLC.

Ryan, J. and McClure, C. R. (2003) *Economic Impact of the Hawaii State Public Library System (HSPLS) on the Business and Tourism Industries Study: final report*, Hawaii State Public Library System.

Stephens, M. (2007) Web 2.0 and Libraries, Part 2: trends and technologies, *Library Technology Reports*, **43** (September–October).

Van House, N., Lynch, M. J., McClure, C. R., Zweizig, D. L. and Rodger, E. J. (1987) *Output Measures for Public Libraries: a manual of standardized procedures*, American Library Association.

11

Measuring the quality of academic library electronic services and resources

JILLIAN R. GRIFFITHS

Introduction

Walk into any lecture theatre in a UK higher education institution and ask what students use to find information and the majority will shout 'Google' – a situation we refer to as the 'Googling phenomenon' (Griffiths and Brophy, 2005). Students' use of search engines influences their perception and expectations of all electronic resources but, although the preference for very simple search engine approaches is prevalent, it does not mean that students are necessarily best served by this approach. Exclusive use of any commercial search engine, coupled with a lack of awareness and understanding of peer-reviewed, quality resources, is not in the best interest of students or academic staff.

This issue of 'quality' plays a key role in professional discussions regarding electronic (and other) services and resources and as a result sophisticated approaches to quality assurance have been developed, such as peer review (largely for journal articles) and publisher reputation (for monographs) and relating these to the known interests of the user community, present and future. As a profession we are constantly striving to ensure that we provide the best services and resources possible to our users and this concern has resulted in a myriad of approaches and methods being used in an attempt to establish the quality of services and resources and lead to improvements in them. Online resources in particular have been the focus of much research in recent years, with work being undertaken in many areas including, for example, information retrieval, information-seeking behaviour and usability studies.

Evaluation of comparative online systems, services and resources has a long tradition of improving the state of the art in information retrieval (IR) technology. The criterion for the evaluation of performance effectiveness has largely been based on the overall goal of a retrieval system, that is, the retrieval of relevant documents and suppression of non-relevant items. Such evaluations adopt the Cranfield experimental model based on relevance, a value judgement on retrieved items, to calculate recall and precision. These dual measures are then presented together where recall is a measure of effectiveness in retrieving all the sought information and precision assesses the accuracy of the search.

Many and varied criticisms and concerns have been levelled at the validity and reliability of a Cranfield approach to IR evaluation (for example, Ellis, 1984). The core concern centres on the compromise necessary in the definition of relevance for such experimentation. That is, it is necessary to assume that relevance judgements can be made independently and that a user will assess each document without being affected by their understanding of any previous items read. In addition, there is a basic assumption that relevance can ignore the many situational and psychological variables that in the real world affect it (Large, Tedd and Hartley, 1999). The appropriateness of this traditional model has also been questioned when used in the internet environment, the major limitation being that the internet does not provide for a controlled environment. As a result many studies in this area use the precision measure only (Clarke and Willett, 1997; Leighton and Srivastava, 1999).

The quality attributes approach allows for a holistic assessment of the quality of services or resources and encompasses usability and evaluation of a user-centred view of performance effectiveness using the user's own perception of relevance and satisfaction with items retrieved and of the resource as a whole. The quality attributes approach has been adapted for use in libraries and information services by a number of authors: Marchand (1990), Brophy and Coulling (1996), Brophy (1998) and Griffiths and Brophy (2002, 2005). The aim of this paper is to reflect on the work that has been undertaken in this field and to offer some observations on possible future directions. It explores the quality attributes approach pioneered by Garvin and presents the development of this approach from its original conception by Garvin to its latest adaptation by Griffiths and Brophy (2002, 2005).

Garvin's original quality attributes

In the general management literature, the classic definitions of quality emerged from the work of a number of researchers and writers, known collectively as the quality gurus (see Brophy and Coulling, 1996, Chapter 2). They developed a series of statements about and definitions of the concept of quality, of which the most commonly quoted are 'quality is fitness for purpose' and 'quality is conformance to requirements'.

Interest in quality management among librarians reached its peak in the 1990s.

Researchers and practitioners across a number of countries undertook research in relation to applying the more general quality management approaches and practices to libraries. This interest was epitomized by a conference on total quality management held as part of the Library Technology Fair at Hatfield, UK, in 1993. Other examples of work in the field include the UK Institute of Management guide to ISO 9000, the international quality management standard (Ellis and Norton, 1993) and Hernon and Altman's (1998) exploration of the application of quality management approaches.

The classic definitions of quality, concerned with 'fitness for the user's purpose', clearly relate to the benefits that customers perceive as arising from a service or product that they purchase or use, and are more concerned with measures of impact and outcome rather than performance measures or indicators. Garvin recognized that the classic definitions of quality were too simplistic and set about developing a more sophisticated approach in the USA in the 1980s. He recognized that quality is a complex and multifaceted concept and suggested that there are eight critical dimensions or attributes that can be used as a framework for determining the overall quality of a product or service (Garvin, 1987).

Garvin (1984) suggested that many of the problems of defining and recognizing quality arise because the concept can be approached from many different perspectives. He suggested that at least five views can be identified in the literature and in practice:

- the transcendental view: quality can be recognized, but cannot be defined
- the customer view: quality as fitness for the customer's purposes or conformance to the customer's requirements
- the manufacturer view: quality as conformance to specification
- the product view: quality is related to inherent characteristics of the product
- the value-based view: quality is dependent on what a customer is willing to pay for it.

Quality attributes adapted

While Garvin's quality attributes approach was originally intended mainly for manufacturing industries it has subsequently been adapted for use in libraries and information services by Marchand (1990), Brophy (1998), Griffiths and Brophy (2002) and Griffiths and Brophy (2005). The latter team suggested that library and information services might be assessed on the basis of ten quality attributes. Other work has suggested that this approach is also applicable to web pages (for example, Abels, White and Hahn, 1997; Madu and Madu, 2002).

Griffiths and Brophy adapted the quality attributes further by changing the emphasis of one attribute, changing the concept of one attribute, and introducing two additional attributes (currency and usability), thus producing a set of ten attributes, which can be used to assess the quality, usability and impact of services and resources (see Table 11.1). These attributes are: performance, conformance, features, reliability, durability, currency, serviceability, aesthetics, perceived quality and usability. Usability, often used as an assessment criterion in its own right, has been defined by ISO 9241-11 as 'the extent to which a product can be used by specified users to achieve specified goals with effectiveness, efficiency and

Table 11.1 Garvin's original attributes (1984) contrasted with adaptations by Brophy (1998) and Griffiths and Brophy (2002, 2005)

Garvin (1984)	Brophy and Griffiths (1998, 2002 and 2005)
Performance, the primary purpose of the product or service and how well it is achieving that primary purpose.	*Performance*, concerned with establishing confirmation that a library service meets its most basic purpose, such as making key information sources available on demand.
Features, secondary characteristics that add to the service or product without being of its essence.	*Features*, aspects of the service that appeal to users but are beyond the essential core performance attributes, such as alerting services.
Reliability, the consistency of the product or service's performance in use.	*Reliability*, which for information services would include availability of the service. Such problems as broken web links, lack of reliability and slowness in speed of response would be measured as part of this attribute.
Conformance, whether or not the product or service meets the agreed standard, which may be internally or externally generated.	*Conformance*, whether the service meets the agreed standard, including conformance questions around the use of standards and protocols such as XML, RDF, Dublin Core, OAI, Z39.50 etc.
Durability, the amount of use the product or service can provide before it deteriorates to a point where it needs replacement.	*Durability*, related to the sustainability of the information or library service over a period of time.
	Currency of information, that is, how up to date the information provided is when it is retrieved.
Serviceability, how easy it is to repair a product or correct a service when it goes wrong, including the level of inconvenience experienced by the customer.	*Serviceability*, which may translate to the level of help available to users during, for example, information retrieval, or otherwise at the point of need. The availability of instructions and prompts throughout an online service, context sensitive help and the usefulness of that help could be measured in order to assess performance under this attribute.
Aesthetics, the appearance of the product or service.	*Aesthetics* and image, both of the physical library and of web-based services based on it.
Perceived quality, in essence the reputation of the product or service among the population, especially those with whom the potential customer comes into contact.	*Perceived quality*, the user's view of the service as a whole and the information retrieved from it. It may be useful to measure perceptions both before and after a service is used.
	Usability, which is particularly relevant to electronic services and includes issues of accessibility.

satisfaction in a specified context of use' and, as Neilsen points out, 'It is important to realize that usability is not a single, one-dimensional property of a user interface. Usability has multiple components and is traditionally associated with these five usability attributes: learnability, efficiency, memorability, errors, satisfaction' (1993, 26).

The following describes in detail the quality attributes as adapted by Griffiths and Brophy (2002, 2005) in the context of measuring the quality of academic library electronic services and resources:

- *Performance* is concerned with establishing confirmation that a service meets its most basic requirement. These are the primary operating features of the product or service. For example, an electronic information service would be expected to retrieve a set of documents that matched a user's query. The most basic quality question is then 'Does the service retrieve a list of relevant documents?'. In the Evaluation of the Distributed National Electronic Resource (EDNER) study (Brophy et al., 2003) the performance attribute was measured using the criteria 'Are you satisfied that the required information was retrieved?' and 'Are you satisfied with the ranking order of retrieved items?', and was primarily concerned with eliciting information about the user's relevance assessment of the items retrieved.

- With *conformance* the question is whether the product or service meets the agreed standard. This may be a national or international standard or locally determined service standard. The standards themselves, however they are devised, must of course relate to customer requirements. For information services there are obvious conformance questions around the use of standards and protocols such as XML, RDF, Dublin Core, OAI, Z39.50 and so on. Many conformance questions can only be answered by expert analysts since users are unlikely to have either the expertise or the access needed to make technical or service-wide assessments: thus users in the EDNER study did not evaluate this attribute.

- *Features* are the secondary operating attributes, which add to a product or service in the user's eyes but are not essential to it. They may provide an essential marketing edge. It is not always easy to distinguish performance characteristics from features, especially as what is essential to one customer may be an optional extra to another, and there is a tendency for features to become performance attributes over time – inclusion of images into full text databases is an example of a feature developing in this way. The attribute was measured by asking participants which features appealed to them most on each individual service and by identifying which search option/s they used to perform their searches.

- Users place high value on the *reliability* of a product or service. For products this usually means that they perform as expected (or better). For electronic information services a major issue is usually availability of the service. Therefore broken links, unreliability and slowness in speed of response can have a detrimental effect on a user's perception of a service. Users were asked if they found any dead links while searching each service and, if so, whether these dead links impacted on their judgement of the service. Participants were also asked if they were satisfied with the speed of response of the service, a measure which has previously been reported as being important to users by Dong and Su (1997), who put forward that response time is becoming a very important issue for many users.

- Garvin uses the term *durability*, defined as 'the amount of use the product will provide before it deteriorates to the point where replacement or discard is preferable to repair'. In the case of electronic information services this will relate to the sustainability of the service over a period of time. In simple terms, will the service still be in existence in three or five years? This is more likely to be assessed by experts in the field than by end users (although they may have useful contributions on the assessment of the attribute based on comparisons with similar services), and therefore was not evaluated during the EDNER testing.

- For most users of electronic information services an important issue is the *currency* of information, that is, how up to date the information provided is when it is retrieved.

- *Serviceability* relates to when things go wrong and is concerned with questions such as 'How easy will it then be to put things right?', 'How quickly can they be repaired?', 'How much inconvenience will be caused to the user?', and 'How much will it cost?' For users of an electronic information service this may translate to the level of help available to them during the search and at the point of need. The availability of instructions and prompts throughout, context sensitive help and usefulness of help were measured in order to assess responses to this attribute.

- Although *aesthetics* and image is a highly subjective area, it is of prime importance to users. In electronic environments it brings in the whole debate about what constitutes good design. In a web environment the design of the home page may be the basis for user selection of services and this may have little to do with actual functionality. A range of criteria were used to measure user responses to this attribute, these being satisfaction with the interface and presentation of features, familiarity with the interface or elements of the interface, and how easy it was to understand the content of retrieved items from the hit list.

- *Perceived quality* is one of the most interesting of attributes because it recognizes that all users make their judgements on incomplete information. They do not carry out detailed surveys of hit rates or examine the rival systems' performance in retrieving a systematic sample of records. Most users do not read the service's mission statement or service standards and do their best to by-pass the instructions pages. Yet, users will quickly come to a judgement about the service based on its reputation among their colleagues and acquaintances, their preconceptions and their instant reactions to it. Perceived quality in the studies undertaken by Griffiths and Brophy (2002) related to the user's view of the service as a whole and the information retrieved from it. This was measured twice, before using the service (pre-perceived quality, where participants were aware of the service prior to testing) and after using the service (post-perceived quality). This allows investigation of how a user's perception of a service changes pre- and post-use.

  The notion of quality is a concept that many students seem to struggle with. In the work undertaken for the EDNER study it was found that 74% of students did not agree that the criterion 'refereed' was an indicator of quality. 89% agreed that 'accurate' was an indicator of quality, 81% agreed that 'current' was an indicator of quality and 52% that 'reliable' was an indicator of quality. Students were also asked what quality meant to them and criteria such as speed, relevancy, useful, links to related areas, understanding language used, valuable, referenced, presentation, timeliness, accessible, clear information and source were listed (Brophy et al., 2003). Clearly there is confusion here.

- The addition of *usability* as an attribute is important in any user-centred evaluation. User-centred models are much more helpful when personal preferences and requirements are factored in. Participants were asked how user friendly the service was, how easy it was to remember what the features and commands meant and how to use them, how satisfied they were with the input query facility and how satisfied they were with the ease with which they could modify their query.

Quality attribute measurement in practice

Table 11.2 presents examples of measures designed to provide responses to enable assessment of the service or resource for each quality attribute. These measurement instruments were developed to assess existing and developing services of the UK Joint Information Systems Committee (JISC) Information Environment as part of the EDNER and EDNER+ projects (Griffiths, 2003; Griffiths and Brophy, 2005). This research used a user-centered approach, but could be tailored to different contexts and stakeholders, thus enabling a holistic approach to the evaluation of digital library services.

Table 11.2 Examples of quality attribute measurement instrument

Quality attribute	Measurement
Performance Basic requirements, primary operating features	• Are you satisfied that you found the required information on this service? • How satisfied were you with the order of the items retrieved (e.g. most relevant first, least relevant last)?
Conformance Agreed standard	• Not evaluated by end users, could be assessed by expert user or service provider
Features Secondary operating attributes, added value, subjective	• There can be many different search options that you could have used to search for the information on this service. Which did you use (please list)? • Were there any features that you particularly liked about this service?
Reliability High user value	• Did you find any dead links when using this service? • If Yes, does the finding of dead links in your search session make you think that the service is unreliable, reliable or doesn't it affect your judgement? • How satisfied were you with the speed of response of this service?
Durability Sustainability of the service	• Not evaluated by end users, could be assessed by expert user
Currency How up to date is the information?	• Do you think that the information from this service is up to date?
Serviceability How easy will it be to put things right?	• Did you find on-screen instructions and prompts helpful or unhelpful? • Did you select Help at any stage? • If Yes, how helpful did you find it?
Aesthetics Highly subjective area of prime importance	• How satisfied were you with the interface and features of this service? • Were there any features or aspects of the interface that you were familiar with? • How easy is it to understand what each item is about from the retrieved list?
Perceived quality Users' judgements	• Please rate the overall quality of the items you found on this service
Usability Important in any user-centred evaluation	• How user-friendly did you think this service was? • How easy was it to remember which features to use? • How satisfied were you with the facility to input your query? • How satisfied were you with the facility to modify or change your query, e.g. find similar, related searches, refine search, etc.?

Benefits of this approach

One of the major benefits of the quality attributes approach is that they allow investigation of how a user's perception of a resource changes pre- and post-use, and show that although preconceived notions of a service may be negative it is possible to change these perceptions if the resource performs well across a number of the attributes. If pre-use perceptions do not alter it is possible to identify which aspects of a resource need to be improved by examining those attributes that users have scored lower. For example, in Figure 11.1 a participant has used a service and then indicated their satisfaction across a range of attributes.

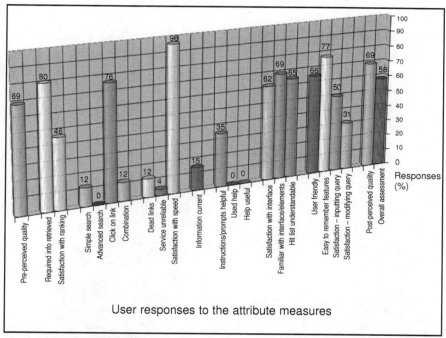

Figure 11.1 Example of a participant's assessment of resource

For this resource participants indicated high levels of satisfaction that the required information was retrieved (80%) but satisfaction with ranking was much lower (46%). The majority of users navigated to information by clicking on links (76%), with only 12% using the simple search option and 12% using a combination of techniques. A small number of participants (12%) found dead links and of these 4% felt the service was unreliable as a result. Satisfaction with speed of response was very high at 96%. Low levels of satisfaction were recorded on the currency attribute (15%). Instructions and prompts were found to be helpful by 35% of participants and the Help facility was not used in any of the cases. 69% of participants reported that they were familiar with the interface, or elements of the interface and 62% of participants were satisfied with it. 65% felt that the hit list was understandable. On the usability attribute 65% of students felt that the service was user friendly and 77% found features and commands easy to remember and use. 50% of participants reported that they were satisfied with the facility to input their query but only 31% were satisfied with the facility to modify their query. The preferred method of obtaining information was by navigating via click on link as opposed to engaging with a search option. Perceived quality, pre- and post-searching, remained static at 69% and overall satisfaction was recorded at 58%.

These results provide a detailed demonstration that measures other than just performance play an important role in student evaluation and help resource developers, providers and educators to understand a user's reaction to individual components of a resource.

Assessment does not just have to be conducted on an individual resource; data gathered from assessments of a number of resources and services can assist in the identification of those which are underperforming. In Figure 11.2 (looking just at performance, usability, aesthetics and perceived quality) it is possible to make comparisons that can inform collection development and retention.

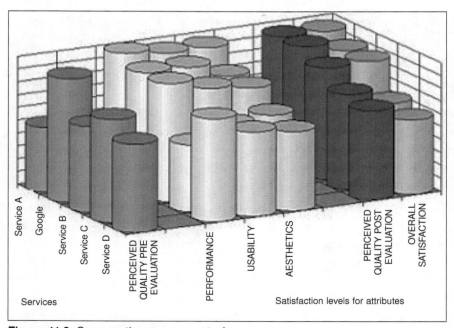

Figure 11.2 Comparative assessment of resources

Results show varying degrees of satisfaction across each of the services and each of the attributes. On Service D, perceived quality pre and post searching remained static (and relatively low), despite high levels of satisfaction with performance. In conjunction with this performance score, satisfaction with usability and aesthetics were lower. Overall satisfaction was also relatively low. This seems to indicate that users' perceptions of quality are driven by factors other than performance of a system. It also raises interesting questions as to how fixed preconceptions about quality may affect the results of the evaluation of a system or service.

On the Service C post-search perceived quality dropped only very slightly (2%), despite low levels of satisfaction with performance. Satisfaction with usability and aesthetics was slightly higher than with performance. This again may indicate that factors (or quality attributes) such as user friendliness and interface design may be at least as important as evaluation criteria as performance.

Users expressed an increase in post-search perceived quality on Services A and B, coupled with high levels of satisfaction overall and across each of the attributes. In this instance actual use of the service appears to have changed the preconceptions of the users.

Results for Google were high across all the measures used in the test. However, satisfaction with aesthetics was lower than satisfaction with aesthetics on Service B, and had lower overall satisfaction ratings.

It is interesting to note that in each instance satisfaction overall corresponded very closely with post perceived quality.

Conclusion

Previous research (Griffiths and Brophy, 2005) has indicated that students are confused as to the meaning of quality when it comes to assessing academic resources. Viewed in the light of the findings of Cmor and Lippold (2001), who stated that students will give the same academic weight to discussion list comments as peer-reviewed journal articles, it would seem that students are poor evaluators of the quality of academic online resources. The original premise of the perceived quality attribute is that users make their judgements about a service based on incomplete information and that they will come to this judgement based on its reputation among their colleagues and acquaintances and their preconceptions and instant reactions to it. If the notion of quality conveys so many different meanings to students, it poses something of a challenge to the academic community in encouraging students to understand and use quality-assured electronic resources.

It is also apparent, from a methodological perspective, that further work is needed to explore the meaning of perceived quality and the interpretation of user responses to this area of enquiry. Fundamentally different understandings of information quality could otherwise lead to questionable conclusions being drawn by researchers and service providers. Measures of impact should also be taken into account and future work is planned to include this as an eleventh attribute. And so the quality attributes approach to assessment of library services and resources continues to evolve and change.

The assessment of service and resource quality has developed significantly in recent years. We have robust sets of performance indicators, which provide the basic 'picture' of library performance and, beyond that, we have ways to explore the customer experience, to find out how users feel about the services and resources they use and to use these insights to provide better managed services.

Brophy (2004) has ruminated that, as a profession, we may be moving beyond individual techniques in an attempt to synthesize the different approaches towards measurements of impact, to get back to the essential question of 'do libraries and their services do any good?'. As Brophy concludes, our challenge is to strive to seek, and understand, the evidence that they do.

References

Abels, E. G., White, M. D. and Hahn, K. (1997) Identifying User-based Criteria for Web Pages, *Internet Research: Electronic Networking Applications and Policy*, **7** (4), 252–62.

Brophy, P. (1998) It May Be Electronic But Is It Any Good? Measuring the performance of electronic services, *Robots to Knowbots: the wider automation agenda, Proceedings of the Victorian Association for Library Automation 9th Biennial Conference*, 28–30 January, VALA, 217–30, www.vala.org.au/valaweb/num511.pdf.

Brophy, P. (2004) The Quality of Libraries. In Hilgermann, K. and te Borkhorst, P. (eds), *Die effektive Bibliothek*, K. G. Saur, 30–46.

Brophy, P. and Coulling, K. (1996) *Quality Management for Information and Library Managers*, Gower.

Brophy, P., Fisher, S., Griffiths, J. R. and Markland, M. (2003) *EDNER: formative evaluation of the Distributed National Electronic Resource: DNER service evaluation* (Deliverable MDA 2, EDNER Project), The Centre for Research in Library and Information Management (CERLIM), www.cerlim.ac.uk/edner/dissem/dissem.html.

Clarke, S. J. and Willett, P. (1997) Estimating the Recall Performance of Web Search Engines, *Aslib Proceedings*, **49** (7), 184–9.

Cmor, D. and Lippold, K. (2001) Surfing vs. Searching: the web as a research tool, paper presented at the *21st Annual Conference of the Society for Teaching and Learning in Higher Education*, June 14–16, Newfoundland, http://staff.library.mun.ca/~DCmor/stlhe/.

Dong, X. and Su, L. (1997) Search Engines on the World Wide Web and Information Retrieval from the Internet: a review and evaluation, *Online and CDROM Review*, **21** (2), 67–81.

Ellis, D. (1984) The Effectiveness of Information Retrieval Systems: the need for improved explanatory frameworks, *Social Science Information Studies*, **4**, 261–72.

Ellis, D. and Norton, B. (1993) *Implementing BS5750/ISO 9000 in Libraries*, Aslib.

Garvin, D. (1984) What Does 'Product Quality' Really Mean?, *Sloan Management Review*, **26** (1), 25–43.

Garvin, D. A. (1987) Competing on the Eight Dimensions of Quality, *Harvard Business Review*, November–December, 108–9.

Griffiths, J. R. (2003) Evaluation of the JISC Information Environment: student perceptions of services, *Information Research*, **8** (4), http://informationr.net/ir/8-4/paper160.html.

Griffiths, J. R. and Brophy, P. (2002) Student Searching Behaviour in the JISC Information Environment, *Ariadne*, **33**, www.ariadne.ac.uk/issue33/edner/intro.html.

Griffiths, J. R. and Brophy, P. (2005) Student Searching Behaviour and the Web: use of academic resources and Google, *Library Trends*, Spring, 539–54.

Hernon, P. and Altman, E. (1998) *Assessing Service Quality: satisfying the expectations of library customers*, American Library Association.

Large, A., Tedd, L. A. and Hartley, R. J. (1999) *Information Seeking in the Online Age: principles and practice*, Bowker Saur.

Leighton, H. V. and Srivastava, J. (1999) First 20 Precision Among World Wide Web Search Services (search engines), *Journal of the American Society for Information Science*, **50** (10), 870–81.

Madu, C. N. and Madu, A. A. (2002) Dimensions of Equality, *International Journal of Quality and Reliability Management*, **19** (3), 246–59.

Marchand, D. (1990) Managing Information Quality. In Wormell, I. (ed.), *Information Quality: definitions and dimensions*, Taylor Graham, 7–17.

Nielsen, J. (1993) *Usability Engineering*, Academic Press.

12

Influential leadership for academic libraries

JENNIFER ROWLEY AND SUE ROBERTS

Introduction

Libraries are at the forefront of the turbulent environment of the digital age. Academic libraries, more specifically, are wrestling with changing student, staff and researcher expectations about access to information resources to support learning, teaching and research. The 'Google generation' of students expect fast and straightforward access to information and are intolerant of interfaces that require multiple stages to arrive at the full text of a document. They are not impressed by the need for authentication or barriers imposed by organizational structures and licensing arrangements. Taking this further, Von Hippel (2006) talks about the democratization of innovation in access to information and the shift in power from information providers to users. In addition, and with potentially serious consequences for providing ready access to research information, there are major changes taking place in the scholarly communication processes.

Open access publishing and institutional repositories are vying with more traditional publisher-controlled means of publication in what were print, and are now, e-journals and e-books. Information professionals not only need to respond to changing user expectations and relationships between stakeholders in scholarly publishing, they are also required to work in different partnership models with other academic services and other professional groups, which can take them far beyond the traditional concept of libraries, creating new models of holistic student support, learning environments and teaching and research collaborations. Consequently, the academic information profession has no option but to continuously change. As Mech suggested as long ago as 1996, 'academic transformation will not be the result of a committee decision. Higher education and academic librarianship are being re-shaped by the actions of professionals and the institutions in which they work. These individuals are not super-heroes. They are ordinary people who decide to exercise leadership' (345). Unless the information profession is prepared to sell out to the technocrats and to relinquish the very important role of working with communities and organizations to facilitate their access to information in the face of overwhelming complexity and, some might suggest, chaos, the information profession and its members have no choice but to exercise influential leadership.

Yet, there is concern that too many members of the information profession may be challenged to offer any kind of leadership, let alone influential leadership. O'Connor (2007) has even made the contentious suggestion that perhaps professional librarians are not the best people to act as leaders due to their potential lack of a wider, strategic view. This is supported by research undertaken by Mullins (2005) in the public library sector that indicates a scarcity of leadership qualities with senior managers focusing too much on 'library' skills and not enough on leadership. Both Mullins and O'Connor (2007) suggest that the library and information profession has been too 'narrow', too focused on 'the ordinary and the mundane' and that staff need to consider the intelligences that they require to pursue their work and lives and to succeed as leaders. Consequently, if there is to be significant change in perceptions on library leadership and the attributes and behaviours needed for the future, we will require a 'mental shift'. There is a need for information professionals to commit to leadership and leadership development and to refresh their notion of and engagement with leadership in general, and influential leadership more specifically.

Accordingly, we offer this chapter on leadership to mark the contribution of an information leader, Peter Brophy, who has over many years, in different contexts, and playing different roles, been a leader not only in the specific job roles that he has held, but also to the profession as a whole. He has been an examplar of the influential leader. In common with all leaders, he has influenced people and situations in multiple ways, sometimes after much effort, but on other occasions almost unwittingly as a consequence of a seemingly unrelated action. Although he will undoubtedly know when management responsibility has necessitated specific leadership actions, in many other situations he will be largely unaware of his influence and impact. Like all authentic leaders, a strong value set is part of his self-identity, and among these values is a concern for others. Others recognize him as a 'superior leader' (Kouzes and Posner, 2003) for his honesty, competency, and capacity for forward thinking. Finally, and most importantly, as an authentic leader, he is 'an original not a copy', and one from whom others learn.

This chapter outlines our understanding of influential leadership in an academic library and information service context. We take influential leadership to mean leadership across the profession through engagement with professional networks, as well as leadership beyond the profession across the university. We feel this is of particular importance in today's organizations where libraries and library and information professionals are often working – and indeed are expected to work – beyond traditional boundaries and in doing so can provide added value. This blurring of boundaries brings multiple opportunities for wider influence and greater impact, but clearly requires a high level of influential leadership. This involves understanding and capitalizing on the leadership, management and information competencies that working in an information service or information industry environment can develop.

Later in this chapter we develop the notions of leadership and influence further, and specifically differentiate between the influence that is a normal part of any leadership activity, and wider influential leadership. It is our thesis that although influential leadership is a must for every leader, in times of change and complexity such as those currently faced by the information profession and by the education sector, it becomes a priority. On the other hand, those who are able to exercise wider influence will not succeed if they only seek to lead beyond their own team or organization. They must be able to influence at home as well as away! Accordingly, the next section in this chapter develops further the characteristics of the changing context for the academic information profession, and this is followed by a section that outlines our perspective on the nature and importance of leadership. Later sections of the chapter outline in more detail the link between leadership and influence, and the importance of understanding politics and power in dynamic environments. The chapter concludes with a vision for the future.

The changing context for academic libraries

The changing context for academic libraries is highlighted throughout this collection. We would like to emphasize the key challenges that require influential leadership. The information environment and learning environment in an academic context have become increasingly complex and sophisticated, requiring holistic approaches and solutions to meet diverse needs. This has required a shift in philosophy and emphasis, from 'patch protection' and fighting for 'library' resources, to collaborative working and taking a helicopter view of strategic priorities. Many authors have stressed the need for information professionals to act as 'enabling partners' within universities – traversing the silos of an organization to bring different groups together (Levy and Roberts, 2005). This is evident in the leadership of converged information services that comprise libraries and a range of other related services, for example IT, student skills support, media services. The aim is often to provide an integrated experience for staff and students and a one-stop-shop approach to learning services (see Hanson, 2005).

Academic library leaders are also expected to act in a more entrepreneurial style, seeking out ways in which to add value and make significant contributions to the organization's goals that go beyond the traditional parameters of an information service. Bundy tells us to go beyond the 'self-limited role focused justs on information identification' (2003). There are many examples of how different library and information services, and the individuals involved, have taken on a wider leadership role to influence their organizations to change or to influence wider communities. Library and information professionals have taken on broader portfolios of responsibility as a result, for example:

- Information professionals within different contexts who have taken on extended responsibilities for knowledge management and information management. As Hart (2007) highlights, 'Evolution of the information professional role requires a knowledge of context and an understanding of how technology can help differentiate your organization.'
- Individual library and information professionals who have become champions for particular issues that have wide ranging influence; for example, the open scholarship movement, which encourages web publishing by academics to make research more accessible, or the importance of graduate attributes and their development through the student experience.

In a context where leadership is crucial, it is disconcerting to read about recruitment problems, crises of confidence and the growing need for strategic interventions to ensure leadership development occurs. The HIMSS (Hybrid Information Management: Skills for Senior Staff) project (Parsons, 2004) explored recruitment, training and succession planning issues for heads of information services. Challenges identified included obstacles to recruitment, skills gaps, training and development needs, the increased pace of change for managers and the increase in hybrid roles that encompassed diverse services, not simply libraries. The key management skills found to be lacking were:

- strategic management and leadership
- ability to manage change
- customer focus orientation.

Since this research was undertaken, there is no evidence in the literature to suggest that the situation has improved. Indeed Noon (2004) highlights that succession planning for leadership remains a key concern for academic libraries, a concern that has been reinforced by recent conference themes and proceedings (see Ritchie and Walker, 2007). There is an implicit sense in some authors' works that library and information professionals are reluctant to become leaders, not seeing this as their domain. O'Connor (2007) has even made the contentious suggestion that perhaps professional librarians are not the best people to act as leaders due to their potential lack of a wider, strategic view and also the skills and perspective they would bring. There are examples of individuals from outside the library profession being recruited to leadership positions, for example, corporate IT directors who have been recruited to lead converged IT and library services in the academic sector.

In response to the challenge to develop current and future leaders – for it is not just about succession planning but developing current leaders to their fullest potential – there now exists a diverse range of leadership development programmes and institutes worldwide targeted at the library and information professional. Some are very specific in their focus, for example, academic library leaders in the USA. Others take a cross-sectoral approach, while some also include a cross-section of related professionals, for example IT and library professionals in higher education (see the SCONUL/UCISA/British Library Future Leaders Programme). The motivation to establish such programmes or institutes is powerfully articulated by Billy Frye:

> Many of the elements that are needed to make a great university are in short supply: money, books and journals for the library, a sound technology base, staff, better supported services. But the resource that is most valuable and in shortest supply is leadership. So as we plan for the future we must make provision for the recruitment and development of potential leaders – persons who are capable of seeing the big picture and understanding institutional relationships: persons who welcome change and have the vision, imagination and courage to take carefully considered risks; and who are unselfish in their goals, fair in their dealings, and trusted by the colleagues at all levels with whom they work.
>
> (www.fryeinstitute.org/)

It should also be stressed that leadership is a concern right across library organizations, required in all levels and functions, and not simply in senior roles, which is the primary focus of leadership programmes. Eastell (2003) highlights this non-hierarchical approach in a public library context, 'It's much less about finding the next head of library service and far more about finding ways of offering library staff at all levels the opportunity to demonstrate and develop their leadership skills.' This philosophy is also required in the academic library environment.

What is leadership?

In common with a range of other commentators we argue that the information profession, and more specifically academic libraries, need leadership at all levels, but in this chapter we have yet to reflect on what is really meant by leadership. Handy (1993) suggests that seeking to understand leadership is like 'the quest for the holy grail', and the wide range of leadership theories variously describing leadership traits, styles, behaviours, experiences and competencies is further evidence that there is unlikely to be a simple answer to the question: 'What is leadership?'. Certainly, leadership is a complex phenomenon, which is executed in different ways by different people in different contexts. As a basis for discussion later in the chapter, we offer a definition of leadership, introduce the key facets of leadership through the Leadership Diamond, and discuss four key topical themes currently being debated in leadership theory: transformational leadership, dispersed leadership, leadership competencies and leadership development, and authentic leadership.

Defining leadership

We propose that leadership is when someone else is following! The more prosaic version of this statement is to define leadership as influencing others. Kouzes and Posner (2003) investigated the expectations that followers have of leaders. On this basis, the characteristics of superior leaders can be identified as honesty, competency and being forward-thinking (visionary) and inspiring, a mix of personal attributes, values and specific skills. Goffee and Jones (2001) offer another perspective on what followers want of their leaders: significance (to feel valued), community (to feel part of something) and excitement (to feel challenged). Taken together these perspectives suggest that leadership is very much concerned with people and relationships, even in situations where the figurehead leader is not in direct person-to-person contact with all of those that they lead.

The Leadership Diamond

Some leadership theories emphasize the vision and direction setting role of leaders, while others, for example, emphasize the need to work with and lead people. The real skill of being a leader is to work on several fronts at the same time and we propose the Leadership Diamond (Figure 12.1) as a model that summarizes the four facets of leadership behaviour and competencies.

The Leadership Diamond identifies the following four facets of leadership:

- *Personal qualities* – Leaders have a range of personal qualities that will provoke followership; they understand their own abilities and strengths and weaknesses. They continually seek to develop their leadership, managerial and professional capabilities and have a commitment to learning and development both for themselves and others.

- *Working with others* – Leaders need to work effectively with others and to develop successful relationships both within teams and across the wider organization. They adopt a style and approach that motivates, inspires and empowers others, and facilitates effective team working. Further, they establish and embed values and cultures and support others in developing their capabilities and confidence for and in the future in dynamic and changing environments.

- *Vision and direction* – Leaders take the wider perspective looking to the context and the longer term future. They scan the horizon, and engage in networking and influencing outside the organization so that they are able to make intelligent and well informed decisions about strategic direction. They encourage others to do the same, and are able to formulate visions that can be shared but also position their organization or team for the future. In particular, leaders are prepared to formulate vision in an often unknown and fragmented future, and accept the personal risk that this involves.

- *Managing performance and implementation* – Leaders make sure that things happen. There is no point in having vision, good working relationships and effective leadership qualities without harnessing these to appropriate action. Earlier leadership theories discuss the balance between being task centred and people centred. This facet can also be viewed as 'delivering the service'. At the practical level this facet involves: quality management; day-to-day working; energizing; communicating and reiterating performance expectations; making effective plans for implementation; and attending to budgets and resource allocation and management.

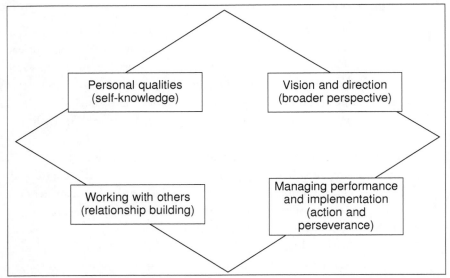

Figure 12.1 The Leadership Diamond

New leadership theories

Leadership theory has been refreshed with some new perspectives. We have chosen four topics to mention here, all of which we believe to be important to influential leadership for academic library and information services. All of these speak to important aspects of influential leadership, and promote philosophical stances about the nature of leadership which can provide a useful basis for reflection on leadership processes and journeys.

Transformational leadership

'New leadership' theory (Burns, 1978) proposed the idea of transformational leadership and differentiated it from transactional leadership. Transformational leadership is particularly appropriate in changing times, and is appropriate when an organization needs to undergo significant stepwise change. The transformational leader is an inspirational visionary who is concerned to build a shared sense of purpose and mission and to create a culture in which everyone is aligned with the organization's goals and is skilled and empowered to achieve them. Transformational leaders are characterized as charismatic individuals who inspire and motivate others to perform beyond their contract; they focus on motivation, commitment, influencing and inspiring followers. For example, Castiglione (2006) suggests that although the transactional library administrator is assignment- and task-oriented, and expects employee compliance, the transformational library administrator motivates and facilitates strategic renewal by empowering staff to question old assumptions, and encouraging staff to construct a compelling vision of the future.

Dispersed leadership

Dispersed leadership, and associated concepts such as self-directed teams and team and individual empowerment, proposes that there is a need for informal leadership at all levels and associated with a variety of roles in an organization (e.g. Mason and Wetherbee, 2004; Stephens and Russell, 2004). The concept derives from the observation that leadership is best exercised by those who have the interest, knowledge, skills and motivation to perform specific leadership functions and roles. Dispersed leadership theory could seem to be diametrically opposed to the search for and development of transformational and charismatic leaders, but Bennis and Nanus (1997) have argued that the two can be coupled together. They suggest that a 'super leader' develops leadership capacity in others, empowering them, reducing their dependence on formal leaders and stimulating their motivation, commitment and creativity. Moore (2004) describes facilitative leadership, in which the leader blends their role of visionary decisive leader with that of listening and empowering leader.

Leadership competencies and leadership development

Early leadership theories focused on leadership traits, styles and behaviours, sometimes taking into account the context (contingency theories). Such theories make statements about what a leader is and how they should behave, with very limited reference to how a leader achieves such behaviours; they offer limited insight into how leadership capacity can be developed and enhanced. By identifying leadership competencies, it is possible to identify the areas to be targeted in leadership development programmes and activities. Competencies have been variously described as sets of behaviours that are instrumental in the delivery of desired outcomes (Bartram, Robertson and Callinan, 2002), and 'observable behaviours that reflect knowledge, skills and attitudes learned by individual staff' cited in Mason and Wetherbee, 2004). In particular, in leadership development it is important to focus on the leader in context and to consider the impact of specific leadership competencies and behaviours on the organization. For example, 3M, an organization that aims to reflect knowledge management principles in its culture and working context, identified 12 leadership competencies, which are grouped into three categories:

- *Fundamental principles* – ethics, integrity, intellectual rigour, and moral judgement
- *Essential processes* – customer orientation, people management and performance
- *Visionary leadership* – the development of a global outlook, strategic perspective, encouraging innovation, building relationships, and encouraging flexibility and adaptability.　　　　(Allredge and Nilan, 2000).

Authentic leadership

Authentic leadership, like leadership competencies, comes out of the leadership school that focuses on the experience of being a leader. Authentic leadership recognizes that all leaders are on a leadership journey, which may start with very small beginnings, and that evolves through leadership experiences, provided that the leader is proactive about their own leadership development. Authentic leadership is achieved through self-awareness, self-acceptance, authentic actions and relationships, while remaining cognizant of one's own vulnerabilities (Luthans and Avolio, 2003). Authentic leadership is concerned with owning one's own experiences, including thoughts, emotions, needs, wants and preferences, acting in accordance with one's own true self, expressing what one thinks, and feeling and behaving accordingly. Theorists in this area suggest that authentic leaders are highly self-aware, have clearly defined and therefore strongly articulated values, what they say is consistent with what they believe, and they have ongoing drive and motivation towards natural goals and the ability to harness followership. The Authentic Leadership Framework (Gardner et al., 2005) has three key elements: trigger events (key events in the leadership journey), a strong value set (grounded in experience), and emotions (which are acknowledged, shown and experienced, but carefully regulated).

Leadership and influence

Leaders at all levels use their influence to lead and motivate people, to implement change, to lead teams and to shape values and culture. Many authors write about 'influencing skills' and suggest that we can simply learn these skills in order to manage and lead people effectively. Although we can definitely develop and perfect our skills of communication and impression management, we would argue that true and extensive influence stems from authenticity and congruence and cannot be simply reduced to a competencies based approach. The literature on influencing often focuses on techniques that require you to be a kind of chameleon rather than showing your own inner values, qualities and beliefs.

Authenticity and congruence, as touched on previously in this chapter, involve understanding yourself and then behaving and communicating in ways that reflect – are congruent – with this. Burton and Dalley (2007) summarize the 'art of influencing' in the following way:

- understanding who you are and what you stand for
- having congruence and authenticity (the link between our identity and values and the behaviour we exhibit generates trust)
- having empathy with others
- being able to communicate (questioning, listening, feedback)
- having intent (most successful influencers are those who operate from values such as truth, trust and integrity)
- being at ease with uncertainty
- being at ease with interdependence.

Conceptualizing influence in this way is challenging as it does not provide easy answers or techniques but begins with self-exploration and questioning. This does not mean that there aren't influencing tactics available to leaders that can have powerful results. Yukl (2002) summarizes these under nine headings, represented in Table 12.1.

Table 12.1 Influencing tactics available to leaders (Yukl, 2002)	
Rational persuasion	Logical arguments, facts and figures in support of particular objectives
Inspirational appeals	Focus on values, ideals, aspirations
Consultation	Participation, willingness to adjust a viewpoint or approach
Ingratiation	Praise, flattery, friendship
Personal appeals	Calling on loyalty, friendship
Exchange	Offers of reciprocation or sharing benefits to meet joint objectives
Coalition tactics	Seeking the aid of others to exercise persuasion
Pressure	Demands, threats, constant checking or reminders
Legitimating tactics	Claiming authority, verifying a request in line with organizational policy

As Yukl highlights, the point is to use the right tactics in the right circumstances and it could be argued that in academic contexts consultation, rationalization and inspiration are the most persuasive. We don't disagree that being aware of different approaches, and understanding what could work in different contexts, can be valid and valuable. However, in comparison with beginning with personal authenticity and congruence, the tactical approach could appear manipulative and shallow.

Politics and power

'The political role of the information service manager is to make things happen' (Bryson, 2006, 119). In order to influence, leaders at any level – not just managers – must know how to get things done within their organization and know how to use power constructively. Skilled political leaders understand what the organization wants (even if the organization cannot identify and articulate this!) and how they and their service and staff can create solutions to the problems facing the organization. Consequently, leaders must interpret the political environment correctly, identify supporters, build networks and gain commitment. In this section we will explore briefly the different elements of working with power and politics, beginning with French and Raven's model of power bases (Roberts and Rowley, 2003).

Leaders must be aware of the different bases of power and use them appropriately and ethically. As Adair highlights, 'Leadership is the intelligent and sensitive use of power' (2003, 157) and within the context of modern leadership there is a strong emphasis on developing and enabling the power of others through participative leadership and empowerment. Yukl (2002) also stresses that 'researchers have begun to examine the specific types of behaviour used to exercise influence, rather than focus exclusively on power as a source of potential influence'. Undoubtedly, the concept and model of power expressed in Table 12.2 is shifting as notions of leadership change. This links back to our previous discussion around influencing tactics and authenticity.

Table 12.2 French and Raven's bases of power (taken from Roberts and Rowley, 2003)

Position power	Reward power	Being able to grant favours or benefits
	Coercive power	Through punishment, threats or control
	Legitimate power	Through authority or your status or role
Personal power	Expert power	Through your skills and competencies
	Referent power	Through being attractive to someone else who wishes to please you

Our ability to influence remains closely linked to how we engage with organizational politics, which has been defined as the ways in which individuals 'acquire, develop, and use power and other resources to obtain one's outcome in a situation.' (Bryson, 1990, 251). Research on academic library leadership by Pors and Johannsen (2003) highlighted political action on the part of the senior leader as central and stressed the role of the director:

- The director has to make the library visible in the political system.
- The director's political legitimacy will be very important.
- The director must create political contacts and networks.

We would stress the need for staff at other levels to be aware of the political context and to work on all three of the above, for example developing their own networks within and beyond the organization. The political positioning of the library and information service should also not be the end in itself but should be motivated by the desire to enhance services to customers and for the good of the organization as a whole. We would argue once again that if a leader is authentic and congruent in their approach – and has a clear intent that is focused on achieving the goals of the organization – they will be in a positive position to influence without it appearing that they are 'empire building' or focused on personal agendas. In the context of the need for increased partnerships both within organizations – between libraries and other areas such as information technology, research, education and training – and externally across libraries to maximize access and resources, library leaders must be expert and ethical influencers and negotiators. The need for awareness and engagement in the wider environment and agendas is reflected in the topics covered by the Frye Leadership Institute:

- Perspectives on issues in higher education
- Innovation in higher education
- Issues in scholarly communication
- Teaching and learning
- Intellectual property: legal and societal framework
- Government information policy and its influence on access to information within the university
- Public policy and higher education
- Impact of technology on college and university economics, budgeting, and organization
- Leadership in an era of transformational change.

The vision . . .

There has been extensive discussion about the future for libraries and information professionals and the leadership approaches required to shape this future. In this section we seek to outline our vision for academic library leadership roles and how these might be facilitated to ensure that information professionals in the academic sector can confidently exercise influential leadership.

Developing leadership capacity

Both the broader literature on leadership, and specific recent contributions on library leadership, emphasize the lack of consensus on the nature of leadership, 'library' leadership competencies, and optimal approaches to leadership development (e.g. Mason and Wetherbee, 2004; Stephens and Russell, 2004; Storey, 2004). Although over the last decade there has been increasing interest in leadership for the information profession – the catalogue of leadership development courses in the US is truly impressive (Mason and Wetherbee, 2004) – there remains little consensus of the competencies that such courses should develop. Further, there is a question as to whether such programmes, whether they be residential training programmes or in-house coaching and mentoring schemes, are actually delivering enhanced leadership capacity. As Mason and Wetherbee (2004) indicate, evaluation of such programmes is too often superficial and short term. Furthermore, there needs to be a concerted effort to ensure that such programmes embrace current thinking on leadership, and, in particular, recognize the need for the development of dispersed leadership. Accordingly, there is considerable scope for more focused debate and sharing of practice in the general area of building leadership capacity. This might fruitfully focus on:

- understanding leadership competencies for the information profession (taking into account the need for influential leadership at all levels in the profession)
- looking beyond competencies to consider authentic leadership and the 'true' self
- design of leadership development opportunities for leaders at all levels in the organization, typically facilitated by leaders who facilitate others to lead

- the potential for adopting a learning organization culture that values learning about leadership, alongside individual and organizational learning in other areas of knowledge and skills (Giesecke and McNeil, 2004).

Innovation, entrepreneurship and creativity

Innovation and the development of new ideas, devices, systems, processes, products or services needs to be ongoing. Leaders need to continually monitor and engage in potential improvements, developments and enhancements in all aspects of their organization. Riggs (1989) is a significant, if somewhat dated, collection, which emphasizes the importance of creativity, innovation and entrepreneurship in libraries. Roberts and Rowley (2008) have discussed that a focus on innovation and creativity might be more appropriate than thinking in terms of change and its management. Change management has undertones of being imposed from above, while appropriately managed innovation, supported by the cultivation and accommodation of corporate entrepreneurship, can capitalize on a wider pool of skills and abilities. Deiss (2004) discusses the challenges associated with promoting innovation to create customer value in user-centred libraries. She acknowledges that the mature nature of most library organizations makes it more difficult to take risks, experiment and accommodate creativity and generate innovation. The task is not easy, but by being more innovative, creative and entrepreneurial than other organizations, libraries will be in a strong position to act as 'leading organizations', influencing and impacting on their stakeholder organizations and communities.

Playing centre stage in managing knowledge

Ferguson (2004) suggested that 'most librarians are still too close to the periphery of their organization's core business to provide the kind of leadership required in the knowledge management environment' (5). Influential leadership is rarely achieved from the sidelines. Too many leaders of the information profession have been dismissive of knowledge management. Yet academic librarians have a pivotal role to play in shaping knowledge production and scholarly communication. There are two strands to this. The first relates to their involvement in the evolution of traditional scholarly communication and dissemination processes relating to Mode 1 knowledge, where research typically precedes application. The second agenda arises from the increasing importance of Mode 2 knowledge. Mode 2 knowledge is differentiated from Mode 1 knowledge by its link to application; the application and usefulness is fundamental to the process of its creation. Knowledge production increasingly becomes a factor that differentiates a successful organization and knowledge is not simply the preserve of universities. In their search for relevance, universities are increasingly seeking the productive ways in which to facilitate, manage and integrate Mode 1 and Mode 2 knowledge creation, often under terms such as academic enterprise.

Concluding thoughts

The information landscape is changing beyond all recognition as a result of broader trends that require a change in thinking in terms of the role of libraries. An additional challenge is the sense of an unknown and fragmented future. As O'Connor (2007) states, 'The future is often not continuous with or in a linear relationship to the present or the past. We do not have only one future; we have many and we are, in our personal lives, constantly choosing between them. Organisations are the same; they are not what they were; they will not be the same into the future' (2007, 69). Anyone working in 21st-century academic institutions will recognize this vision of a disruptive and uncertain future.

Academic library and information professionals must work and thrive within this context; moreover, if we pay sufficient attention and dedicate considerable energy to leadership development for ourselves and for others, we have the potential to influence across boundaries and to 'create a more assertive vision of the way in which academic librarians will shape future learning environments' (Levy and Roberts, 2005, 228). We have explored in this chapter approaches to influential leadership, arguing that developing the capacity for influencing is crucial for academic library and information services and for their wider organizations. The art of true influencing begins with the authentic self; consequently, 'the work is from the inside out – develop yourself and you develop your world' (Burton and Dalley, 2007).

References

Adair, J. (2003) *Not Bosses but Leaders*, 3rd edn, with P. Reed, Kogan Page.

Allredge, M. E. and Nilan, K. J. (2000) 3M's Leadership Competency Model: an internally developed solution, *Human Resources Management*, **39** (2 & 3), 133–45.

Bartram, D., Robertson, I. T. and Callinan, M. (2002) Introduction: a framework for examining organizational effectiveness. In Robertson, T., Callinan, M. and Bartram, D. (eds), *Organizational Effectiveness: the role of psychology*, Wiley, 1–12.

Bennis, W. and Nanus, B. (1997) *Leaders: strategies for taking charge*, 2nd edn, Harper Business.

Bryson, J. (1990) *Effective Library and Information Centre Management*, Gower.

Bryson, J. (2006) *Managing Information Services: a transformational approach*, 2nd edn, Ashgate.

Bundy A. (2003) A Window of Opportunity: libraries and higher education, *Library Management*, **24** (8/9), 393–400.

Burns, J. M. (1978) *Leadership*, Harper and Row.

Burton, L. and Dalley, B. (2007) Beyond Influencing, leadership seminar.

Castiglione, J. (2006) Organizational Learning and Transformational Leadership in the Library Environment, *Library Management*, **27** (4/5), 289–99.

Deiss, K. J. (2004) Innovation and Strategy: risk and choice in shaping user-centred libraries, *Library Trends*, **53** (1), 17–32.

Dewe, A. J. (2005) Knowledge Leadership in a University Context, *Proceedings of Educause Australasia, 2005*, www.educause.auckland.ac.nz/interactive/papers/A15.pdf.

Eastell, C. (2003) The Key to Ciara and the Next Generation of Public Library Leaders, *Library and Information Update*, (April), 40–1.

Ferguson, S. (2004) The Knowledge Management Myth: will the real knowledge managers please step forward?, *Challenging Ideas: ALIA 2004 Biennial Conference*, Australian Library and Information Association.

Gardner, W. L., Avolio, B. J., Luthans, F., May, D. R. and Walumbra, F. (2005) Can You See The Real Me? A self based model of authentic leader and follower development, *The Leadership Quarterly*, **16**, 343–72.

Giesecke, J. and McNeil, B. (2004) Transitioning to the Learning Organization, *Library Trends*, **53** (1), 54–67.

Goffee, R. and Jones, G. (2001) Followership: it's personal too, *Harvard Business Review on Breakthrough Leadership*, Harvard Business School Press.

Handy, C. (1993) *Understanding Organisations*, 4th edn, Penguin Books.

Hanson, T. (ed.) (2005) *Managing Academic Support Services in Universities: the convergence experience*, Facet Publishing.

Hart, C. (2007) Take Opportunities to Get Ahead, says Hart, *Library + Information Gazette*, 18–31 May, 1–2.

Kouzes, J. M. and Posner, B. Z. (2003) *Credibility: how leaders gain and lose it, why people demand it*, Jossey-Bass.

Levy, P. and Roberts, S. (2005) *Developing the New Learning Environment: the changing role of the academic librarian*, Facet Publishing.

Luthans, F. and Avolio, B. J. (2003) Authentic Leadership: a positive development approach. In Cameron, K. S., Dutton, J. E. and Quinn, R. E. (eds), *Positive Organizational Scholarship*, Barrett-Koehler, 241–61.

Mason, F. M. and Wetherbee, L. V. (2004) Learning to Lead: an analysis of current training programs for library leadership, *Library Trends*, **53** (1), 187–217.

Mech, T. (1996) Leadership and the Evolution of Academic Librarianship, *Journal of Academic Librarianship*, September, 345–53.

Moore, T. L. (2004) Facilitative Leadership: one approach to empowering staff and other stakeholders, *Library Trends*, **53** (1), 230–1.

Mullins, J. (2005) Are Public Libraries Led or Managed?, *Library Review*, **55** (4), 237–48.

Noon, P. (2004) Developing the Academic Library Managers of the Future. In Oldroyd, M. (ed.), *Developing Academic Library Staff for Future Success*, Facet Publishing, 41–60.

O'Connor, S. (2007) The Heretical Library Manager for the Future, *Library Management*, **28** (1–2), 62–71.

Parsons, F. (ed.) (2004) *Recruitment, Training and Succession Planning in the HE Sector: findings from the HIMSS project*, The University of Birmingham.

Pors, N. O. and Johannsen, C. G. (2003) Library Directors Under Cross-pressure Between New Public Management and Value-based Management, *Library Management*, **24** (1/2), 51–60.

Riggs, D. E. (1989) *Creativity, Innovation and Entrepreneurship in Libraries*, Haworth Press; also *Journal of Library Administration*, **10** (2/3).

Ritchie, A. and Walker, C. (eds) (2007) *Continuing Professional Development: pathways to leadership in the library and information world*, IFLA Publications 126, K. G. Saur.

Roberts, S. and Rowley, J. (2003) *Managing Information Services*, Facet Publishing.

Roberts, S. and Rowley, J. (2008) *Leadership: the challenge for the information profession*, Facet Publishing.

Stephens, D. and Russell, K. (2004) Organizational Development, Leadership, Change, and the Future of Libraries, *Library Trends*, **53** (1), 238–57.

Storey, J. (2004) Changing Theories of Leadership and Leadership Development. In Storey, J. (ed.), *Leadership in Organizations: current issues and key trends*, Routledge, 11–37.

Von Hippel, E. (2006) Democratizing Innovation, MIT Press, www.web.mit.edu/evhippel.

Yukl, G. (2002) *Leadership in Organisations*, 5th edn, Prentice Hall.

Peter Brophy: a selected bibliography

Brophy, P. (2008) The Integration of Physical and Virtual Environments to Support HE Learners: the European perspective. In Weaver, M. (ed.), *Transformative Learning Support Services in Higher Education: educating the whole student*, Facet Publishing, 119–33.

Brophy, P. (2008) Issues for Library and Information Services. In Craven, J. (ed.), *Web Accessibility: practical advice for the library and information professional*, Facet Publishing, 97–112.

Brophy, P., Craven, J. and Markland, M. (eds) (2008) *Libraries Without Walls 7: exploring 'anytime, anywhere' delivery of library services*, Facet Publishing.

Brophy, P. (2008) *Narrative-based Practice*, Ashgate (in press).

Brophy, P. (2008) Telling the Story: qualitative approaches to measuring the performance of emerging library services, *Performance Measurement & Metrics*, **9** (1), 7–17.

Brophy, P. (2007) Communicating the Library: librarians and faculty in dialogue, *Library Management*, **28** (8/9), 515–23.

Brophy, P. (2007) *The Library in the Twenty-First Century*, 2nd edn, Facet Publishing.

Brophy, P. (2007) Narrative-based Practice, *Evidence Based Library and Information Practice*, **2** (1), 149–58, http://ejournals.library.ualberta.ca/index.php/EBLIP/article/view/137/248.

Brophy, P. and Butters, G. (2007) Creating a Research Agenda for Local Libraries, Archives and Museums Across Europe, *New Review of Information Networking*, **13** (1), 3–21.

Brophy, P. and Craven, J. (2007) Web Accessibility, *Library Trends*, **55** (4), 950–72.

Brophy, P., Butters, G. and Hulme, A. (2007) Supporting Creativity in Networked Environments: the COINE Project, *Ariadne*, **51**, www.ariadne.ac.uk/issue51/brophy-et-al/.

Brophy, P., Markland, M. and Butters, G. (2007) The History of the Future: evaluating projects and service developments before they begin, *Performance Measurement and Metrics*, **8** (1), 34–40.

Brophy, P. (2006) The eLibrary and Learning. In Weiss, J. et al. (eds), *International Handbook on Virtual Learning Environments*, Springer, 895–913.

Brophy, P. (2006) *Measuring Library Performance: principles and techniques*, Facet Publishing.

Brophy, P. (2006) Projects Into Services: the UK experience, *Ariadne*, **46**, February, www.ariadne.ac.uk/issue46/brophy/.

Brophy, P., Craven, J. and Markland, M. (eds) (2006) *Libraries Without Walls 6: evaluating the distributed delivery of library services*, Facet Publishing.

Brophy, P. (2005) *The Academic Library*, 2nd edn, Facet Publishing.

Brophy, P. (2005) The Development of a Model for Assessing the Level of Impact of Information and Library Services, *Library and Information Research*, **29** (93), 43–9.

Brophy, P. (2005) The Formative Evaluation of the 5/99 Programme and its Broader Environment: the EDNER project, *VINE*, **35** (1/2), 105–12.

Brophy, P. (2005) The Policy Framework: a critical review. In Levy, P. and Roberts, S. (eds), *Developing the New Learning Environment: the changing role of the academic librarian*, Facet Publishing, 1–23.

Griffiths, J. R. and Brophy, P. (2005) Student Searching Behaviour and the Web: use of academic resources and Google, *Library Trends*, **53** (4), Spring, 539–54.

Brophy, P. (2004) Beyond the Mainstream of Library Services. In Brophy, P., Fisher, S. and Craven, J. (eds), *Libraries Without Walls 5: the distributed delivery of library and information services*, Facet Publishing, 7–15.

Brophy, P. (2004) Evaluating the Joint Information Systems Committee's Information Environment – the EDNER and EDNER+ projects, *VINE*, **34** (4), 143–7.

Brophy, P. (2004) Narrative-based Librarianship. In *The Area of Information and Social Communication: Festschrift for Professor Wanda Pindlova*, Studies in Library and Information Science 10, Jagiellonian University Press, 188–95.

Brophy, P. (2004) Networked Learning and Networked Information: towards a theoretical basis for the development of integrated information environments. In *Networked Learning 2004: a research based conference on e-learning in higher education and lifelong learning*, Lancaster University and University of Sheffield, 216–21.

Brophy, P. (2004) *The People's Network: moving forward,* Museums, Libraries and Archives Council,
www.mla.gov.uk/resources/assets/lid1414rep_pdf_4287.pdf.

Brophy, P. (2004) The Quality of Libraries. In Hilgermann, K. and te Borkhorst, P. (eds), *Die effektive Bibliothek*, K. G. Saur, 30–46.

Brophy, P. and Craven, J. (2004) Evaluating the Longitudinal Impact of Networked Services in UK Public Libraries: the Longitude II project, *Performance Measurement and Metrics,* **5** (3), 112–17.

Brophy, P., Fisher, S. and Craven, J. (eds) (2004) *Libraries Without Walls 5: the distributed delivery of library and information services,* Facet Publishing.

Brophy, P., Fisher, S., Jones, C. R. and Markland, M. (2004) *EDNER: Final Report,* Manchester, CERLIM (Centre for Research in Library and Information Management),
www.cerlim.ac.uk/edner/dissem/x3.doc.

Brophy, P. (2003) Marketing and Quality: using dimensional analysis to achieve success. In Gupta, D. K. and Jambhekar, A. (eds), *An Integrated Approach To Services Marketing: a book of readings on marketing of library and information services,* Allied Publishers Private, 84–91.

Brophy, P. (2003) *The People's Network: a turning point for public libraries: first findings,* Resource: The Council for Museums, Archives and Libraries.

Brophy, P. (2003) Synchronised Object Retrieval: the enhancement of information retrieval performance in multimedia environments using synchronisation protocols, *Information Research,* **8** (4),
http://InformationR.net/ir/8-4/paper161.html.

Brophy, P. and Craven, J. (2003) *Non-visual Access to the Digital Library: the use of digital library interfaces by blind and visually impaired people: Library and Information Commission Report 145,* CERLIM (Centre for Research in Library and Information Management), Manchester Metropolitan University,
www.cerlim.ac.uk/projects/nova.html.

Brophy, P., Fisher, S., Griffiths, J. R. and Markland, M. (2003) *EDNER: Formative Evaluation of the Distributed National Electronic Resource: DNER service evaluation* (Deliverable MDA 2, EDNER Project), CERLIM (The Centre for Research in Library and Information Management),
www.cerlim.ac.uk/edner/dissem/dissem.html.

Brophy, P. (2002) La bibliothèque hybride, *Bulletin des Bibliothèques de France,* **47** (4), 14–20.

Brophy, P. (2002) Cultural Objects in Networked Environments – COINE, *Cultivate Interactive*, **7**, July, www.cultivate-int.org/issue7/coine/.

Brophy, P. (2002) Digital Resources in Higher Education: some issues arising from the formative evaluation of a national initiative in the United Kingdom, *European Journal of Engineering for Information Society Applications*, September, www.ejeisa.com/sys/code/journal_issue/journal_issue_main.php?action=view _journal_issue_article&journal_id=42&volume_id=5&issue_id=12&volume_ ignore=&volume_current=1.

Brophy, P. (2002) Evaluating the Distributed National Electronic Resource: the EDNER Project, *VINE*, **126**, 7–11, http://litc.sbu.ac.uk/publications/vine.html.

Brophy, P. (2002) *Longitude Project Final Evaluation Report*, Library and Information Commission Research Report 139, Resource: The Council for Museums, Archives and Libraries, www.resource.gov.uk/documents/lic121_eval.pdf.

Brophy, P. (2002) New Models of the Library in a Digital Era. In *International Yearbook of Library & Information Management*, Facet Publishing.

Brophy, P. (2002) Performance Measures for 21st Century Libraries. In Stein, J., Kyrillidou, M. and Davis, D. (eds), *Proceedings of the 4th Northumbria International Conference on Performance Measurement in Libraries and Information Services, Pittsburgh, USA, 12–16 August 2001*, Association of Research Libraries, 1–8.

Brophy, P. (2002) The Role of the Professional in the Information Society. In Hornby, S. and Clarke, Z. (eds), *Challenge and Change in the Information Society*, Facet Publishing, 217–32.

Brophy, P., Fisher, S. and Clarke, Z. (eds) (2002) *Libraries Without Walls 4: the delivery of library services to distant users*, Facet Publishing.

Brophy, P. and Griffiths, J. R. (2002) Student Behaviour in the JISC Information Environment, *Ariadne*, **33**, www.ariadne.ac.uk/issue33/edner/intro.html.

Brophy, P. (2001) Assessing the Performance of Electronic Library Services: the EQUINOX project, *The New Review of Academic Librarianship*, **7**, 3–18.

Brophy, P. (2001) Electronic Library Performance Indicators: the EQUINOX project, *Serials*, **14** (1), 5–9.

Brophy, P. (2001) The Historical Context of eLib: practice-based library research in the UK, *Library Management*, **22** (1/2), 15–18.

Brophy, P. (2001) *The Library in the Twenty-First Century*, Library Association Publishing.

Brophy, P. (2001) Library Research: a perspective from the UK, *Bulletin des bibliothèques de France*, **46** (4), 78–80.

Brophy, P. (2001) Networked Learning, *Journal of Documentation*, **57** (1), 130–56.

Brophy, P. (2001) Strategic Issues for Academic Libraries, *Relay, the journal of the University, College and Research Group*, **52**, 4–5.

Brophy, P. (2000) *The Academic Library*, Library Association Publishing.

Brophy, P. (2000) Library and Information Services for Off-site Users: the future looks bright. In Lock, D., Downham, G. and Haddon, K. (eds), *Library and Information Services for Off-site Users: the future looks bright: proceedings of the seminar held at the University of Central Lancashire in collaboration with the University of Surrey*, University of Surrey Information Services, 3–9.

Brophy, P. (2000) Performance Indicators for the Electronic Library, *SCONUL Newsletter*, **21**, Winter, 25–8.

Brophy, P. (2000) Progettare la qualità: le nuove frontiere del management in biblioteca, *Biblioteche Oggi*, **XVIII** (4), 8–15.

Brophy, P. (2000) Towards a Generic Model of Information and Library Services in the Information Age, *Journal of Documentation*, **56** (2), 161–84.

Brophy, P. and Eve, J. (2000) VITAL Issues: the perception, and use, of ICT services in UK public libraries, *LIBRES: Library and Information Science Research*, **10** (2), http://libres.curtin.edu.au/libres10n2/vital.htm.

Brophy, P., Eskins, R. and Oulton, A.J. (2000) *Synchronised Object Retrieval: a feasibility study into enhanced information retrieval in multimedia environments using synchronisation protocols*, CERLIM, Manchester Metropolitan University, www.cerlim.ac.uk/projects/sync.htm.

Brophy, P., Fisher, S. and Clarke, Z. (eds) (2000) *Libraries Without Walls 3: the delivery of library services to distant users*, Library Association Publishing.

Brophy, P. (1999) Digital Libraries in Europe: an educational perspective, *Proceedings of the 8th Panhellenic Conference of Academic Libraries, Rhodes, Greece, 20–22 October*, 81–90.

Brophy, P. (1999) *Digital Library Research Review: final report*, Library & Information Commission, www.lic.gov.uk/.

Brophy, P. (1999) The eLib Programme, *Relay*, **47**, 5–7.

Brophy, P. (1999) Extremism and the Internet, *British Library Research & Innovation Centre Research Bulletin*, **22**, Spring, 9.

Brophy, P. (1999) The Integrated, Accessible Library: building a national accessible library service, *Library Hi-Tech News*, Spring, 15.

Brophy, P. and Craven, J. (1999) *The Integrated, Accessible Library: a model of service development for the 21st century: the Final Report of the REVIEL (Resources for Visually Impaired Users of the Electronic Library) Project*, British Library Research & Innovation Report 168, CERLIM, Manchester Metropolitan University.

Brophy, P. and Halpin, E. (1999) Through the Net to Freedom: information, the internet and human rights, *Journal of Information Science*, **25** (5), 351–64.

Brophy, P., Craven, J. and Fisher, S. F. (1999) *Extremism and the Internet*, British Library Research & Innovation Report 145, CERLIM, Manchester Metropolitan University.

Brophy, P. (1998) It May Be Electronic But Is It Any Good? Measuring the performance of electronic services. In *Robots to Knowbots: the wider automation agenda, Proceedings of the Victorian Association for Library Automation 9th Biennial Conference, January 28–30*, VALA, 217–30, www.vala.org.au/valaweb/num511.pdf.

Brophy, P. (1998) Libraries Without Walls: from vision to reality. In Brophy, P., Fisher, S. and Clarke, Z. (eds), *Libraries without Walls 2: the delivery of library services to distant users*, Library Association Publishing, 2–13.

Brophy, P. (1998) Management Information. In Hanson, T. and Day, J. (eds), *Managing the Electronic Library*, Bowker-Saur.

Brophy, P. and Craven, J. (1998) Lifelong Learning and Higher Education Libraries: models for the 21st century, *Eighth Off-Campus Library Services Conference, Providence, Rhode Island, USA, April 22–24*.

Brophy, P. and Fisher, S. F. (1998) The Hybrid Library, *The New Review of Information & Library Research*, **4**, 3–15.

Brophy, P. and Wynne, P. (1998) *Management Information Systems and Performance Measurement for the Electronic Library: final report*, eLib/LITC, South Bank University, www.ukoln.ac.uk/dlis/models/studies/mis/mis.doc.

Brophy, P., Craven, J. and Fisher, S. (1998) *The Development of UK Academic Library Services in the Context of Lifelong Learning, A supporting study in the JISC Electronic Libraries (eLib) Programme*, eLib/LITC, South Bank University.

Brophy, P., Fisher, S. and Clarke, Z. (eds) (1998) *Libraries Without Walls 2: the delivery of library services to distant users*, Library Association Publishing.

Brophy, P. (1997) *A Comparable Experience? Library support for franchised courses in higher education, paper presented to the Library Association UC&R and CoFHE Sections* (West Midlands) Seminar, Leicester, 26 November.

Brophy, P. (1997) Conference Review, *2nd Northumbria International Conference on Performance Measurement in Libraries and Information Services, 7–11 September*.

Brophy, P. (1997) Distributing the Library to the Learner, *Beyond the Beginning*, Joint nSC/CAUSE Conference, London, 16–17 June.

Brophy, P. (1997) *Future Challenges, paper presented at the CAM/LE (Concerted Action on Management Information for Libraries in Europe CEC-DGXIII PROLIB/CAMILE) National Workshop, Athens College, Athens, Greece, 15 September.*

Brophy, P. (1997) *Lifelong Learning, paper presented at the Expert Seminar on the Development of Library Services in the Context of Lifelong Learning Committee of Vice-Chancellors and Principals, 9 July.*

Brophy, P. (1997) *Management Information for the Electronic Library: key issues, paper presented at the Expert Workshop on Management Information for the Electronic Library, Preston, 16 May.*

Brophy, P. (1997) The SELF Project: an investigation into the provision of self-service facilities for library users, *VINE*, **105**, 8–13.

Brophy, P. (1997) TQM. In Baker, D. (ed.), *Resource Management in Academic Libraries*, Library Association Publishing.

Brophy, P. (1997) UK Library Research, *Research Seminar*, University of Victoria, British Columbia, 10 October.

Brophy, P. and Coulling, K. (1997) Quality Management in Libraries. In Brockman, J. (ed.), *Quality Management and Benchmarking in the Information Sector: results of recent research*, Bowker-Saur, 33–119.

Brophy, P. with Goodall, D. (1997) *A Comparable Experience? Library support for franchised courses in higher education*, British Library Research & Innovation Report 33, University of Central Lancashire.

Brophy, P. and Goodall, D. (1997) The Role of the Library in Franchised Higher Education Courses, *Library & Information Briefing*, **72**, July.

Brophy, P. and Wynne, P. (1997) Performance Measurement and Management Information for the Electronic Library, paper given at *2nd Northumbria International Conference on Performance Measurement in Libraries and Information Services, 7–11 September.*

Brophy, P., Clarke, Z. and Wynne, P. (1997) *EQLIPSE: Evaluation and Quality in Library Performance: system for Europe*, CERLIM, University of Central Lancashire.

Brophy, P., Fisher, S., Hare, G. and Kay, D. (1997) *National Agency for Resource Discovery (NARD): scoping study*, Report to the British Library Research and Innovation Centre (BLRIC) and the Joint Information Systems Committee (JISC).

Brophy, P., Goodall, D. and Wynne, P. (1997) Library Services to Distant Learners: research and operational developments in a UK and European context. In Watson, E. F. and Jagannathan, N. (eds), *Library Services to Distance Learners in the Commonwealth*, The Commonwealth of Learning, 55–9.

Brophy, P., Wynne, P. and Butters, G. (1997) Delivering the Library to its Users: from the BIBDEL project to the virtual academic library of the north-west, *Interlending and Document Supply*, **25** (4), 166–74.

Brophy, P., Wynne, P. M. and Butters, G. (1997) An Examination of the Costs and Benefits of an Experimental Extension of Academic Library Services to Remote Users, *The New Review of Academic Librarianship*, **3**, 25–37.

Brophy, P. (1996) *Case Studies on Opportunities for Libraries in Europe (OPLES)*, British Library Library and Information Reports 107, British Library.

Brophy, P. (1996) The Concept of Libraries Without Walls. In Irving, A. and Butters, G. (eds), *Proceedings of the first 'Libraries without Walls' Conference, Mytilene, Greece, 9–10 September 1995*, University of Central Lancashire, 16–21.

Brophy, P. (1996) Resourcing the Learning Experience. In Abramson, M., Bird, J. and Stennett, A. (eds), *Further and Higher Education Partnerships: the future for collaboration*, Society for Research into Higher Education & Open University Press, 46–57.

Brophy, P. and Allred, J. (1996) *Open Distance Learning in Public Libraries*, Office of Official Publications of the European Communities.

Brophy, P. and Coulling, K. (1996) *Quality Management for Information and Library Managers*, Gower.

Brophy, P. with Brinkley, M., Butters, G., Butters, M., MacDougall, A., Papachiou, P. and Vlachou, E. (eds) (1996) *Access to Campus Library and Information Services by Distant Users: final report*, University of Central Lancashire.

Brophy, P. (1995) The Electronic Library (keynote address). In Collier, M. and Arnold, K. (eds), *Electronic Library and Visual Information Research: ELVIRA 1*, Aslib, 6–12.

Brophy, P. (1995) From Understanding Off-Campus Learners to the Virtual Library. In *Proceedings of the Seventh Off-Campus Library Services Conference, San Diego, California, USA, October 25–27*, Central Michigan University Libraries, 25–32.

Brophy, P. (1995) *Opportunities for Libraries in Europe (OPLES)*, British Library Library and Information Reports 103, British Library.

Brophy, P. (1995) Quality Management and Benchmarking for Library and Information Services. In Evans, M. (ed.), *Quality Management and Benchmarking for Library & Information Services, proceedings of a seminar held in Stamford, Lincolnshire, 7 June*, Capital Planning Information, 9–18.

Brophy, P. (1995) Quality Management in Libraries. In *Proceedings of the 1st Northumbria International Conference on Performance Measurement in Libraries and Information Services, 31 August to 4 September*, Information North, 77–81.

Brophy, P. (1995) Quality Management in Libraries: a UK perspective. In *Kvalitetssikring av Bibliotektjenester: NVBF's 9. medlemsmfJte 1 Lillehammer (Norway), 19–22 juni*, Nordiske Vitenskapelige Bibliotekforeningers Forbund, 129–48.

Brophy, P. (1994) BS5750: implementation in an academic library. In *BS5750/ISO9000 in Libraries and Information Centres: why bother? Proceedings of a Seminar held in London on 12 April*, Effective Technology Marketing.

Brophy, P. (1994) The Quality Program of the Library and Learning Resources Service at the University of Central Lancashire, *Inspel*, **28** (2), 240–7.

Brophy, P. (1994) The Service-oriented Library. In Mackenzie, G. and Feather, J. (eds), *Librarianship and Information Work Worldwide 1994*, Bowker-Saur, 93–114.

Brophy, P. (1994) Towards BS5750 in a University Library. In *Quality Management: towards BS5750: proceedings of a seminar held in Stamford, Lincolnshire, on 21 April*, Capital Planning Information, 3–10.

Brophy, P. and Irving, A. (1994) Awareness and Understanding: issue 1. In *Networks, Libraries and Information: progress on priorities for the UK 1992–1994*, Library & Information Briefings 55/56, 3–7.

Brophy, P. (1993) Franchising Higher Education: the library's role. In Lessin, B. (ed.), *Proceedings of the Off-Campus Library Services Conference, Kansas City, Missouri, October*, Central Michigan University.

Brophy, P. (1993) Networking in British Academic Libraries, *British Journal of Academic Librarianship*, **8** (1), 49–60.

Brophy, P. (1993) What's in a Name?, *New Library World*, **94** (4).

Brophy, P. with Coulling, K. and Melling, M. (1993) Quality Management: a university approach, *Aslib Information*, **21** (6), 246–8.

Brophy, P. (1992) Distant Libraries: the support of higher education students who study off-campus, *Library Management*, **13** (6), 4–7.

Brophy, P. (1992) Distributed Higher Education – Distributed Libraries?, *New Library World*, **93** (1), 22–3.

Brophy, P. (1992) The Effective Library: a British perspective. In Cecconi, M., Manzoni, G. and Salvetti, D. (eds), *La Biblioteca efficace: tendenze e ipotesi di sviluppo biblioteca negli anni '90 ed*, Editrice Bibliografica, 22–8.

Brophy, P. (1991) Budgeting in Academic Libraries: the polytechnic perspective, *Library Management*, **12** (4), 4–9 (reprinted in *Serials: the Journal of the United Kingdom Serials Group*, **5** (1), 35–41).

Brophy, P. (1991) The Mission of the Academic Library, *British Journal of Academic Librarianship*, **6** (3), 135–47.

Brophy, P. (1991) Strategic Planning for Academic Libraries: policy and process. In Ashcroft, M. and Wilson, A. (eds), *Strategic Planning for Academic Libraries: policy and process: proceedings of a seminar held in Stamford, Lincolnshire. on 30 October*, Capital Planning Information, 3–15.

Brophy, P. (1990) Information, Technology and Management, *Agenda*, May/June, 40–1.

Brophy, P. (1990) Introduction to the Use of Workstations for Library and Information Management, paper presented at the Third Dawson's Research Seminar, University of Loughborough, June, *Aslib Proceedings*, November.

Brophy, P. (1990) The Long Arm of the Librarian, professorial lecture delivered at Lancashire Polytechnic, 23 May, *Library Management*, **11** (6), 18–25.

Brophy, P. (1990) Organising for Change in Polytechnic Libraries. In *Libraries and Academic Excellence: Coals to Newcastle? Library Association UC&R Conference, April 1990, UC&R Newsletter*, **32**, Autumn, 10–16.

Brophy, P. (1990) *Towards the Millennium: library catalogues for the nineties, keynote address to the Annual Conference of the Library Association, Cataloguing & Indexing Group, Edinburgh, 13–16 July*.

Brophy, P. and Storey, C. et al. (1990) *The IBM DOBIS/LIBIS Integrated Library System: a guide for librarians and systems managers*, Gower.

Brophy, P. (1989) Performance Measurement in Academic Libraries: a polytechnic perspective, *British Journal of Academic Librarianship*, **4** (2), 99–110.

Brophy, P. and Hayter, M. (1989) *The Use of Information Technology by Senior Managers in UK Academic Libraries: final report*, British Library Research Paper 64, British Library.

Brophy, P. (1988) Influencing the Systems Designer: strategy for change. In *Online Public Access to Library Files: proceedings of the Third National Conference held at the University of Bath, 12th to 15th September 1987*, Elsevier Advanced Technology Publications, 15–25.

Brophy, P. (1987) Management Information Needs: the academic library. In Harris, C. (ed.), *Management Information Systems in Libraries and Information Services*, Taylor Graham, 29–41.

Brophy, P. (1986) *Management Information and Decision Support Systems in Libraries*, Gower.

Brophy, P. (1985) *Computers Can Read: machine-readable codes and their applications*, Gower.

Brophy, P. (1985) Managing the System Implementation Process. In Crowley, J. (ed.), *The Management of Academic Libraries*, Gower, Chapter 4.

Brophy, P. (1985) The Place of Special Collections in Polytechnic Libraries, *COPOL Newsletter*, **38**, December, 37–40.

Brophy, P. and Moorhouse, P. (1984) The Operation of a Variable Loan Policy Within an Automated Library System, *Program*, **18** (2), (April), 166–9.

Brophy, P. (1983) Critical Path Analysis: a library management tool, *Program*, **17** (4), 204–16.

Brophy, P., Moss, R. and Hargreaves, P. (1982) *Time Factor Classification and Relegation: final report*, British Library Research and Development Department, project SI/G/258.

Brophy, P. (1981) COPOL and BSI: the work of the BSI technical committees, *COPOL Newsletter*, June, 17–20.

Brophy, P. (1978) The Management of Cataloguing, *Library Management News*, August, 9–15.

Brophy, P. (1977) Teesside Polytechnic Library's Acquisitions Information System, *Program*, **11** (3), 83–93.

Brophy, P. (1976) *COBOL Programming: an introduction for librarians*, Bingley.

Brophy, P. (1976) The Techniques of Operations Research: a tutorial. In Brophy, P., Buckland, M. K. and Hindle, A. (eds), *Reader in Operations Research for Libraries*, Information Handling Services.

Brophy, P. and Ford, G. (1976) The Library Research Unit, University of Lancaster. In Schofield, J. L. and Cooper, A. (eds), *Library Management Research in Britain*, 103–16.

Brophy, P., Buckland, M. and Hindle, A. (eds) (1976) *Reader in Operations Research for Libraries*, Information Handling Services.

Brophy, P. with Daly, J. et al. (1976) *The Use of Gaming in Education for Library Management: final report on a research project*, University of Lancaster Library Occasional Papers 8, University of Lancaster Library.

Brophy, P. and Buckland, M. K. (1972) Simulation in Education for Library and Information Science Administration, *Information Scientist*, **6** (3), 93–100.

Brophy, P. et al. (1972) *A Library Management Game: report on a research project*, University of Lancaster Library Occasional Papers 7, University of Lancaster Library; available as ERIC Report ED 071 700. Also issued as *Computer-aided Instruction in Scientific and Technical Systems Management: report to OSTI on project SI/14/67*.

Index